The Slave Catchers

STANLEY W. CAMPBELL is Associate Professor of History at Baylor University.

The Slave Catchers

ENFORCEMENT

OF THE

FUGITIVE SLAVE LAW,

1850–1860

STANLEY W. CAMPBELL

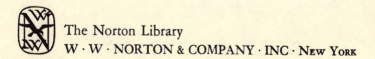

The Norton Library
W · W · NORTON & COMPANY · INC · NEW YORK

Books That Live
The Norton imprint on a book means that in the publisher's
estimation it is a book not for a single season but for the years.
W. W. Norton & Company, Inc.

SBN 393 00626 3

PRINTED IN THE UNITED STATES OF AMERICA

1 2 3 4 5 6 7 8 9 0

To Ella

Preface

For over one hundred years the Fugitive Slave Law of 1850 has been considered a failure, largely because of hostile public opinion in the northern states during the decade preceding the Civil War. Many Southerners justified secession from the Union in part on their belief that the North, hostile to the institution of slavery, had failed to live up to its obligations under the Constitution and the Compromise of 1850. Historians in their treatment of the subject have generally concluded that the law was not enforced, and in fact was unenforceable.

While engaged in research on the problem of fugitive slaves in Virginia in a seminar directed by Professor Fletcher Melvin Green, I discovered that very little basic research in contemporary and official sources had been done on the Fugitive Slave Law. Further research seemed to indicate that the generally accepted interpretations about enforcement of the law were based upon unsystematic and insufficient research. With the exception of a few local studies, not a single monograph has been written on the enforcement of the Fugitive Slave Law since the Civil War. Most conclusions seem to have been based on the work of Henry Wilson, James Ford Rhodes, and Allan Nevins, and their research, perhaps out of necessity, was superficial.

My thesis is that while most citizens residing in the North were opposed to the institution of slavery, only a few citizens in isolated communities engaged in active opposition to enforcement of the

Fugitive Slave Law. But in spite of hostility and opposition, the law was enforced by those charged with responsibility for enforcement, namely, officers of the federal courts. Moreover, the personal liberty laws, to which the South reacted so violently, did not prevent even one slave from being returned to the South where the claim was legitimate.

While completing the research and writing of this manuscript, I have incurred many debts of gratitude. Especially I should like to thank Professor Fletcher Melvin Green for his inspiration and critical judgment. Professor John G. Barrett read the entire manuscript, and his comments were most helpful. Without the aid of the staffs in the Justice and Executive Branch and the Fiscal Branch of the National Archives, the research would have been most difficult if not impossible. For postponing their vacations to complete the tedious job of typing the manuscript I am very grateful to Mrs. Martha Dudley and Mrs. Nancy Hostetter of Lexington, Virginia.

Stanley W. Campbell
Lexington, Virginia

Table of Contents

The Slave Catchers

Chapter I

Background and Passage
of the
Fugitive Slave Law

In Washington, the nation's capital, the spring and summer of 1850 were long, hot, and trying for members of the Thirty-first Congress. Questions of great importance to the Union were being debated both in and out of Congress during that session, and men, tempers already short from protracted and intemperate discussions of seemingly insoluble problems, were becoming irascible. Men of good will from all sections of the country had reached an apparent impasse in the controversies over such problems as the admission of California into the Union as a free state, extension of slavery into the territories, organization of the territory recently acquired from Mexico, the Texas boundary dispute, abolition of the slave trade in the District of Columbia, and a more effective law for the reclamation of fugitive slaves. A great part of the southern minority, sensing the majority was hostile to it, felt that the section had its back against the wall and must now resist. Talk of disunion was rife among certain groups of Southerners, and, although many Northerners scoffed at the idea, there were men in the North who would have rejoiced to see the slave states withdraw from the Union. Extremist elements from neither section were dominant in Congress, but a potentially dangerous crisis had developed which would require the utmost in statesmanship to allay.

The leadership of President Zachary Taylor was faltering, but there were men in the United States Senate with sufficient knowledge of statecraft to steer the nation through this perilous moment, notably Henry Clay, Daniel Webster, and Stephen Arnold Douglas. When Clay rose to address the Senate on January 29, he must have been aware that to overcome the challenge confronting the nation's lawmakers would require consumate political skill. "In his blandest mood, with a conciliatory gleam playing over his visage," wrote Allan Nevins, "Clay came now not to plead, but to direct; not to defer to the Administration, but to force it to take a truly national stand; not to conciliate individuals, but to marshal groups and interests into an irresistible phalanx." [1]

The plan which Clay presented to the Senate was simple enough. It consisted of eight steps which incorporated the ideas of separate bills, most of which had already been introduced by Senator Douglas, the chairman of the Committee on Territories. Clay proposed: (1) that California should be admitted to the Union as a free state; (2) that, as slavery was "not likely to be introduced into the territory" acquired from Mexico, governments should be established there "without the adoption of any restriction or condition on the subject of slavery"; (3) that the western boundary of the state of Texas should be drawn to exclude "any portion of New Mexico"; (4) that the public debt of Texas contracted prior to annexation be assumed by the government of the United States; (5) that without the consent of Maryland and just compensation to the owners, it would be "inexpedient" to abolish slavery in the District of Columbia; (6) that it would be "expedient," however, to abolish the slave trade in the District; (7) that a more effective fugitive slave law ought to be passed; and (8) that Congress had no power to prohibit the slave trade between the states. In "fairness and candor," said Clay in conclusion, "I now ask every Senator . . . to examine the plan of accomodation which this series of resolutions proposes, and not to pronounce against them until convinced after a thorough

1. Allan Nevins, *Ordeal of Union*, 2 vols. (New York: Charles Scribner's Sons, 1947), 1:265 (hereafter cited as Nevins, *Ordeal of Union*).

examination." [2] With that statement he sat down. The road to compromise had been opened, but it would be September before the deep-seated differences could be adjusted to the satisfaction of a majority in the Congress.

Only the seventh of Clay's resolutions which called for the passage of a more effective fugitive slave law will be evaluated here. It must be remembered, however, that the Fugitive Slave Law was only a part of the Compromise of 1850. To some extent, the vehement demands for effective enforcement can be accounted for in that many Southerners felt the Fugitive Slave Law was the only concession made to the South. "This law," wrote the editor of *De Bow's Review,* "was the only 'tub thrown to the whale of the South, out of the whole series of *compromise* measures. . . .' " [3] The South was particularly anxious for the law to be enforced. In fact, by December 1850, "faithful execution" of the Fugitive Slave Law was to become the fifth plank of the Georgia Platform upon which "the preservation of our much loved Union" rested.[4] If the solemn compact embodied in the compromise were breached by the North, the South would no longer be bound by it. During the debates on Clay's resolutions, southern advocates of compromise made it exceedingly clear that the successful adjustment of the problems arising from the slavery question depended upon the passage of an effective, stringent, enforceable law for reclaiming fugitive slaves.

The history of the fugitive slave problem from the adoption of the Constitution to the Compromise of 1850 provides ample evidence that the demands of the South for a more rigorous law were not unreasonable. Southern claims were based upon the Constitution of the United States. It explicitly provided that "No person held to service or labor in one State, under the laws thereof, escaping into another, shall, in consequence of any law or regulation therein, be discharged from such service or labor; but shall be delivered up on claim of the party, to whom such service or labor may be due." [5]

2. Debates and Proceedings, 1833–73, *Congressional Globe,* 31st Cong., 1st sess., 21:246 (hereafter cited as *Congressional Globe*).

3. *De Bow's Review,* 28 (1860) : 519.

4. Herman V. Ames, ed., *State Documents on Federal Relations: The States and the United States,* no. 4 (Philadelphia: Department of History, University of Pennsylvania, 1906), pp. 31–32 (hereafter cited as Ames, *State Documents*); *New York Tribune,* November 29, 1851.

5. U.S., *Constitution,* Art. 4, Sec. 2, clause 3.

Demands for a more stringent law were widespread in the South, but the states of the Deep South lost fewer slaves to the North than the four border states of Maryland, Virginia, Kentucky, and Missouri. In fact, these four states proclaimed a greater annual loss than all the remaining southern states.[6] But there was practically no agreement on the annual loss of absconding slaves. The *Louisville Journal* reported that the state of Kentucky lost thirty thousand dollars worth of slave property to the North each year.[7] Senator James Murray Mason believed Virginia was losing slaves to the value of one hundred thousand dollars a year; Senator Thomas George Pratt asserted that Maryland suffered an annual loss of eighty thousand dollars, while South Carolina's Andrew Pickens Butler estimated the annual loss of slaves from all the southern states to be in excess of two hundred thousand dollars.[8] According to the United States Census, the number of slaves reported as having escaped into the free states in 1850 was 1,011, or about one in each 3,165 of the slave population.[9]

Southerners were convinced that one of the principal causes of the fugitive slave problem was the activities of abolitionists in the North. Public meetings, at which fugitive Negroes were openly exhibited, had become a common occurrence. Antislavery leaders in the North and Northwest took advantage of every opportunity to declaim against the institution of slavery. Moreover, the activity of the antislavery societies was not confined by geographical limits. "The fact is notorious and undeniable," reported a special committee of the Virginia legislature, appointed to investigate the effectiveness of existing legislation for reclaiming runaway slaves, "that their emissaries have penetrated into the very hearts of the slaveholding states, and aided the escape of slaves whom they had seduced from the service of their owners."[10] Abolitionist newspapers, such as the *Liberator* in Boston, flaunted the Constitution and railed against slaveholders as agents of the devil. In some of the northern states,

6. *New York Tribune*, August 28, 1851.

7. *Congressional Globe*, 31st Cong., 1st sess., Appendix, p. 79.

8. Ibid., pp. 79, 1605; Nevins, *Ordeal of Union*, 1:243.

9. James Ford Rhodes, *History of the United States from the Compromise of 1850 to the Final Restoration of Home Rule at the South in 1877*, 7 vols. (New York: The Macmillan Company, 1904–6), 1:378 (hereafter cited as Rhodes, *History of the United States*).

10. *Acts of the General Assembly of Virginia, 1849–1850*, p. 247.

vigilance committees were formed to give aid and succor to Negroes who had fled their masters and to make it as difficult as possible for the owners of slaves to reclaim their property. The New York State Vigilance Anti-Slavery Committee, for example, reported that in 1849 it assisted 151 fugitives in escaping from servitude.[11] Describing the "war of ambition against the South," the Virginia legislative committee reported:

Fugitive slaves were harbored and protected, vexatious suits and prosecutions were instituted against the owner or his agent, resulting sometimes in imprisonment for want of bail, irresponsible mobs, composed of fanatics, ruffians and fugitive slaves, who had already found asylum abroad, were permitted by local authorities to rescue recaptured slaves in the lawful custody of their masters, and to imprison, beat, wound and even put to death citizens of the United States, seeking to enforce by lawful proceedings, the rights guaranteed to them by the constitution.[12]

The first Fugitive Slave Law had been passed by Congress in 1793. Before that date, the southern states had relied upon the good faith of those states which were freeing their bondsmen to live up to the compromises of the Constitution. Initially, it was thought that the presence of this class of persons in the free states would provide ample motivation for the white majority in northern communities to cooperate with the slaveholders in recapturing their runaways. "For it was to be expected," said the report of Virginia's legislative committee, "that the enlightened and sagacious people of the North would see at a glance, that the violation of that compact would create, and continually recruit on their soil, a class of paupers like the Parias of Hindostan; of outcasts from society; of men who are neither slaves nor citizens; a wen on the body politic; an anomaly on their institutions, and a pestilent curse to them and their posterity." [13]

The Fugitive Slave Law of 1793 did not result from a complaint of the South for legislation on this subject; it grew incidentally from a call for remedial statutes to facilitate the surrender of fugitives from justice. A free Negro residing in Pennsylvania had been captured by three white men and taken to Virginia. The three white men were

11. Seth Barton, *The Randolph Epistles* (Washington: n.p., 1850), p. 3. Quotes the official report of the committee.
12. *Acts of the General Assembly of Virginia, 1849–1850*, pp. 246–47.
13. Ibid., p. 245.

charged with kidnapping, and the governor of Pennsylvania attempted to have them extradited. On the ground that there was no statute providing for the rendition of fugitives from justice, the governor of Virginia refused to comply with the request of her sister state. Unable to obtain satisfactory cooperation from Virginia, the governor of Pennsylvania presented the facts of the case to President George Washington who relayed them to the Congress. The result was passage of the Fugitive Slave Law of 1793. The first two sections of this law concerned the surrender of fugitives from justice, and the last two sections pertained to the rendition of fugitive slaves.[14]

In light of experience and a hostile public opinion in the North, Southerners found many weaknesses in this law. The law provided that the slave owner could apply to a district or circuit judge of the United States for a certificate to enable him to return his slave to the state from which he had fled. However, at the time the law was passed, many states had only one district judge, and the circuit judges were resident in only nine states. With the fugitive slave in tow, extensive travel and expense were usually necessary before a slave's owner came under the protection of the federal courts. The law did not authorize federal judges to issue a warrant for the arrest of the fugitive slave, nor did it permit the slaveholder to demand of federal marshals aid in the pursuit of their fugitive property. In Virginia, it was noted that before the law could operate

the master . . . a stranger, must go into a free state, seize his slave without form or process of law, and unaccompanied by a single civil officer, must carry that slave, in the face of a fanatical and infuriated population, perhaps from the centre of extremists of the state, a distance of two or three hundred miles to the place where the judge may happen to reside, before he can have any legal or judicial action in his case; and suppose that he had passed through the almost insuperable barriers incident to such an undertaking, and had succeeded in bringing his slave before the judge, and had obtained the certificate which the law prescribes, there is no provision in that law by which the judgment can be enforced, or the power of the national government be invoked, through its marshals and officers, to sustain the rights of property thus adjudicated in his favor.[15]

14. Rhodes, *History of the United States,* 1:24; Henry Wilson, *History of the Rise and Fall of the Slave Power in America,* 3 vols. (Boston: J. R. Osgood and Company, 1872–77), 1:69–78 (hereafter cited as Wilson, *Rise and Fall of Slave Power*). See also C. W. A. David, "The Fugitive Slave Law of 1793 and Its Antecedents," *Journal of Negro History* 9 (January 1924): 18–25.
15. *Acts of the General Assembly of Virginia, 1849–1850,* pp. 251–53.

As antislavery sentiment in the North became more intense, opposition to enforcement of the Fugitive Slave Law of 1793 became more pronounced. When active contravention by extremist elements had made the law a virtual dead letter in certain northern communities, southern congressmen attempted to secure a more effective law for the reclamation of fugitive slaves. In December, 1817, James Pindall of Virginia, Philemon Beecher of Ohio, and Richard C. Anderson of Kentucky were appointed to a committee in the House of Representatives and charged with the responsibility of devising a more efficient fugitive slave law. A bill was reported and placed on the calendar for consideration January 26, 1818. However, opposition forces were already at work.

As soon as the bill had been explained on the floor by the chairman of the committee, Charles Rich of Vermont offered an amendment which would have required proof before a court of record, under penalty of a ten-thousand-dollar fine, that the person being claimed was actually a slave before he could be removed from the state. Henry R. Storrs, congressman from New York, submitted a new section in lieu of Rich's amendment which provided that, if any person made a false claim for a fugitive slave, he should suffer imprisonment for fifteen years and a fine not exceeding five thousand dollars. Storr's amendment was adopted by a large majority. After a motion to recommit the bill to the committee had failed, John Sergeant of Pennsylvania proffered an amendment which would have permitted the judges in the state where the fugitive was arrested to determine whether such person owed service or labor. Southern leaders were unanimously opposed to such a proposal, and the amendment was defeated. By a majority of fifteen, the bill then passed the House of Representatives and was sent to the Senate. The bill passed the Senate with amendments which the Conference Committee was unable to resolve, so it was tabled.[16] Until 1850, frequent attempts were made by southern congressmen to overcome northern opposition and pass a more effective law, but such efforts proved futile. In many sections of the North, a hostile public opinion had rendered as nugatory any efforts to secure a more stringent law for reclaiming fugitive bondsmen.

Generalizations of northern opposition to the Fugitive Slave Law of 1793 were largely overdrawn, but there is no doubt that in certain

16. Wilson, *Rise and Fall of Slave Power*, 1:74–77.

areas such as northern Ohio, Wisconsin, Michigan, western Pennsylvania, northern New York, Vermont, Connecticut, Massachusetts, and Rhode Island antislavery feeling was at times intense. Nor can it be denied that opposition to enforcement of the law was frequently militant.

In some of the northern states, antislavery sentiment found expression in the passage of personal liberty laws. For the most part, the personal liberty laws relative to the Fugitive Slave Law of 1793 were not enacted until after the famous decision of the Supreme Court in *Prigg* v. *Pennsylvania*.[17] Before that date, Connecticut had passed a law which forbade her judges and justices of the peace to take cognizance of such cases. Indiana, New York, and Vermont had passed legislation which provided for trial by jury in cases involving fugitive slaves; Pennsylvania and Ohio had placed on their statute books laws to prevent kidnapping.[18]

Because the Fugitive Slave Law of 1793 permitted a slaveholder or his agent to go into a free state, arrest his fugitive property, and take the fugitive back to the state from which he had fled without due process of law, many northern citizens feared for the safety of free Negroes living in their communities. Several southern states passed laws providing lucrative rewards for the return of fugitive slaves, a result of which was that the kidnapping of free Negroes residing in the free states had become an all too frequent occurrence.[19] Hence, personal liberty laws were passed by northern states to protect Negroes living within their borders.

Before the Prigg decision, most of the northern states had not enacted personal liberty laws, and some of the free states lived up to their constitutional obligations, at least as they interpreted them. In 1806, for example, the state of Ohio passed a law which required every sheriff and jailer in the state "to receive all prisoners committed to his custody by the authority of the United States," and this included fugitive slaves.[20] In the following year, Negroes were pro-

17. Prigg v. Pennsylvania, 16 Peters 539 (1842).

18. For a summary of the personal liberty laws see Marion Gleason McDougall, *Fugitive Slaves 1619–1865* (Boston: Ginn & Company, 1891) (hereafter cited as McDougall, *Fugitive Slaves*).

19. See, for example, *Acts of the General Assembly of Virginia, 1855–1856*, pp. 43–44.

20. *Statutes of the State of Ohio* (1854), pp. 106–7.

hibited from settling in the state unless within twenty days they had secured a five-hundred-dollar bond ensuring their good behavior; a hundred-dollar fine was the penalty for harboring or concealing fugitive slaves, and Negroes were barred from testifying against white persons. This law was amended in 1809 so that Negroes with a "fair certificate of actual freedom" from a court of the United States could settle in the state.[21] In 1831, the antislavery forces gained a majority in the legislative and passed an antikidnapping law, but the tide turned the other way in 1839, and the law was repealed.[22] An Ohio statute enacted in 1839 established a system by which state officers superintended the arrest, trial, and delivery of fugitive slaves to their owners. But this law was also of short duration for, in 1843, it was repealed and the law of 1831 re-enacted.[23]

As regards interstate responsibility for cooperation in the rendition of fugitive slaves, the year 1842 was an important turning point. During this year three events occurred which were to have far-reaching effects. The first was the decision of the Supreme Court which upheld the constitutionality of the Fugitive Slave Law of 1793, relieved the states of all legal responsibility for recapturing and returning runaway slaves, and declared that the Personal Liberty Law of Pennsylvania was unconstitutional and void. The second was the Van Zandt case in Ohio, and the third was the Latimer case in Massachusetts.

By 1826, abolitionists in Pennsylvania had gained enough influence in the legislature to push through a law which provided stiff penalties for anyone "who should take or carry away from the State any negro with the intention of selling him as a slave, or of detaining or causing to be detained such negro as a slave for life." The primary purpose of this law was to prevent kidnapping of free Negroes residing within the state and selling them as slaves, but the provisions of this statute extended also to fugitive slaves who "had sought refuge within its borders."[24] In 1837, Margarette Morgan was arrested as a fugitive slave in the state by Edward Prigg, agent for the owner. With her children, the Negro woman was taken back to

21. *Congressional Globe*, 31st Cong., 1st sess., Appendix, p. 532.
22. *Statutes of the State of Ohio* (1854), pp. 306–7; *Congressional Globe*, 31st Cong., 1st sess., Appendix, p. 532.
23. *Congressional Globe*, 31st Cong., 1st sess., Appendix, p. 532.
24. Wilson, *Rise and Fall of Slave Power*, 1:471.

Maryland. Under the provisions of the act of 1826, Prigg was arrested, tried, and convicted. The judgment of the lower court was upheld on appeal to the Supreme Court of Pennsylvania. The case was then appealed to the Supreme Court of the United States.

The issue before the Court was the constitutionality of the act under which Prigg was prosecuted. Before rendering its decision on this point, the Court endeavored to ascertain the nature of the right which the Constitution intended to secure to masters of persons escaping from service or labor. First it was to determine whether the power to legislate under the fugitive slave clause of the Constitution was vested in the state or national legislatures and, second, whether Congress held this power exclusively. The opinion of the Court, delivered by Justice Joseph Story, held that the power of legislation upon this subject was "exclusive in the national government" and was "not concurrent in the states. . . ." The Court also ruled that no state was bound to provide means to carry the provisions of the fugitive slave clause into effect "either by its courts or magistrates; but that the national government was bound, through its own proper departments, legislative, judicial, and executive, to enforce all the rights and duties growing out of this clause in the constitution." [25] The object of this constitutional provision, the Court declared, "was to secure to the citizens of the slaveholding states the complete right and title of ownership in their slaves, as property, in every state in the union into which they might escape. . . ." Justice Story thus laid down the rule that the right of the master in the free states was the same as in the slave states. "We have not the slightest hesitation," said the Court, "in holding, that . . . the owner of a slave is clothed with entire authority in every State in the Union, to seize and recapture his slave, whenever he can do it without any breach of the peace, or any illegal violence." The Court then ruled that the Pennsylvania statute was unconstitutional.[26]

On a return trip from Cincinnati, John Van Zandt, a resident of

25. Prigg v. Pennsylvania, 16 Peters 539 (1842); see also Joseph Story, *Commentaries on the Constitution of the United States: With a Preliminary Review of the Constitutional History of the Colonies and States, Before the Adoption of the Constitution,* 2nd ed, 2 vols. (Boston: Charles C. Little and James Brown, 1851), 2:547 (hereafter cited as Story, *Commentaries on the Constitution*).

26. Prigg v. Pennsylvania, 16 Peters 539, 613, 638 (1842).

Hamilton County, Ohio, picked up and concealed in his wagon nine fugitive slaves who had just escaped from Kentucky. The owner's agents, who had been pursuing the fugitives, caught up with the party and stopped the wagon. Two of the slaves again managed to escape, but the remaining seven were returned to Kentucky without process of law and were lodged in the Covington jail. Indicted by a grand jury in Ohio, the "kidnappers," were acquitted.[27] Van Zandt did not fare so well. He was indicted by a federal grand jury and tried before a circuit court of the United States, Justice John McLean presiding. Ably defended by Thomas Morris and Salmon Portland Chase, Van Zandt was none-the-less made the victim of his own philanthropy. Having been charged by Justice McLean in accordance with the doctrines of the Prigg decision, the jury brought in a verdict of guilty. The slaves' captors collected a large reward, but Van Zandt was fined twelve hundred dollars. On appeal, the case was argued before the United States Supreme Court in 1846 by William Harris Seward and Salmon P. Chase. The opinion of the Court, delivered by Justice Levi Woodbury, sustained the constitutionality of the Fugitive Slave Law of 1793 and affirmed the decision of the lower court. Van Zandt's conviction stood.[28]

The city of Boston was the site of the Latimer case. At the request of James B. Grey of Norfolk, Virginia, George Latimer was arrested without a warrant as a fugitive slave. Counsel for the fugitive, Samuel E. Sewall and Amos B. Merrill, attempted to secure his release through a writ of habeas corpus. Chief Justice Lemuel Shaw, of the Massachusetts Supreme Court, denied the writ on the ground that the Fugitive Slave Law authorized the owner to seize his fugitive property in any state to which he might have fled and, after proving his claim before a court of the United States, return him to the state from which he had escaped. In behalf of the claimant, Elbridge Gerry Austin, attorney for the city of Boston, applied to Justice Joseph Story for a certificate of removal and then moved for time to procure evidence from the city of Norfolk. The motion was granted, and Latimer was placed in the custody of Grey until the time of the trial. The city jailer consented to act as Grey's agent, and Latimer was lodged in the city jail.

27. Wilson, *Rise and Fall of Slave Power*, 1:475–76.
28. Jones v. Van Zandt, 5 Howard 215 (1847).

Great indignation was aroused by Latimer's arrest and detention. Public meetings were held, large crowds gathered to hear impassioned speeches, the city and state were condemned for their part in the proceedings. Petitions signed by influential citizens demanded that the sheriff dismiss the jailer or be removed himself. Because of the public clamor, Grey agreed to release Latimer for a price. The Reverend Nathaniel Colver, fearing that Latimer might be "smuggled" out of the state, agreed to pay four hundred dollars. Grey accepted the offer, and Latimer was released from custody a free man. Subsequently, more than sixty-five thousand signatures were affixed to a petition submitted to the state legislature by Charles Francis Adams and requesting a law that would bar state officers from aiding in the arrest and detention of fugitive slaves and would prohibit the use of state jails for their confinement.[29]

Largely because of the indignation and resentment kindled by the decisions in the Prigg, Van Zandt, and Latimer cases in 1842, new personal liberty laws were enacted, and old statutes were strengthened. Several of the northern states passed laws which prohibited state officers from participating, and state jails from being used, in the process of returning fugitive slaves. Massachusetts, Vermont, and Ohio in 1843, Connecticut in 1844, Pennsylvania in 1847, and Rhode Island in 1848 passed laws characterized by a Virginia legislative committee as a "disgusting and revolting exhibition of faithless and unconstitutional legislation" and as "palpable frauds upon the South, calculated to excite at once her indignation and her contempt." [30]

The lines had now been drawn, but the bonds of union were weakened. On the one hand, the Prigg decision had affirmed the position Southerners had taken since the adoption of the Constitution, namely, that a slaveholder could pursue his fugitive slave into any state or territory of the Union and capture and return with him without process of law. On the other hand, the decision exempted the states from all responsibility for enforcement of the Fugitive Slave Law, thus fortifying the abolitionists to a far greater degree than they reasonably could have hoped for under the circumstances.[31] The

29. Wilson, *Rise and Fall of Slave Power*, 1:477–80.

30. *Acts of the General Assembly of Virginia, 1849–1850*, pp. 248–50.

31. Julius Yanuck, "The Fugitive Slave Law and the Constitution" (Ph.D. diss., Columbia University, 1953), pp. ii–v (hereafter cited as Yanuck, "The Fugitive Slave Law").

owner of fugitive slaves could legally go into the free states in pursuit of his property, but the abolitionists, under the new personal liberty laws, could legally harass the slaveholder until costs for rendition sometimes exceeded the slave's value. Hence, if the slaveholder or his agent were compelled to pursue his slave beyond the southern sections of the northern border states, he quite frequently abandoned pursuit. Even after a successful rendition, the captured slaves were generally sold to cover the expenses incurred in travel, court costs, bail bonds, and rewards.[32]

Understandably the South concluded that the Fugitive Slave Law of 1793 was inadequate, that the North was not living up to its constitutional pledge, and that a new law was necessary if the slave states were to receive justice at the hands of the free states.

On January 3, 1850, Senator James Mason of Virginia stood up in the Senate and "gave notice of his intention . . . to introduce a bill to provide for the more effectual execution" of the fugitive slave clause of the Constitution. On the following day, Senate Bill No. 23 was read twice, ordered printed, and referred to the Judiciary Committee. Andrew P. Butler, senator from South Carolina and chairman of the Judiciary Committee, reported the bill favorably on January 16, and debate was scheduled to begin January 24.[33]

As reported from the Judiciary Committee, the bill had four sections. The first section provided that the owner or his agent, after arresting his fugitive slave, could take him "before any judge of the circuit or district courts of the United States, or before any commissioner, or clerk of such courts, or marshal thereof, or any postmaster . . . or collector of customs" residing within the state where the arrest was made. If satisfactory proof were offered that the fugitive owed service or labor to the claimant, these officers were required to issue a certificate which would be "sufficient warrant for taking and removing such fugitive . . . to the State or Territory from which he or she had fled." Upon proper application, the second section stipulated that with the exception of the marshal the above named officers were to issue a warrant to a federal marshal for the arrest of the fugitive slave. The third section provided that anyone attempting to harbor, conceal, or rescue a fugitive slave would be liable to a one-thousand-dollar fine. The last section required that, if the fugi-

---

32. Ibid., p. 9, note 3.
33. *Congressional Globe*, 31st Cong., 1st sess., 21:99, 103; appendix, p. 79.

tive were arrested by a federal marshal, the officers listed in the first section proceed in the same manner as if the slave had been arrested by the owner or his agent.[34]

Debate on the bill was opened by Senator Andrew P. Butler on an extremely pessimistic note. "I have no very great confidence," he said, "that this bill will subserve the ends which seem to be contemplated by it. The Federal Legislature . . . has too limited means to carry out the article of the Constitution to which this bill applies. . . . And I know," he continued, "that the cardinal articles of the Constitution are not to be preserved by statutory enactments upon parchment. They must live and be preserved in the willing minds and good faith of those who incurred the obligation to maintain them." He then reiterated the evils which he felt the South had suffered because of the northern personal liberty laws.[35]

Senators from both sections of the country were opposed to the new fugitive slave bill. Some Southerners argued that the bill did not go far enough to protect their property adequately. Northern opponents maintained that it did not go far enough to protect the liberty of free Negroes residing in the North. Senator Mason, sponsor of the bill in the Senate, offered two amendments: one made anyone guilty of obstructing execution of the act liable to a fine of one thousand dollars; the other barred testimony of the fugitive from being admitted as evidence. On January 28, Senator William H. Seward, advocate of the higher law doctrine, presented an amendment which, in effect, was a substitute for the bill already before the Senate. It provided for the right of trial by jury in fugitive slave cases and a stiff penalty for judges who would disallow the writ of habeas corpus in such cases. Seeing no reason to hesitate at this point, Mason submitted his own substitute carrying the demands for a more stringent law still further.[36] The amendments were received and laid on the table.

In the meantime, Henry Clay had proposed his compromise plan and, on February 5, stood before a crowded Senate to defend it. Not until the second day did Clay speak on the fugitive slave question. On this issue, he sided with his southern colleagues. He said:

34. Ibid.
35. Ibid.
36. Ibid., 21:210, 236, 270.

. . . upon this subject, I go with him who goes furthest in the interpretation of that clause in the Constitution which relates to this subject. In my humble opinion, that is a requirement by the Constitution of the United States which is not limited in its operation to the Congress of the United States, but which extends to every State in the Union. And I go one step further. It extends to every *man* in the Union, and devolves upon him the obligation to assist in the recovery of a fugitive slave from labor, who takes refuge in or escapes into one of the free States.[37]

In Clay's opinion, the demands of the South on the subject of fugitive slaves were right and just.

Extensive support was generated for the compromise measures by Clay's oratorical powers, but the ultras promptly flocked to the attack. In resolutions adopted by its legislature, the state of Georgia threatened secession if Congress admitted California as presently organized, passed the Wilmot proviso, abolished slavery in the District of Columbia, or if the northern states continued to impede the rendition of fugitive slaves.[38] Jefferson Davis, senator from Mississippi, spoke in opposition to Clay's proposal, dismissing the plan with "contemptuous brevity." [39] On the resolutions respecting popular sovereignty in the territories and the fugitive slave question, Mason found that he could support the idea of compromise; to the remainder of the scheme he was utterly opposed. On March 4, John C. Calhoun entered the Senate, supported on the arms of James Hamilton and Senator Mason. Too ill to deliver an extended address, the senator from South Carolina sat wrapped in his cloak as Mason read his speech. Following through on earlier extremist statements, Calhoun's discourse was essentially disunionist.

Three days later, on March 7, Daniel Webster gave vent to his own oratorical talent, throwing his support to Henry Clay and the Union. With regard to the problem of fugitive slaves, the senator from Massachusetts agreed with Clay that the complaints of the South were just. He said that "there has been found at the North, among individuals and among the Legislatures of the North, a disinclination to perform, fully, their constitutional duties, in regard to the return of persons bound to service, who have escaped into the free States. In

37. Ibid., Appendix, p. 122. See also Glyndon G. Van Deusen, *The Life of Henry Clay* (Boston: Little, Brown and Company, 1937), p. 401 (hereafter cited as Van Deusen, *Henry Clay*).

38. Ames, *State Documents*, pp. 259–61.

39. Nevins, *Ordeal of Union*, 1:276.

that respect, it is my judgment that the South is right, and the North is wrong." [40] Despite the furious attacks this speech elicited from abolitionists, Webster's influence was to be of tremendous importance in the passage of the compromise measures. Webster was able to swing great blocs of northern public opinion in support of the compromise, particularly from northern industrialists.[41] From this time, disunionist sentiment "rapidly subsided. . . . A crisis had been reached and passed, and this blustery week marked a reversion of the tide." [42]

From March through June, debate on the fugitive slave bill was intermittent but fierce. On March 18 and 19, Senator George Edmund Badger of North Carolina spoke on the slavery question. As regards the fugitive slave bill, he argued in support of the amendment offered by Mason but was absolutely opposed to Seward's amendment which provided for trial by jury in the state where the fugitive was captured. William Lewis Dayton, senator from New Jersey, was just as vehement in his support of a jury trial. Attempting to show that northern juries could be trusted to do their duty, Dayton cited several cases in point. In his own state, two slaves had recently been tried in Burlington County, "where I should think three-fourths of all the population are of Quaker blood or connection, and . . . adverse to slavery." But the slaves were remanded to the claimant and returned to Maryland.[43] If a jury trial was extended to fugitive slave cases, most Southerners feared that, because of widespread antislavery sentiment, runaway slaves would be freed by the juries. Hence, Southerners opposed jury trials in such cases on principle.

Speaking against vesting judicial power in the hands of "petty commissioners," Connecticut's Roger Sherman Baldwin scored the bill reported by the Judiciary Committee and argued for jury trials in the state where the fugitive was found. This is a question, he said, "affecting the liberty of an individual who has a right to remain where he is, and to assert his freedom in the State where he happens to be, until his right is disproved by evidence. . . . He will have no

40. *Congressional Globe*, 31st Cong., 1st sess., Appendix, p. 274.

41. Rhodes, *History of the United States*, 1:157; Van Deusen, *Henry Clay*, pp. 402–3.

42. Nevins, *Ordeal of Union*, 1:297.

43. *Congressional Globe*, 31st Cong., 1st sess., Appendix, pp. 382–92, 438–41.

trial if delivered to the claimant. . . ." In reply, Clay's colleague Joseph Rogers Underwood said: "If we are to have a new tribunal, judges, and jurors—a regularly organized court, ignorant of the laws of the State from which the fugitive escapes, and upon which . . . the rights of the parties depend—then the cost of the pursuit of a slave, with the expense, delay, and harassments incident to a protracted litigation before such a tribunal, will be more than the slave is worth, and the master will be the loser, even should he *win* the suit. . . ." [44] Having reached an impasse in the discussion of the compromise measures, the Senate agreed to a resolution by Mississippi's Henry Stuart Foote to submit the proposals for compromise to the select Committee of Thirteen.

On April 19, the committee was elected, and Clay was made chairman. Lewis Cass of Michigan, Daniel Stevens Dickinson of New York, and Jesse David Bright of Indiana represented northern Democrats. Massachusett's Daniel Webster, Vermont's Samuel Shethar Phelps, and Pennsylvania's James Cooper were the northern Whig choices. Southern Democrats were represnted by William Rufus de Vane King of Alabama, James M. Mason of Virginia, and Solomon Weathersbee Downs of Louisiana. Southern Whigs elected to the committee were Willie Person Mangum of North Carolina, John Bell of Tennessee, and John Macpherson Berrien of Georgia. To the committee were referred the compromise resolutions and the subsequent amendments which had been offered in the Senate, but Clay was able to forestall resolutions offering special instructions. [45]

On May 8, Clay presented to the Senate the report of the Committee of Thirteen. Two amendments were offered by the committee to the fugitive slave bill. In order that Negroes living in the North might be protected from false arrest as fugitive slaves, the committee proposed that the owner of a fugitive slave be required to obtain a record from a competent tribunal in the state from which the fugitive had fled, "adjudicating the facts of elopement and slavery, with a general description of the fugitive." This record, when taken to the state where the fugitive was found, was to be held as "sufficient evidence of the facts which had been adjudicated," and would "leave nothing more to be done than to identify the fugitive." To meet the

44. Ibid., pp. 421, 526.
45. Ibid., p. 526.

northern demands for a jury trial, and at the same time get around southern fears that antislavery juries would free runaway slaves, the committee suggested a jury trial in the state from which the fugitive fled only in "cases where he declares to the officer giving the certificate for his return that he has a right to his freedom." The claimant would be placed under bond and required to return the fugitive to his home state in order that his freedom might be established before a jury. In the county where the master resided, the United States district attorney would have the responsibility for seeing that the trial was carried out.[46]

Aligning himself with the strongest advocates of state rights, Pierre Soulé of Louisiana objected to the amendments submitted by the Committee of Thirteen. He argued that the provisions of the report dealing with fugitive slaves "would greatly embarrass, delay, and add to the expenses of reclamation, to say nothing of the absence of constitutional authority in this Government to exercise jurisdiction over *State Courts* of the South, enlarge their jurisdiction, assign them new duties, or require at their hands *records* of matters to which their functions do not pertain . . . of exercising *a federal jurisdiction within the slave States upon the subject of slavery,* under the guise of a penal bond *payable to the* United States. . . ." The courts of the southern states were already open, he said, to any Negro held in bondage who avowed that he was free "without the promptings or encroachments of these federal requisitions."[47]

On June 12, Senator Dayton again addressed the Senate. He too was opposed to the amendments, offered by the committee, to the fugitive slave bill. As regards the provision requiring the slaveholder to bring a record of a state court with him, Dayton argued that this would make the free states "the mere executive, the mere ministerial officers of the slave States, for the purpose of carrying their judgments into effect." Dayton preferred the amendment offered by Webster on June 3 which provided for a jury trial in the state where the fugitive was arrested.[48] For the next two months, debate in the Senate was confined to the other compromise proposals.

Not until August 19 did the fugitive slave bill again come up for

46. Ibid., 21:946.
47. Ibid., Appendix, pp. 630–31.
48. Ibid., pp. 816–17.

consideration. Now, discussion would continue until the bill was passed. The bill reported by the Judiciary Committee was rejected. Mason took this opportunity to offer his substitute for the original bill which incorporated many of the changes thus far presented, including the Committee of Thirteen's first amendment requiring the slaveholder to obtain a record from the courts in his home state.[49] But no action was taken on his bill at this time. Persistent in his efforts to extend trial by jury to fugitive slave cases, Senator Dayton submitted an amendment similar to Webster's, but it was submitted in vain. His resolution was voted down twenty-seven to eleven. Amendments submitted by Senator Chase providing for jury trial "on the question of claim or no claim" and by Senator Robert Charles Winthrop, extending the right of habeas corpus to fugitive slaves, were quickly set aside.[50]

The next two days were devoted to one of the most hotly contested issues in the course of arguing the bill. Thomas George Pratt, senator from Maryland, proposed an amendment which would have given the owner of a fugitive slave the right to institute suit in the district or circuit courts of the United States to recover from the United States Treasury the value of the fugitive and the legal expenses incurred when a slave was not delivered on a legitimate claim. A proviso was added that should the slave be delivered to the owner after he had received payment from the federal treasury, the master would be liable to the United States for the current value of such fugitive.[51] Jefferson Davis had no great interest in the fugitive slave bill because he had no hope that it would ever be "executed to any beneficial extent." But, because the senators from the border states wanted such a law, he gave his support to the measure with certain state rights reservations. Davis was consistently opposed to any measure that would extend the authority of the federal government over the states. "Our safety," he said, "consists in a rigid adherence to the terms and principles of the federal compact. If, for considerations of temporary or special advantage, we depart from it, we, the minority, will have abandoned our only reliable means of safety." Pratt's amendment, he

49. *Washington Daily National Intelligencer*, August 20, 1850 (hereafter cited as *National Intelligencer*).
50. *Congressional Globe*, 31st Cong., 1st sess., Appendix, pp. 1582–83, 1589.
51. Ibid., pp. 1616, 1237, 1609.

felt, was a plea for "special advantage" which would lead to consequences not to be desired by any southern man. If the federal government were given the "power to assume control over the slave property," or to "interpose its legislative and financial power between the individual owning that property and the property itself," there would be no end "to the action which anti-slavery feeling will suggest." Davis could not support Pratt's amendment.[52] Tennessee's Hopkins Lacy Turney asserted that, if the federal government was liable for the value of fugitive slaves that could not be recovered, no great effort would be made to recapture them. The effect of such a proposition would be to "emancipate the slaves of the border States and to have them paid for out of the Treasury of the United States." The slaveholders, said Senator Turney, would thus be forced to pay for half of their own property, and the balance of the nation would be taxed to pay the other half.[53] Pro and con, the debate was continued at great length by Senators Pratt, Winthrop, Yulee, Cass, Dayton, Badger, Butler, Underwood, and Sturgeon. The amendment was finally rejected twenty-seven to ten.

Final passage of the bill was now in sight, but Mason's substitute was still to be considered. A regular flury of amendments was introduced by both sides.

Senator Joseph Rogers Underwood, wishing merely to strengthen the Fugitive Slave Law of 1793 rather than write and a new law, submitted a substitute for Mason's bill.[54] Jefferson Davis presented a series of amendments designed to make the Virginian's bill more acceptable to the strong state rights advocates in the South. The first would strike out the clause providing compensation for escaped slaves. The second would provide for civil action against anyone who concealed or rescued a fugitive slave and would permit the owner to recover one thousand dollars for each slave lost in such a manner. "With that remedy, and with another amendment which I shall offer," said Davis, "requiring the delivery of the slave into the State of the owner, under the hands of a marshal, and the summoning of a posse to aid him at the expense of the Government, the bill, I think will be effectual." The Davis amendments were accepted and incorpo-

52. Ibid., p. 1614.
53. Ibid., p. 1616.
54. Ibid., p. 1609.

rated into Mason's bill. Senator Chase introduced an amendment to Underwood's bill to prevent slaves in the territories from being restored by federal commissioners, but it was rejected forty one to one.[55]

On August 23, the Senate voted on Underwood's substitute bill. It was rejected twenty-two to fourteen. Mason then moved to insert the first three sections of Underwood's amendment into his own bill. The Senate agreed to the motion and adopted Mason's bill.[56] The bill was ordered engrossed for a third reading and, on August 24, was read a third time and passed by a vote of twenty-seven to twelve. Two days later, the title of the bill was amended by Mason to read: "An act to amend, and supplementary to the act, entitled 'An act respecting fugitives from justice, and persons escaping from the service of their masters,' approved February 12, 1793." [57] Senate Bill No. 23 was then sent to the House of Representatives where it was scheduled for a first reading on September 12.

On schedule, the bill was read the first and second time by its title. James Thompson, Democrat from Pennsylvania, obtained the floor and requested that the entire bill be read. After the clerk had finished reading, Thompson addressed the House in support of the "great plan which had been devised for the pacification of the country," and then, in good partisan fashion, moved the previous question which would close debate if the House concurred. When Thompson refused to rescind his motion, a motion to table the bill was offered by Thaddeus Stevens of Pennsylvania. A division was called for, and the motion to table the bill was voted down 113 to 67. Demand for the previous question then recurred, and was seconded; the main question was ordered: "Shall the bill pass?" The yeas and nays were ordered and, by a vote of 109 to 76, the bill was passed and returned to the Senate.[58] On September 18, after receiving a favorable report on the constitutionality of the bill from his attorney general, President Millard Fillmore signed the Fugitive Slave Law of 1850.[59]

This act was composed of ten sections. The duties and powers

55. Ibid., pp. 1619, 1623.
56. Ibid., p. 1625.
57. Ibid., 21:1660.
58. Ibid., 21:1806–7: *House Journal No. 566,* 31st Cong., 1st sess., pp. 1289, 1448–53.
59. *U.S. Statutes at Large,* 9:462–65.

conferred by the law were to be exercised by commissioners appointed by the United States Circuit Courts, and commissioners in the territories were to be appointed by the superior court of each territory where "reasonable facilities to reclaim fugitives from labor" were to be maintained. The jurisdiction of the commissioners was to be concurrent with that of the circuit and district judges, and they had authority to grant certificates for the return of fugitive slaves.

United States marshals and deputy marshals who refused to act under the law were liable to a fine of one thousand dollars, "to the use of [the] . . . claimant . . ." If a fugitive should escape from the marshal's custody, the marshal was liable for the slave's full value. Under this law, the commissioners were authorized to appoint special officers and to call out the *posse comitatus*.

The owner of a fugitive slave, or his agent, was authorized to "pursue and reclaim such fugitive person," either by procuring a warrant from a judge or commissioner, "or by seizing and arresting such fugitive, where the same can be done without process. . . ." The claimant could take the fugitive before such judge or commissioner, and, if the identity of the prisoner could be established, the judge or commissioner was authorized to grant a certificate to the claimant which would allow the removal of the slave "back to the State or Territory from whence he or she may have escaped. . . ." And "reasonable force or restraint as may be necessary under the circumstances of the case" could be used to ensure the fugitive's return. Under no circumstances was testimony of the fugitive to be accepted as evidence. All molestation of the claimant in the removal of his slave "by any process issued by any court, judge, magistrate, or other person whomsoever," was prohibited. The right of habeas corpus, therefore, did not extend to fugitive slaves.

Any person who obstructed the arrest of a fugitive or attempted to rescue, aid, harbor, or conceal a fugitive, knowing him to be such, was liable to a fine not to exceed one thousand dollars and imprisonment of not more than six months.

Marshals, deputies, clerks, and special officers were to receive their usual fees, but the commissioners were to receive ten dollars if the fugitive were remanded to his owner; otherwise, the fee was to be five dollars. The fees were to be paid by the claimant.

If the claimant made an affidavit that he feared a rescue attempt would be made, the officer who made the arrest was required to return the slave to the place from which he had escaped and was authorized to employ as many persons as necessary to prevent a rescue. The expenses of assistance and transportation were to be paid from the federal treasury.

The tenth section was the catch-all provision of the act. Whenever a slave escaped, if the owner could present "satisfactory proof" of his ownership of such slave, the court in his home state was required to issue an authenticated copy of the testimony, with a description of the fugitive, which, upon being presented to any judge, commissioner, or other officer authorized by this act, was to be held as conclusive evidence of the escape and of the claimant's right to the fugitive.[60]

After a grueling, hot summer's work, the Fugitive Slave Law had become a part of the Compromise of 1850. The new law for the more effective reclamation of fugitive slaves was the only real concession made to the South, and Southerners would take a wait-and-see attitude as to whether it would be enforced. Not wishing to see the Union torn asunder, perhaps the majority of Southerners hoped the new law would be enforced, but many remained skeptical. The initial reaction in the North to passage of the law did little to assuage the fear in the South that the effort at compromise had been a waste of time. As public meetings were called in city after city proclaiming the hostility of certain groups in the North to the law, and their opposition to its enforcement, there was reason to fear for the fate of the Union. This fear was felt also in the North, and while the abolitionists screamed their defiance and worked to make the Fugitive Slave Law a dead letter, the more sober-minded citizens in the North would realize the danger to the Union and would reluctantly acquiesce in the law's enforcement. Acquiescence to enforcement of the law would take time, however. Meanwhile, great effort was expended in an attempt to show the nation that the Fugitive Slave Law conflicted with the Constitution of the United States and should not be enforced. The constitutionality of the Fugitive Slave Law was debated by some of the most prominent lawyers in the country.

60. Ibid.

Chapter II

The Constitutionality
of the
Fugitive Slave Law
of 1850

The avowed purpose of the Fugitive Slave Law of 1850 was to render the Act of 1793 "adequate to the constitutional guarantees" which had been given to the owners of fugitive slaves.[1] This was to be done by providing more effective execution of the law and by freeing the slaveholder, or his agent, from molestation. That Southerners felt justified in demanding such guarantees can hardly be denied. For abolitionist elements and antislavery advocates in the North, however, the question remained: Did the desire to placate the South, and the dangers inherent in the crisis which faced the nation in the summer of 1850, cause Congress to exceed the limitations placed upon it by the Constitution? Among certain groups in the North, answers to this question, pro and con, were highly significant in the development of public opinion toward the compromise measures in general and the Fugitive Slave Law in particular.

1. Allen Johnson, "The Constitutionality of the Fugitive Slave Acts," *Yale Law Journal* 31 (November 1921): 169–70 (hereafter cited as Johnson, "The Constitutionality of the Fugitive Slave Acts").

In the decade of the 1850's, the Fugitive Slave Law was supported vigorously in some quarters, but the number of writers who questioned its constitutional validity is impressive. Many of the detractors were abolitionists; most of them were honorable, law-abiding men; several were highly respected in the legal profession. Horace Mann, for example, feeling himself perfectly competent to interpret the Constitution, made no apology whatever for doubting the handiwork of Congress with regard to fugitive slaves. He wrote: "The constitutionality or unconstitutionality of the Fugitive Slave law is not a question to be determined solely by any single and simple provision of the fundamental law. . . . It presents a case where commentators and expounders must appeal to precedents and analogies, and to general principles respecting the nature of government and the object of all law. It is therefore a question of construction and interpretation." Mann objected to the law for reclaiming fugitive slaves as a transition from freedom under the Constitution to "despotism"; it was a law which warred against the "fundamental principles of human liberty." [2] Charles Sumner, an avowed abolitionist and one of the most active opponents of the Fugitive Slave Law, wrote a letter to a public meeting in Syracuse, New York to celebrate the "Jerry Rescue." Regretting that he could not attend the meeting, he said: "You know well how much I sympathize with you personally, and also how much I detest the Fugitive Slave Bill, as a flagrant violation of the Constitution, and of the most cherished human rights, —shocking to Christian sentiments, insulting to humanity, and impudent in all its pretentions." [3] Gerrit Smith, merchant, lawyer, philanthropist, and abolitionist from New York, found seventeen reasons for holding that the law was unconstitutional. [4]

Arguments propounded for the unconstitutionality of the Fugitive Slave Law may be summarized as follows: (1) the fugitive slave clause of the Constitution was a compact between the states which

2. Horace Mann, *Slavery: Letters and Speeches* (Boston: B. B. Mussey & Co., 1853), p. 400, 470 (hereafter cited as Mann, *Letters and Speeches*).

3. Charles Sumner, *The Works of Charles Sumner*, 15 vols. (Boston: Lee and Shepard, 1875–83), 5:271 (hereafter cited as Sumner, *Works*). The fugitive slave "Jerry" was rescued from the custody of federal officers in October, 1851. The event was celebrated each year thereafter in Syracuse until the Civil War.

4. Gerrit Smith, *Abstract of the Argument on the Fugitive Slave Law . . . On the Trial of Henry W. Allen, U.S. Deputy Marshal, for Kidnapping* (Syracuse: Daily Journal, 1852) (hereafter cited as Smith, *Abstract of the Argument*).

conferred upon Congress no power to enact laws for the reclamation of fugitive slaves; (2) as interpreted by the United States Supreme Court, the constitutional clause provided for the absolute delivery of the runaway slave to his owner rather than the limited right of removal for which the law seemed to provide; (3) the rendition of fugitive slaves was not comparable to the extradition of fugitive criminals, thus the summary proceedings before a fugitive slave tribunal were final rather than preliminary; (4) fugitive slave commissioners rendered judgments which could properly be rendered only by United States judges exercising national judicial power; (5) the commissioners were compensated by fees rather than by fixed salaries; (6) fugitive slaves were denied the right of trial by jury; (7) fugitives did not have the right to confront and cross-examine witnesses and could therefore be remanded to slavery on *ex parte* testimony; and (8) the summary nature of the proceedings before the fugitive slave tribunal impaired the right of habeas corpus.

The authority for the Fugitive Slave Law rested upon a single clause in the Constitution: "No person held to service or labor in one State, under the laws thereof, escaping into another, shall, in consequence of any law or regulation therein, be discharged from such service or labor; but shall be delivered up on claim of the party, to whom such service or labor may be due." [5] In the period before the Civil War, there was no essential agreement as to the force of this particular clause and the imperatives that it placed upon Congress. On the one hand, important men in the legal profession believed that the Union could not have been created unless this clause were included in the Constitution. Justice Joseph Story asserted that "it cannot be doubted that it constituted a fundamental article, without the adoption of which the Union could not have been formed." [6] The venerable Justice William Tilghman, of Pennsylvania, declared that "our southern brethern would not have consented to become parties to a constitution . . . unless their property in slaves had been secured." [7] Also in accord with this view was Justice John McLean. He stated that "The clause was deemed so important that, as a matter

5. U.S. *Constitution*, Art. 4, Sec. 2, clause 3.
6. Prigg v. Pennsylvania, 16 Peters 611 (1842). See also Story, *Commentaries on the Constitution*, 2:549.
7. Commonwealth *ex rel*. Wright v. Deacon, 5 Sergeant & Rawle (Pa.) 63 (1819).

of history, we know the Constitution could not have been adopted without it." [8] On the other hand, many students of the Constitution claimed that no such importance was attached to this clause of the Constitution by those who framed it.

After a careful study of the records of the federal convention, Charles Sumner found no evidence that this provision "was regarded with any peculiar interest." "It was introduced tardily, at a late period of the convention, and adopted with very little and most casual discussion." [9] Professor Allen Johnson's investigation supported Sumner's view.[10] The argument that the fugitive slave clause was not considered by the Founding Fathers as one of the fundamental compromises of the Constitution seems to be valid. If this conclusion is correct, the averment that the fugitive slave clause was a compact between the states, which looked to the states rather than to the national government for a remedy, has considerable weight.

Although the compact theory was held valid by many abolitionists,[11] it had currency in other quarters as well. Daniel Webster, no abolitionist, admitted in his March 7 speech that until the Prigg case he had believed that the fugitive slave clause limited the states without conferring power on Congress. Pessimistic about the utility of federal power in recapturing runaway slaves, the fiery Robert Barnwell Rhett of South Carolina seems to have been converted to the compact theory.[12] He called for "reinvesting in the states responsibility for the recovery of fugitive slaves." [13] Despite the compact theory's plausibility, it had been rejected by the Supreme Court.[14] Its

8. Giltner v. Gorham, 10 Federal Cases 425 (1848).

9. Sumner, *Works*, 3:136.

10. Johnson, "The Constitutionality of the Fugitive Slave Acts," p. 161. See also Max Farrand, ed., *Records of the Federal Convention of 1787*, rev. ed., 4 vols. (New Haven: Yale University Press, 1911–37), 2:446, 3:325.

11. *Trial of Henry W. Allen, U.S. Deputy Marshal, for Kidnapping, with Arguments of Counsel & Charge of Justice Marvin, on the Constitutionality of the Fugitive Slave Law, in the Supreme Court of New York* (Syracuse: Daily Journal Office, 1852), p. 29; William Hosmer, *The Higher Law, in its Relation to Civil Government: With Particular Reference to Slavery, and the Fugitive Slave Law* (Auburn, N.Y.: Derby and Miller, 1852), p. 158. See also the remarks of Charles Sumner in *Congressional Globe*, 32nd Cong., 1st sess., Appendix, p. 1113.

12. *Congressional Globe*, 32nd Cong., 1st sess., Appendix, p. 274; 2nd sess., Appendix, p. 317.

13. Yanuck, "The Fugitive Slave Law," p. 255.

14. Prigg v. Pennsylvania, 16 Peters 539 (1842).

dismissal cut the ground from under one of the major arguments against the validity of the Fugitive Slave Law. In addition, the state courts of Massachusetts, New York, Pennsylvania, Ohio, Indiana, and Illinois concurred with this view.[15] It was necessary to concede, therefore, that the Constitution did confer upon Congress the power to legislate upon the subject of fugitive slaves.

Some of the law's opponents were willing to assume that Congress had the power to enact legislation implementing the provision in the Constitution with regard to fugitive slaves, but the opponents insisted that there was in the language of that clause an absolute test for the validity of the Fugitive Slave Law. For example, Thomas H. Talbot, of the Cumberland Bar in Maine, asserted that if the law did not perform what the clause required, it was unconstitutional.[16] What then did the fugitive slave clause explicitly require?

In the opinion of Justice James Moore Wayne, the clause contained four substantive declarations: (1) the fugitive must owe service or labor under the law of the state from which he escaped; (2) he must have fled from that state; (3) he could not be discharged from service by any law passed in the state to which he had fled; and (4) the states were obliged to "deliver up" the fugitive on claim "to whom such service or labor" was due.[17] "This clause," said the Court, "contemplated the existence of a positive unqualified right on the part of the owner of a slave which no State law could in any way regulate, control or restrain. Consequently the owner of a slave had the same right to seize and repossess him in another State, as the local laws of his own State conferred upon him. . . ."[18] The Constitution guaranteed to the slaveholder the right to "an unqualified

15. Commonwealth v. Aves, 18 Pickering (Mass.) 193 (1836); Glen v. Hodges, 9 Johnson (N.Y.) 67 (1817); Jack v. Martin, 14 Wendell (N.Y.) 507 (1836); Wright v. Deacon, 5 Sergeant & Rawle (Pa.) 62 (1819); Caufmann v. Oliver, 10 Barr (Pa.) 514 (1848); State v. Hoppess, 2 Western Law Journal (Ohio) 289 (1845); Graves v. State, 1 Carter (Ind.) 368 (1849); *In re* Thornton, 11 Illinois 332 (1849).

16. Thomas H. Talbot, *The Constitutional Provision Respecting Fugitives from Service or Labor, and the Act of Congress, of September 18, 1850* (Boston: Bela Marsh, 1852), p. 9 (hereafter cited as Talbot, *Constitutional Provision*).

17. Prigg v. Pennsylvania, 16 Peters 638 (1842).

18. *The Constitution of the United States of America: Analysis and Interpretation Annotations of Cases Decided by the Supreme Court of the United States to June 30, 1952* (Washington: Government Printing Office, 1953), p. 696 (hereafter cited as *Annotated Constitution*, 1952).

delivery of his property . . . a right so unlimited, that, wherever he may find the slave, he may seize him, and carry him away as a piece of property." [19] According to the Court's ruling then, once the fugitive slave was captured the master's possession and property in the reclaimed slave was perfect and needed no further act on his part and no further judicial proceedings to complete it. A delivery of property, as property, to its owner, absolutely and without restriction, is what the Constitution required.

An act of Congress for the reclamation of fugitive slaves must provide for the master the same remedy established by the Constitution. The legal status of the fugitive before the tribunal must correspond to the constitutional requirement, and the decision of the commissioner must show that the claimant and captive "mutually sustain the relation named therein." After this relationship had been established, no court or law could limit its legal force. It could not be required of a man, said Talbot, "to establish by process of judicial investigation a certain right, and then refuse to allow him the full legal scope of that right." [20]

The Fugitive Slave Law of 1850 did not seem to provide for the unlimited right of delivery which would restore to the owner his property in the fugitive's labor and control over his person. In Talbot's opinion, it attempted to substitute the limited right of removal back to the state from which the slave had escaped. The fourth, sixth, ninth, and tenth sections of the law provided for the removal of fugitive slaves. These sections seemed to require the claimant to transport his repossessed slave back to the state from which he had fled.

During the trial of Thomas Sims, a fugitive slave arrested in Boston in April, 1851, Robert Rantoul, Jr., counsel for the defendant, asked Commissioner George Ticknor Curtis whether any restrictions were placed upon the claimant after the fugitive was remanded to his custody. Curtis replied: "Certainly! In the sixth section he has authority 'to take and remove such fugitive person back to the State

---

19. Talbot, *Constitutional Provision*, p. 30. The Supreme Court of New York held the right of the master to be "absolute and complete, not conditional and limited." Jack v. Martin, 12 Wendell 321 (1836). The right of the slaveholder to pursue and retake his slave was fully acknowledged by the United States Supreme Court in Jones v. Van Zandt, 5 Howard 215 (1847).

20. Talbot, *Constitutional Provision*, p. 21.

or Territory whence he or she may have escaped,' and no where else." [21] In place of the mere right of removal at the master's own expense, the ninth section provided for removal at the expense of the national government. Delivery of the fugitive was made only after he had been returned to the state from which he had escaped. Only the tenth section provided for the delivery of the escaped slave to the claimant in the state where he was found. This right was also restricted, however, for the certificate authorized the claimant merely to "transport such person to the State or Territory from which he escaped. . . ." [22] The certificate gave no authority to treat the fugitive as a slave. It was "merely a warrant," said Judge Peleg Sprague of the United States District Court in Massachusetts, "to remove him to a certain place. . . . [It] is simply an authority for transportation, nothing more." [23]

Charles G. Loring disagreed. In the Sims trial, Loring argued that if the slaveholder held his escaped slave under his constitutional right, he could take the slave wherever he pleased and sell him wherever he pleased. But, under the ruling of Commissioner Curtis, if a slave escaped from Georgia and was found in Illinois, and if the slaveholder had, in the interim, moved to Missouri, the master would not remove the slave to Missouri but must transport him back to Georgia. [24]

Holding that the Fugitive Slave Law provided only for the limited right of removal, Judge Sprague and Commissioner Curtis indicated how far the requirements of the act varied from the constitutional clause upon which the law was based. If the Constitution required an absolute delivery of the person owing service or labor to the claimant as his property, and if the statute provided a different right, that difference rendered the constitutionality of the law doubtful.

An important issue in the popular debates on the constitutionality of the Fugitive Slave Law was whether the proceedings before a

21. *Trial of Thomas Sims, an Issue of Personal Liberty, on the Claim of James Potter, of Georgia, against Him, as an alleged Fugitive From Service. Arguments of Robert Rantoul, Jr. and Charles G. Loring, With the Decision of George T. Curtis* . . . (Boston: Wm. S. Damrell & Co., 1851), p. 6 (hereafter cited as *Trial of Thomas Sims*).
22. *U.S. Statutes at Large*, 9:465.
23. *Fugitive Slave Law*, 30 Federal Cases 1015 (1851); 1 Sprague 593 (1851).
24. *Trial of Thomas Sims*, p. 31.

fugitive slave tribunal were preliminary or final in their effect upon the fugitive. To sustain the constitutionality of the law, Commissioner Curtis was forced to argue that the statute provided merely for a preliminary hearing in a judicial inquiry designed to accomplish the extradition of the fugitive to the place from which he had escaped. To give force to the argument, he said the "rendition of fugitives from service . . . is an act analogous to the rendition of fugitives from justice, and . . . the two cases, so far as the powers and duties of the general government are concerned, are of the same general character, and may appropriately be provided for by the same general means." [25] In support of this contention, Curtis cited the opinion of Justice Story. In the Prigg decision, Story had asserted:

It is obvious that these provisions for the arrest and removal of fugitives of both classes contemplates summary ministerial proceedings, and not the ordinary course of judicial investigations. . . . In cases of suspected crimes, the guilt or innocence of the party is to be made out at his trial; and not upon the preliminary inquiry, whether he shall be delivered up. All that would seem in such cases to be necessary, is, that there should be *prima facie* evidence before the executive authority to satisfy its judgment, that there is probable cause to believe the party guilty. . . . And in the cases of fugitive slaves, there would seem to be the same necessity of requiring only *prima facie* proofs of ownership, without putting the party to a formal assertion of his rights by a suit at the common law. [26]

That the two clauses of the Constitution were similar seemed "hardly to admit of rational doubt," declared Professor Johnson. "The fact that the Act of 1793 couples the return of the fugitive from service or labor with the extradition of fugitives from justice," said Johnson, "certainly points to this conclusion." [27] Furthermore, it was pointed out that many of the men who sat in the Constitutional Convention of 1787 were members of the Congress that passed the Act of 1793. The evidence supporting the argument of Commissioner Curtis is strong. In the Constitution, however, the language governing rendition and extradition is noticeably different.

By virtue of the clause providing for extradition, no person could be removed from one state to another unless three conditions were

25. Ibid.
26. Story, *Commentaries on the Constitution*, 2:546–47.
27. Johnson, The Constitutionality of the Fugitive Slave Acts," p. 171.

met: (1) that the fugitive be charged in one state with "treason, felony, or other crime"; [28] (2) that he had fled from justice; and (3) that a demand be made for his delivery to the state "having jurisdiction of the crime." [29]

The extradition of criminals was effected by the specific intervention of state governors. The governor of a state was not authorized to make a demand for the surrender of a fugitive unless it was in the course of regular judicial proceedings.[30] In 1861, the Supreme Court of the United States held that the "duty to surrender is not absolute and unqualified." If the laws of the state to which he had fled were "put in force against the fugitive, and he is imprisoned there, the demands of those laws may first be satisfied" before the duty of obedience to the requisition would arise. With regard to the Act of 1793, moreover, the Court held that the obligation to surrender the fugitive from justice was "merely declaratory of a moral duty. . . ." The national government had no power "to impose on a State officer, as such, any duty whatever, and compel him to perform it." [31] Consequently, a federal court could not issue a writ of mandamus to compel the governor of one state to surrender a fugitive criminal to another.[32]

Horace Mann offered a compelling argument demonstrating the differences between the extradition of fugitives from justice and the rendition of fugitives from service or labor. "When the fugitive from justice is *claimed*," said Mann, "he is claimed by a *state* for having violated its law, and when he is delivered up he is delivered into the custody of the law." Custody of the prisoner was transferred from an officer of the law in one state to an officer of the law from another

28. "For the purpose of determining who is a fugitive from justice, the words 'treason, felony or other crime' embrace every act forbidden and made punishable by a law of a State, including misdemeanors." *Annotated Constitution, 1952,* pp. 694–95.

29. *The Constitution of the United States of America Annotations of Cases Decided by the Supreme Court of the United States to January 1, 1938* (Washington: Government Printing Office, 1938), p. 535 (hereafter cited as *Annotated Constitution, 1938*).

30. Ibid.

31. Kentucky v. Dennison, 24 Howard 66, 107 (1861).

32. The loophole exposed by this decision was not closed until 1934 when Congress enacted a law making it unlawful for any person to flee from one state to another in order to avoid prosecution for certain specified offenses. *U.S. Statutes at Large,* 48:782.

state. The alleged criminal was surrendered "not to avoid a trial, but to have one." "The original indictment or charge, the arrest in a foreign state, and the delivery and transportation to the place of trial," were, declared Mann, "separate parts of one legal proceeding." During this whole process, the prisoner had the "solemn pledge of the government, that if not found guilty on the prosecution *then pending*," he would be discharged.[33] The alleged fugitive slave, however, was claimed not by a state, but by an individual. He was delivered into private hands, not into the custody of the law where his rights might be determined by the due process of law. The party, into whose hands the fugitive bondsman was delivered, was not neutral but was an individual who was interested in depriving the alleged slave of all his rights and claimed for himself the right to be "judge, jury, and all the witnesses. . . ."[34] To the extent that antislavery advocates were concerned, there were significant differences between the two clauses in the Constitution, both as to the character of the parties to be delivered under each and the purpose for which they were to be delivered. The proceedings for extradition of fugitives from justice were admittedly preliminary, and the service rendered by the commissioner was definitely ministerial. The delivery of a Negro into the hands of his alleged owner by a federal commissioner seemed to be final.

All persons delivered under authority of certificates issued by fugitive slave commissioners were "thrown upon the procedures of the slave states for relief."[35] The question of whether a Negro arrested under the Fugitive Slave Law was freeman or bondsman had to be determined in the state from which he allegedly had escaped. If a slave claimed that he were free, every state in the South granted the right to a trial to test the allegation. Amendments to the Fugitive

---

33. Mann, *Letters and Speeches*, p. 443. See also the opinion of Judge Whiton of the Wisconsin Supreme Court in *In re* Booth, 3 Wisconsin 70 (1854).

34. Mann, *Letters and Speeches*, pp. 443–44. See also the discussion of the subject in Yanuck, "The Fugitive Slave ·Law," pp. 214–17. John Codman Hurd, in *The Law of Freedom and Bondage in the United States*, 2 vols. (Boston: Little, Brown and Company, 1858, 1862), 2:681, asserted that the argument upholding the parallel between the rendition of fugitive slaves and the extradition of fugitive criminals "fails, because it cannot be shown that the Governors of the States, in making the required ·delivery, have exercised power derived from the United States." (Hereafter cited as Hurd, *Law of Freedom and Bondage*).

35. Yanuck, "The Fugitive Slave Law," p. 215.

Slave Bill had been rejected largely because "the rights of the fugitive were believed to be amply safeguarded in the slaveholding states. . . ." [36] However, few people in the North felt this was a practical remedy. Many slaves did sue for their freedom, some of them successfully, but few cases involved a Negro who had been returned as a fugitive slave.[37]

As long as the courts of the South were open to test an allegation of freedom by a slave, Commissioner Curtis held that the action of the fugitive slave tribunal was not final. The process to reclaim a fugitive slave was "clearly designed to be ministerial and to secure only the limited right of removal. . . ." Congress had obviously intended to leave to state government the right to adjudicate the status of Negroes "upon the faith that it will do justice to its own subject." [38] All that was required of the commissioner was a preliminary examination of a fact for authorizing removal of the alleged fugitive to the jurisdiction most proper for the final adjudication of that fact.[39]

Other prominent authorities argued that the Fugitive Slave Law provided for no such trial. Neither explicitly nor implicitly was such a purpose stated in the Constitution, the statute, or the papers in any particular case. The fugitive slave, Talbot insisted, was "not claimed for trial; nor examined for trial; nor certified for trial; nor sent back for trial. . . . He is claimed as a slave; arrested as a slave, certified as a slave, and removed as a slave." [40] Moreover, Attorney General John J. Crittenden maintained that Congress had "constituted a tribunal with exclusive jurisdiction, to determine summarily, and without appeal," who were fugitives from service or labor under the Constitution. "The judgment of every tribunal of exclusive jurisdiction where no appeal lies, is, of necessity," said Crittenden, "conclusive upon every other tribunal. And, therefore, the judgment

36. Johnson, "The Constitutionality of the Fugitive Slave Acts," p. 180.

37. Yanuck, "The Fugitive Slave Law," p. 9. The unlikelihood of such suits was increased by the fact that slave owners usually sold their runaway slaves as soon as they were recovered. This is one of the reasons Senator John M. Mason objected to jury trials for fugitive slaves even in the slave states. *Congressional Globe*, 31st Cong., 1st sess., Appendix, p. 1611.

38. *Trial of Thomas Sims*, p. 43.

39. See the argument of the counsel for the state of Maryland in Prigg v. Pennsylvania, 16 Peters 563 (1842).

40. Talbot, *Constitutional Provision*, p. 126.

of the tribunal created by this act is conclusive upon all tribunals." [41] Finally, in the considered opinion of Judge Whiton, "the alleged fugitive from labor is taken back to the state from which he is said to have escaped, as a person who has been proved and adjudged to be a slave. . . ." [42]

Although Commissioner Curtis insisted that his function was strictly ministerial, he did not, and could not, know the court to which he was ministering. It was illogical, said Talbot, to deny that the decision of the fugitive slave commissioner was final in a hearing "preliminary to no other proceeding, ancillary to no other trial, ministerial to no other court. . . ." [43] It did seem logical to argue that the proceeding terminated in a final judgment. [44] Opinion on this point was obviously divided, but the question was never resolved by the United States Supreme Court.

If the decision of the commissioner was the final determination of a fact which could not be appealed to a higher court, it appeared to opponents of the Fugitive Slave Law that the power exercised by the commissioners was a part of the national judicial power. Whenever a fugitive was delivered into the custody of a claimant by a fugitive slave commissioner, from that moment the prisoner became the slave of the claimant by force of a judicial decision. In fugitive slave cases, it was pointed out that there was a "distinct subject for adjudication," there were "distinct parties," and the matter was before a tribunal of "competent jurisdiction." [45] "I admit fully," said Commissioner Curtis, "that a claim for a fugitive slave is a case between parties, arising under the Constitution of the United States, and therefore that it belongs to the judicial power of the United

---

41. Benjamin F. Hall et al., eds., *Official Opinions of the Attorneys General of the United States,* . . . *1791–1948,* 40 vols. (Washington: Robert Farnham, 1852–1949), 5:258–59 (hereafter cited as *Opinions of the Attorneys General*). See also *Ex parte* Van Orden, 28 Federal Cases 1060 (1854) in which the court held that there was no appeal from the commissioner's decision to issue the certificate. Even the judge issuing the certificate could not re-arrest the slave thereafter.

42. *In re* Booth, 3 Wisconsin 71 (1854).

43. Talbot, *Constitutional Provision,* p. 52.

44. Hurd, *Law of Freedom and Bondage,* 2:697.

45. *Trial of Thomas Sims,* p. 40. See also *In re* Booth, 3 Wisconsin 44 (1854) and Lysander Spooner, *Ae Defence for Fugitive Slaves, Against the Acts of Congress of February 12, 1793, and September 18, 1850* (Boston: Bela Marsh, 1850), p. 7 (hereafter cited as Spooner, *A Defence for Slaves*).

States." [46] This was in line with Attorney General Crittenden's opinion in which he had held that the fugitive slave commissioners had "judicial power, and jurisdiction to hear, examine, and decide the case." The certificate granted to the owner was "to be regarded as the act and judgment of a judicial tribunal having competent jurisdiction." [47] Furthermore, the fourth section of the Fugitive Slave Law of 1850 gave the commissioners concurrent jurisdiction with the judges of the circuit and district courts of the United States.

With regard to judicial power, two questions were asked by the law's opponents. First, was the power exercised by the fugitive slave commissioners actually a part of the national judicial power? Secondly, did Congress have the authority, under the Constitution, to bestow judicial power upon petty commissioners? If the commissioner's decision were an exercise of judicial power, and it could be shown that Congress had no authority to confer upon these officers such power, then the constitutionality of the Fugitive Slave Law was questionable.

Under the Constitution, the judicial power extends "to all Cases, in Law and Equity, arising under this Constitution, the Laws of the United States, and Treaties made, or which shall be made, under their Authority. . . ." [48] As later defined by Justice Samuel Freeman Miller, judicial power was "the power of a court to decide and pronounce a judgment and carry it into effect between persons and parties who bring a case before it for decision." [49] The Supreme Court of the United States had ruled repeatedly that cases at common law were understood to be suits in which legal rights were to be ascertained and determined. Cases in equity were interpreted as suits in which relief was sought according to "the principle applied by the English Court of Chancery before 1789, as they have been developed in the Federal courts." [50] A case in law or equity consisted, therefore,

46. *Trial of Thomas Sims*, p. 40.

47. Hall, *Opinions of the Attorneys General*, 5:237.

48. U.S. *Constitution*, Art. 3, Sec. 2, clause 1.

49. John Bouvier, *Bouvier's Law Dictionary*, 2 vols., rev. ed., ed. Francis Rawle (Boston: The Boston Book Co., 1897), 2:42. Furthermore, "The term judicial power," said Justice William Johnson, "conveys the idea both of exercising the faculty of judging and of applying physical force to give effect to a decision" (p. 49).

50. *The Constitution of the United States of America (Annotated), Annotations of Cases Decided by the Supreme Court of the United States to Janu-*

"of the right of one party, as well as of the other, and may truly be said to arise under the Constitution or a law of the United States, whenever its correct decision depends on the construction of either." [51] Because the term "suit" was often used interchangeably with "case" or "controversy," the Court understood the term "to apply to any proceeding in a court of justice which the law affords him." [52]

To further clarify the argument that the decision of the commissioner was an exercise of the national judicial power, and therefore unconstitutional, it will be necessary to review the process established by the Fugitive Slave Law of 1850 for reclaiming fugitive slaves. There were three parts to the proceeding. First, an owner whose slave had run away could go to any court of record in his own state and make out an affidavit to that effect. Included in the affidavit were three points: (1) that the fugitive had escaped; (2) that he owed service or labor to the claimant; and (3) a general description of the fugitive. Secondly, if the judge was satisfied that the first two points were established, a record was made of the proceeding, and an official transcript was given to the claimant. The transcript, when presented to a commissioner in the district where the fugitive might be found, was to be received as conclusive evidence that the slave described in the transcript had escaped and owed service or labor to the claimant. The third and remaining part of the process was to be decided by the commissioner, namely, the identity of the alleged fugitive. If the commissioner was convinced that the person brought before him was the slave described in the transcript, he was required to issue a certificate authorizing removal of the fugitive to the state from which he had escaped.

On the basis of the evidence presented, the effect of the commissioner's decision was to remand the fugitive to slavery. A claim was made by a slaveholder for his property in an alleged fugitive from service or labor who would normally claim that he was free.[53] All the

---

ary 1, 1938 (Washington: Government Printing Office, 1952), p. 452 (hereafter cited as *Annotated Constitution, 1938*). See also Robinson v. Campbell, 3 Wheaton 212 (1818); Parsons v. Bedford, 3 Peters 433 (1830); Bennett v. Butterworth, 11 Howard 669 (1850).

51. *Annotated Constitution*, 1938, p. 453.

52. Weston v. Charleston, 2 Peters 449 (1829). See also Cohens v. Virginia, 6 Wheaton 379 (1821).

53. The Supreme Court ruled that "a claim is a challenge by a man of the

elements of a case or controversy arising under the Constitution were present. No court, either federal or state, could review the decision. The responsibility of the commissioner was to decide between the right of property on the one hand and the right of liberty on the other. However, it must be pointed out that, if the captive fugitive was actually the slave described in the transcript, the decision of the commissioner to issue a certificate of removal to the claimant did not remand the fugitive to slavery. Escape into the free states in no way affected the status of a slave in the state where he was held in bondage. But, if the commissioner issued a certificate to remove a Negro who was not the person described in the transcript, the possibility of delivering a free man to perpetual bondage was not as remote as the law's supporters believed. That fugitive slave commissioners did indeed exercise part of the national judicial power seemed perfectly clear to adversaries of the Fugitive Slave Law.[54]

Assuming the commissioners did exercise such judicial power, the question arose as to whether Congress had authority to confer any portion of the judicial power upon mere ministerial officers. In the opinion of the law's assailants, fugitive slave commissioners did not in any way conform to the requirements of the Constitution as regards judicial power. They were not appointed by the president; they did not hold their offices during "good behavior only"; and they did not receive "fixed salaries" for their services.[55] Fugitive slave commissioners were appointed by judges of the circuit courts, their tenure was temporary, and they received fees as compensation in place of fixed salaries. Judges may be removed from the federal courts only by impeachment. The commissioners could be removed without notice by the court that appointed them.[56]

Some of the law's supporters argued that the office of the commis-

---

propriety or ownership of a thing which he has not in his possession, but which is wrongfully detained from him." Prigg v. Pennsylvania, 16 Peters 614 (1842).

54. Spooner, *A Defence for Slaves*, p. 9; *In re* Booth, 3 Wisconsin 68 (1854).

55. "From a negative standpoint," said the United States Supreme Court, "a power is not judicial . . . unless it is exercised by judges appointed by the President with the consent of the Senate, holding their offices during good behavior, and receiving fixed salaries." *In re* Kaine, 14 Howard 120 (1853).

56. In Benner v. Porter, the court held that judges appointed to administer the inferior courts must "possess the constitutional tenure of office before they can become invested with any portion of the judicial power of the Union. There is no exception to this rule in the Constitution." 9 Howard 235 (1850).

sioner was analogous only to that of a judicial officer.[57] The commissioner of patents and masters in chancery were cited as examples of officers who exercised judicial power in a similar capacity. The commissioner of patents did make decisions involving judgments of law and fact. Masters in chancery assisted the courts in preparing questions for decision, but in neither case were their judgments final. The decisions of both were subject to appeal in the federal courts. Fugitive slave commissioners, on the other hand, made judgments of fact and law which were subject to no appeal whatever. Their decisions were final and conclusive upon all other tribunals. To that extent, the analogy between fugitive slave commissioners and other officers who acted in a ministerial or quasi-judicial capacity did not stand up.

In 1921, Professor Allen Johnson suggested that the recent course of legal thought provided a basis for reconsidering the validity of the fugitive slave laws. He maintained that the development of a body of administrative law which had evolved over the preceding fifty years threw "a new light on the determinations left to the commissioners by the Act of 1850." Citing cases where property rights were determined without a jury trial, Johnson concluded that "measured by the developments of a half-century and interpreted in the light of reason, these acts [the fugitive slave laws] must be declared constitutional in every particular."[58] Such relativism is questionable. As pointed out by Julius Yanuck, Johnson's position becomes less tenable when it is asked whether the "Framers of the Constitution or the legalists of the antebellum period would have considered as in conformity with the Constitution all the powers exercised by administrative tribunals in our own day."[59] What the courts have determined as judicially true today has only an incidental relationship to what the courts held to be judicially true in the decade of the 1850's.

One of the most striking points against the constitutionality of the Act of 1850 was the fact that fugitive slave commissioners collected

57. See the opinions of Commissioner Curtis in *Trial of Thomas Sims*, p. 41 and James Augustus Door, *Objections to the Act of Congress, Commonly Called the Fugitive Slave Law Answered, In a Letter to Hon. Washington Hunt* (New York: n.p., 1850), p. 11 (hereafter cited as Dorr, *Objections to the Fugitive Slave Law*).
58. Johnson, "The Constitutionality of the Fugitive Slave Acts," p. 181–82.
59. Yanuck, "The Fugitive Slave Law," pp. 217–18.

fees rather than fixed salaries for their services. That the commissioners did not receive fixed salaries further removed them from the right to exercise the judicial power of the United States. If a fugitive slave was remanded to the custody of his claimant, the commissioner received a ten-dollar fee; he received only five dollars if the fugitive was freed. Lysander Spooner maintained that it was not the double fee for "deciding against liberty" that made the law unconstitutional; it was simply the fact that the commissioners received fees.[60] More recently Julius Yanuck argued that it was the variable fee that ruled against the constitutionality of the law. "To give a commissioner a pecuniary interest in the outcome of a hearing over which he presides and in which he must make findings of fact," wrote Yanuck, ". . . is a violation of the due process clause of the Fifth Amendment." [61] This argument was never settled by the Supreme Court.

Arguments that the Fugitive Slave Law of 1850 contravened the Bill of Rights were the most frequently heard and had the most significant effect on public opinion in the North. In these arguments, it was maintained that the alleged fugitive slave was denied trial by jury, but the prisoner was deprived of the right to confront witnesses and was precluded from cross-examining them by making conclusive a record taken in another court, and that the fugitive slave's right to habeas corpus was impaired by the summary nature of the proceedings before the fugitive slave tribunal.

To Southerners, these arguments were preposterous. It was not intended that the Bill of Rights should protect the rights of slaves, and citizens of the slave states were incensed by suggestions that they should be. In the slave states, there was a legal presumption that all Negroes were slaves; the burden rested with the Negro to prove that he was free. Under the law of slavery, the slave was considered as a chattel, a thing, a piece of property, not a person. As a chattel, the slave had no standing before the federal courts and could not be a party to a suit.

The legal presumption in the North was that all men residing in the free states were free. Many Northerners admitted that escape into

---

60. Spooner, *A Defence for Slaves*, p. 11.
61. Yanuck, "The Fugitive Slave Law," p. 222. Justice John McLean asserted that the additional work involved in issuing the certificate of removal justified the differential fee (p. 59, note 2).

the free states did not change the legal status of the slave under the laws of the state from which he had fled. In order to protect their citizens, however, law in the free states provided that any person claimed as a slave had the right legally to challenge the claim in a court of law. If it was proved that the captive Negro was a slave, the obligation to deliver him to the custody of the claimant was granted, but, no person residing in the free states could be deprived of his freedom without due process of law.

With great heat and considerable logic, the Fugitive Slave Law of 1850 was denounced in the North for not providing trial by jury in fugitive slave cases. It was pointed out that the Seventh Amendment provided for such a trial "In suits at common law, where the value in controversy shall exceed twenty dollars. . . ." The Supreme Court's definition of a suit as "the prosecution or pursuit of some claim, demand or request," apparently included the "claim" referred to in the fugitive slave clause of the Constitution.[62] The Court interpreted the Seventh Amendment "to embrace all suits which are not of equity and admiralty jurisdiction, whatever may be the peculiar form they may assume to settle legal rights." [63] The claim for the delivery of a fugitive slave was made against another person. Since it was made as a right of property "capable of being recognized and asserted before a Court of Justice, between parties adverse to each other," it constituted a controversy between parties arising under the Constitution.[64] Horace Mann averred that the trial by jury was not "determined by the character of the litigants, but by the nature of the action." [65] With regard to the constitutional guarantees in the Bill of Rights, John C. Hurd asserted: "In the eye of the national law, the status of the man who has escaped from a State wherein he was a slave, and who is in a non-slaveholding State, must be given by the law of the latter until the contrary is proved; and how it shall be proved, is to be determined by these guarantees of the Constitution which apply to him as well as to those not liable to such claim." [66] Under the Seventh Amendment, however, whether a fugitive from service was consid-

---

62. Cohens v. Virginia, 6 Wheaton 264 (1821).
63. Parsons v. Bedford, 3 Peters 337 (1830).
64. Talbot, *Constitutional Provision*, pp. 77–78; Prigg v. Pennsylvania, 16 Peters 618 (1842).
65. Mann, *Letters and Speeches*, p. 423.
66. Hurd, *Law of Freedom and Bondage*, 2:727.

ered as a person or property was of minimal concern. If deemed mere property, the slave's value was clearly more than twenty dollars; if a slave were considered as a person, the value of his freedom was incalculable.[67]

Denying that the alleged fugitive from service was guaranteed a jury trial, supporters of the law maintained that the proceedings before the fugitive slave tribunal were preliminary, and the action of the commissioner was ministerial. They contended that trial by jury and available under the laws of the state from which the alleged bondsman had fled.[68] Opponents of the Act of 1850 were quick to make clear, however, that the law contemplated no such trial. The courts of the slave states were indeed open to test the allegation of freedom of an alleged fugitive slave; but, his chances of ever obtaining a review were negligible, and if he did manage to get a trial, it would have been a wholly new proceeding. Thus, assailants of the law concluded that, whatever object the law might have had, its effect was to deliver a person into slavery without a trial before a jury of his peers.[69]

That the Fugitive Slave Law was designed to protect the rights of slaveholders rather than the personal liberty of Negroes living in the free states was a well-known fact. For Congress to ignore the possibility that a free person could be delivered into slavery, having had no opportunity to present evidence in defense of his freedom in the state where he was arrested, was a highly questionable attitude in a society that took pride in its democratic traditions, its concepts of justice, and the dignity of man. Yet, one of the most unjust provisions of the law authorized fugitive slave cases to be decided on *ex parte* testimony.

The Act of 1850 provided for evidence by depositions, or other "satisfactory testimony," to be taken in courts of record in the state in which the fugitive was held to service. This evidence, taken *ex parte*, was to be held as competent proof, before the judge or commissioner in the state where the fugitive was found, that the fugitive did owe service or labor to the claimant and had fled the

---

67. Lee v. Lee, 8 Peters 44 (1834).
68. *Trial of Thomas Sims*, pp. 42–43; Spooner, *A Defence for Slaves*, p. 6; Dorr, *Objections to the Fugitive Slave Law*, pp. 6–10.
69. *In re* Booth, 3 Wisconsin 68 (1854).

state. By this process, the status of the person described in the record was changed instantly under the laws of a state where the legal presumption was against his freedom. The commissioner's responsibility was to determine whether the identity of the prisoner corresponded to the description included in the record. The alleged slave was prohibited from testifying in his own behalf and was precluded from cross-examining the witnesses. A free person could therefore be arrested as a runaway slave and brought before the tribunal, and, if the commissioner decided in favor of the claimant, a certificate was issued which was tantamount to a delivery into bondage.

As pointed out by Horace Mann, if the person arrested was prejudged a slave, there was no need for a trial at all, but if the Negro were *prima facie* a free man, he was "entitled to the most perfect mode of trial." "A man who has a presumptive right to his liberty," said Mann, "has a perfect right to all the means to prove it." [70] This was not to say that the guarantees granted in the Fifth Amendment, which declares that no person shall be "deprived of life, liberty, or property, without due process of law," applied in these cases. It was held generally that the Fifth Amendment limited "the juridical action of the national Government only in the exercise of punitive authority . . . and not in the judicial establishment of rights and obligations existing in relations between private persons." [71] However, if the alleged fugitive was a party to a suit in a case arising under the Constitution before a federal tribunal, his right to present evidence in support of his claim to freedom was equal to the right of the claimant to prove the contrary. The claim imposed no obligation on the commissioner to decide for or against the freedom of the alleged fugitive. The real question to be decided was: Who shall be delivered up, a slave or a free man? That such a grave judgment could be made by a ministerial officer, who was paid a double fee for an affirmative decision, seemed to be a radical miscarriage of justice, if not a deprivation of liberty without due process of law.

The final objection to the Act of 1850 to be considered in this study is the averment that the summary proceedings before the fugitive slave tribunal seemed to impair the fugitive's right of habeas corpus. The law guaranteed to the claimant that the certificate issued

70. Mann, *Letters and Speeches*, p. 419.
71. Hurd, *Law of Freedom and Bondage*, 2:738.

by the commissioner "shall be conclusive of the right of the person or persons in whose favor granted, to remove such fugitive to the State or Territory from which he escaped, and shall prevent all molestation of such person or persons by any process issued by any court, judge, magistrate, or other person whomsoever." [72] This seemed to be in violation of the clause in the Constitution which declares that the "privilege of the writ of habeas corpus shall not be suspended, unless when, in cases of rebellion or invasion, the public safety may require it." [73] Hurd suggested that judicial opinion on this point could be pronounced only in some case in which a court had been asked to grant the writ for the purpose of inquiring whether the judge or commissioner had decided properly in granting the certificate, and in which there was no question of the jurisdiction of such judge or commissioner." No such cases seem to have occurred. In the fugitive slave cases reported, habeas corpus was issued only to try the question of jurisdiction.[74]

Attorney General Crittenden laid down the rule generally followed by the courts. In Crittenden's opinion, "The condition of one in custody as a fugitive slave is, under this law, so far as respects the writ of habeas corpus, precisely the same as that of all other prisoners under the laws of the United States. The 'privilege' of that writ remains alike to all of them but to be judged of—granted or refused —discharged or enforced—by the proper tribunal, according to the circumstances of the case, and as the commitment and detention may appear to be legal or illegal." [75] The attorney general argued that habeas corpus should not be issued if it appeared that the decision to deliver up the fugitive was made by the proper judicial authority. He held that the fugitive slave tribunal had exclusive jurisdiction and its decision was "conclusive upon every other tribunal." If the certificate was shown to the court at the time the fugitive applied for the writ, the writ should not issue; if the certificate were shown on the return, the writ must be discharged.[76] This opinion did not preclude

72. *U.S. Statutes at Large*, 9:463–64, sec. 6.
73. Spooner, *A Defence for Slaves*, pp. 25–26.
74. Hurd, *Law of Freedom and Bondage*, 2:745–46.
75. Hall, *Opinions of the Attorneys General*, 5:258.
76. Ibid., p. 259. See also Justice Grier's reasoning in *Ex parte* Jenkins, 13 Federal Cases 969 (1855), and Justice McLean's opinion in *Ex parte* Robinson, 20 Federal Cases 445 (1853).

the assertion that, if the action of the commissioner was ministerial, Congress could not except custody under it from judicial inquiry by habeas corpus. If his action was judicial, then it was an unconstitutional exercise of the judicial power.[77]

It was assumed by the state courts that they had power to issue a writ of habeas corpus in those cases where persons were in the custody of federal officers and to discharge such persons from federal custody.[78] As regards the custody of persons in cases involving conflict of jurisdiction, the Supreme Court ruled that a writ of habeas corpus issued by a state judge could not effect the custody of a person held under authority of the Act of 1850. The states did have authority to inquire into the cause of commitment, but, if it was shown that the person was held under authority of the United States, the state court could proceed no further.[79]

It is unfortunate that the Supreme Court waited until 1859 to rule on the constitutionality of the Act of 1850 and then only to stem the tide of states rightism in Wisconsin. The burden of the arguments presented by the Court in *Ableman* v. *Booth* were directed at the attempt by the state of Wisconsin to nullify federal law. With regard to the constitutionality of the statute, the Court's decision was *obiter dictum*. The Court declared without argument that "the act of Congress commonly called the fugitive slave law is, in all of its provisions, fully authorized by the Constitution of the United States." [80]

There is little doubt that the great initial ground swell of public opinion favorable to the compromise measures was gradually reduced by the almost constant harping by the abolitionist press against the constitutionality of the Fugitive Slave Law. Many law-abiding citizens residing in the free states were apparently convinced that the law was void; hence, they did not feel compelled to aid in the enforcement of an enactment which was not the supreme law of the land. To some of the advocates of extreme abolitionism and the "higher law" doctrine, the constitutional validity of the Fugitive Slave Law was irrelevant. Regardless of the consequences, such men as Gerrit Smith and Theodore Parker were absolutely opposed to the

77. Hurd, *Law of Freedom and Bondage*, 2:747.
78. Yanuck, "The Fugitive Slave Law," p. 156.
79. Ableman v. Booth, 21 Howard 506 (1859).
80. Ibid., p. 524.

rendition of fugitive slaves.[81] Before passage of the Kansas-Nebraska Act of 1854, the evidence indicates that the bulk of the population residing in the free states was not measurably influenced by the massive attack on the constitutionality of the Fugitive Slave Law.

81. Smith, *Abstract of the Argument;* Theodore Parker, *The Trial of Theodore Parker* (Boston: Theodore Parker, 1855), p. 184.

Chapter III

The Fugitive Slave Law

and

Public Opinion,

1850–1854

Effective law enforcement requires a favorable climate of public opinion. In the period between the adoption of the Compromise of 1850 and the passage of the Kansas-Nebraska Act in 1854, public opinion in the northern states toward the Fugitive Slave Law was ambiguous, but on the whole it was acquiescent. A group composed mostly of abolitionists was opposed to the law under any circumstances and vowed to resist its enforcement in any way it could. There were those who were sympathetic toward southern complaints of noncompliance with the provisions of the Fugitive Slave Law and actively supported its enforcement. By far the greater majority, however, although unsympathetic with the harsh provisions of the law, was willing to acquiesce in the return of fugitive slaves to their owners in order to maintain good relations with the South and to prevent disruption of the Union.

The reaction against passage of the Fugitive Slave Law was generally confined to certain minority groups and geographical areas in the northern states. The reaction was swift and in some cases violent. Several prominent men openly condemned the law. Many of the critics were preachers. Typical of the more extreme statements against the law for the reclamation of fugitive slaves were those made by Theodore Parker, William Cullen Bryant, Ralph Waldo Emerson, and Charles Beecher. In Boston, Theodore Parker, crying out against the wickedness of the law, said that he would do all in his power "to rescue any fugitive slave from the hands of any officer who attempts to return him to bondage. . . . What is a fine of a thousand dollars, and gaoling for six months, to the liberty of a man?" [1] William Cullen Bryant argued that, since there was obviously little chance that the law would be repealed, the people of the free states must make the law "odious, and prevent it from being enforced." [2] Ralph Waldo Emerson said this was a law which "everyone of you will break on the earliest occasion—a law which no man can obey, or abet the obeying, without loss of self-respect and forfeiture of the name of a gentleman." [3] One of the more colorful condemnations of the law was made by the Reverend Charles Beecher. In a sermon published in New York, he said: "This law . . . is an unexampled climax of sin. It is the monster iniquity of the present age, and it will stand forever on the page of history, as the vilest monument of infamy of the nineteenth century. Russia knows nothing like it. Hungary blesses God that *she* never suffered from anything worse than Haynau and nations afar off pause awhile from their worship of blocks of wood and stone, to ask what will those Christians do next." [4]

1. John Weiss, *Life and Correspondence of Theodore Parker, Minister of the Twenty-Eighth Congregational Society, Boston*, 2 vols. (New York: Appleton, 1864), 1:102 (hereafter cited as Weiss, *Theodore Parker*).
2. Rhodes, *History of the United States*, 1:269.
3. Ibid., p. 207.
4. Charles Beecher, *The Duty of Disobedience to Wicked Laws. A Sermon on the Fugitive Slave Law* (New York: J. A. Gray, 1851), p. 13. For examples of other opposition sermons on the Fugitive Slave Law, see Rufus Wheelwright Clark, *Conscience and Law. A Discourse Preached in the North Church, Portsmouth, New Hampshire, on Fast Day, April 3, 1851* (Boston: Tappan & Whittemore, 1851); William Carter, *A Reply to Hon. William Thomas' Exposition and Defence of the Fugitive Slave Law* (Winchester, Illinois: Western Unionist, 1851); Nelson Cobleigh, *Iniquity Abounding. A Sermon: Preached at the Laurel Street Methodist Episcopal Church, On Fast Day, April 10, 1851* (Worcester: J. Burrill & Co., 1851); Nathaniel Colver, *The Fugitive Slave Bill; Or, God's Laws Paramount to the Laws of Men. A Sermon, Preached on*

Opposition to passage of the Fugitive Slave Law was not limited to a few individuals. Much of the early opposition was manifested by large groups of concerned citizens who drew up resolutions denouncing the enactment as unconstitutional and an abomination upon the American people. In Massachusetts, people gathered in Boston, Springfield, Worcester, Lowell, and Lynn to express their outraged feelings against such a cruel law. On October 14, 1850, several hundred people met at Faneuil Hall in Boston. The meeting was presided over by Charles Francis Adams. Moved by the eloquence of Wendell Phillips and Theodore Parker, the people resolved that the Fugitive Slave Law was against "the golden rule of Christianity," contradictory to the Declaration of Independence, and inconsistent with the Constitution. At the same meeting, a vigilance committee of fifty members was organized to protect the Negroes of the city from the new danger.[5] At Springfield, inflammatory speeches were made against the law, and fugitive slaves in the town were encouraged to arm themselves against slave catchers.[6] With shouts of approval, a resolution was adopted at the meeting in Lowell to call back three fugitive slaves who had fled to Canada "with a pledge that they shall be protected from arrest. . . ."[7] On November 6, another meeting was held at Faneuil Hall. The crowd was treated to an oration by Charles Sumner. He said that he did not believe the Fugitive Slave Law would be enforced in Massachusetts; but, he continued, "I counsel no violence. There is another power, stronger than any individual arm, which I invoke; I mean that irresistible public opinion inspired by love of God and man which, without violence or noise, gently as the operations of nature, makes and unmakes laws.

Sunday, October 20, 1850, By Rev. Nathaniel Colver, Pastor of the Tremont St. Church (Boston: J. M. Hewes & Co., 1850); William Henry Furness, *Christian Duty. Three Discourses Delivered in the First Congregational Unitarian Church of Philadelphia May 28th, June 4th and June 11th, 1854 . . . With Reference to the Recent Execution of the Fugitive Slave Law in Boston and New York* (Philadelphia: Merrihew & Thompson, 1854); Nathaniel Hall, *The Limits of Civil Obedience. A Sermon Preached in the First Church, Dorchester, January 12, 1851* (Boston: W. Crosby and H. P. Nichols, 1851); William De Loss Love, *Obedience to Rulers—The Duty and Its Limitations. A Discourse Delivered December 22d, 1850, On the Two Hundred and Thirtieth Anniversary of the Landing of the Pilgrims* (New Haven: Storer & Stone, 1851).

5. Rhodes, *History of the United States*, 1:197.
6. *New York Tribune*, October 5, 1850.
7. Ibid.

Let this public opinion be felt in its might, and the Fugitive Slave bill will become everywhere among us a dead letter." [8] In the Old Bay State, the rural areas and the small towns continued to manifest strong opposition to enforcement of the Fugitive Slave Law.

On October 5, 1850, an estimated five hundred persons met in the city hall at Syracuse, New York and resolved that every citizen should be made "fully aware" of the law's "diabolical spirit and cruel ingenuity" and that they should prepare themselves "to oppose legally all attempts to enforce it." An editorial in the *New York Tribune* stated that the northern people regarded the law as having no constitutional or moral force and commented further that "They will not indeed resist it by violence, they will not rise in arms to nullify it, they will not bluster about dissolving the Union on account of it; but they will burden its execution with all possible legal difficulties, and they will help slaves to escape all the more zealously." [9] The members of the Antislavery Society of Rochester, in resolutions introduced by William Lloyd Garrison, proclaimed that they cared not whether the law was "constitutional or unconstitutional, essential or not to the preservation of the Union. . . ." It is "enough for us," they said, "that it is the cruel mockery of all justice, inhuman, anti-Christian, diabolical, and trampling it under our feet. . . . we declare that as far as in us lies it never shall be executed." [10] Abolitionism and strong opposition to enforcement of the Fugitive Slave Law in New York was confined, for the most part, to the western part of the state.

Pennsylvania had its abolitionist element also. Having gathered to condemn the Fugitive Slave Law, citizens of Lawrence County resolved that the law "is abhorrent to our sense of right and justice" and furthermore that they would use every means under the Constitution to "make war upon that infamous law. . . ." [11] At the National Free Soil Convention in Pittsburgh, Frederick Douglass, addressing a sympathetic audience, said that the only way to make the Fugitive Slave Law a dead letter was "to make a dozen or more dead kidnappers. . . . A half dozen or more dead kidnappers carried down

8. Wilson, *Rise and Fall of Slave Power*, 2:308.
9. *New York Tribune*, October 12, 1850; April 5, 1851.
10. *New York Weekly Tribune*, May 22, 1852.
11. Ibid., July 12, 1851.

South would cool the ardor of Southern gentlemen, and keep their rapacity in check." [12]

Righteous indignation was expressed at several public gatherings in northern Ohio. The Western Reserve was well known as a center of abolitionist sentiment. Perhaps more than any other area in the state its citizens were the most defiant of the Fugitive Slave Law. The region was the center of activity for such militant abolitionists as Charles Bachus Storrs, Elizur Wright, Joshua Reed Giddings, and Benjamin Wade.[13] As regards antislavery sentiment in the Western Reserve, James Ford Rhodes said: ". . . with the exception of the Plymouth, it was the most liberty-loving district in the country." [14] A typical example of antislavery rhetoric in northern Ohio was the resolution adopted at an indignation meeting in Salem. It was there resolved that in "speaking of such a law, the severest language of denunciation becomes tame and insignificant, the most ponderous epithets lighter than the faintest breath of summer air, the most startling expressions of moral indignation but a faint and inaudible whisper; and nothing short of thunder and lightnings, and storms and earthquakes—the dread vocabulary of God himself—could give fit utterance to the righteous displeasure with which every virtuous and manly soul must feel in view of a law whose turpitude is measureless and unfathomable." [15] Of all the northern states, Wisconsin seems to have been the most consistent in its opposition to the Fugitive Slave Law. The entire congressional delegation from Wisconsin had voted against the bill. Among the party leadership, Whigs, Free Soilers and bolting Democrats were "particularly outspoken against it." [16] Antislavery feeling in Wisconsin was intense, and many meetings were called to denounce the Fugitive Slave Law.

12. Philip S. Foner, *The Life and Writings of Frederick Douglass,* 4 vols. (New York: International Publishers, 1950–55), 2:207 (hereafter cited as Foner, *Frederick Douglass*).

13. Mary Land, "John Brown's Ohio Environment," *Ohio State Archaeological and Historical Quarterly,* 57 (January 1948): 25 (hereafter cited as Land, "John Brown").

14. Rhodes, *History of the United States,* 1:117.

15. *New York Weekly Tribune,* July 12, 1851.

16. Vroman Mason, "The Fugitive Slave Law in Wisconsin, With Reference to Nullification Sentiment," *State Historical Society of Wisconsin Proceedings* (1895), p. 119 (hereafter cited as Mason, "The Fugitive Slave Law in Wisconsin").

Citizens from all over the state repeatedly urged that every effort be exerted to secure the law's repeal. The long, drawn-out jurisdictional battle between the federal courts and the Wisconsin Supreme Court in the Booth case did little to assuage feelings in the state against the law.

In northern Illinois, like northern Ohio, abolitionist sentiment was particularly strong. Vehement opposition to the Fugitive Slave Law was manifested in Chicago. Indeed, the *Shawneetown Gazette* reported: "We of the South do not regard Chicago as belonging to Illinois. It is as perfect a sink hole of abolitionism as Boston. . . ." The *Cairo Weekly Times* said "They are undoubtedly the most riotous people in this State. . . . Say nigger and slave-catcher in the same breath and they are up in arms." [17] According to Charles Wesley Mann, there were about five hundred Negroes living in Chicago in 1850. Before the end of the month in which the Fugitive Slave Law was passed, a Negro police system had been organized in the city. Its purpose was to patrol the streets at night and provide an early warning system against surprise by slave catchers. On October 21, 1850, the City Council of Chicago expressed its displeasure by adopting a series of resolutions which nullified the Fugitive Slave Law and released city officials from obedience to it. [18] Extensive excitement had been aroused in the city by passage of the act. However, on October 23, at a mass meeting attended by an estimated five thousand people, Senator Stephen Arnold Douglas assuaged much of the agitation by speaking boldly in favor of the Fugitive Slave Law and against the action of the city council. In fact, he was so persuasive that the crowd adopted a set of resolutions which repudiated the action of the council. [19] The council met the following evening to take further action upon its resolutions. At this meeting one of the councilmen moved that the resolutions adopted on October

17. Verna Cooley, "Illinois and the Underground Railroad to Canada," *Transactions of the Illinois State Historical Society*, no. 23 (1917): 81 (hereafter cited as Cooley, "Illinois and the Underground Railroad"), quoting the *Shawneetown* (Illinois) *Gazette* and the *Cairo Weekly Times*.

18. Charles Wesley Mann, *The Chicago Common Council and the Fugitive Slave Law of 1850. An Address Read Before the Chicago Historical Society at A Special Meeting Held January 29, 1903* (Chicago: n.p., 1903), pp. 68–69, 70–71 (hereafter cited as Mann, *Chicago Common Council*).

19. Stephen Arnold Douglas, *Speech of Hon. Stephen A. Douglas on the "Measures of Adjustment." Delivered in the City Hall, Chicago, October 23, 1850* (Washington: Gideon & Co., 1851), pp. 31–32.

21 be expunged from the records of the council, but his motion was tabled for further action at a later date. On November 29, the council met again, and the motion to expunge from the records the previous series of resolutions was debated, but the motion was lost by a vote of nine to three.[20] Despite the efforts of Senator Douglas, the officials of the city council remained friendly to fugitive slaves and opposed to enforcement of the Fugitive Slave Law.

Although the Fugitive Slave Law was denounced bitterly at public meetings, in editorial comment, and by individuals of great prominence, it must be emphasized that the most extreme opposition was manifested by abolitionists and the strongest of the antislavery organizations. The power of these groups to mold public opinion was greater than their numbers would indicate and cannot be written off as of no consequence. In general, however, their influence before 1854 was confined to those areas which had a history of strong abolitionist sentiment. Abolitionism was not generally popular in the early 1850's. Few people in the North desired disruption of the Union, but disunion seemed imminent unless the slavery controversy was quieted. A great majority of the northern population, therefore, did not actively oppose this unpopular law. In fact, northern responses to the Fugitive Slave Law were, on the whole, in accord with the responses to the other compromise measures.

In New England, with certain exceptions, enthusiasm for the compromise was high. Following adoption of the compromise measures, a national salute of one hundred guns was fired "as a testimonial of joy" on the part of Boston's citizens of both political parties.[21] "Of the humanity of this law," said the *Boston Evening Gazette*, "there is but one opinion . . . but of the upholding of the law on the part of those commissioned to carry it into execution, . . . there can be no faltering. . . ."[22] Even in Faneuil Hall it was resolved by conservatives that the compromise "ought to be carried out in good faith" and that "every form of resistance to the execution of a law, except legal process, is subversive and tends to anarchy." Under the leadership of Franklin Pierce, an avowed supporter of the compromise, citizens at a public meeting in Concord, New Hampshire passed

20. Mann, *Chicago Common Council,* pp. 85–86.
21. *Boston Advertiser,* September 21, 1850.
22. *Boston Liberator,* October 25, 1850, quoting the *Boston Evening Gazette.*

resolutions favoring the recent adjustment and opposing the doctrine of the higher law.[23] In Vermont, traditionally strong in antislavery sentiment, excitement over passage of the Fugitive Slave Law soon abated. "Unpalatable as it may be to us here in Vermont where human freedom is so much cherished," said the editor of the *Vermont Journal*, "the letter and purport of the Constitution in this regard are plain and imperative. As citizens of a free and enlightened Government we have no escape from obedience to the authority of this high instrument." At a Union meeting in Bath, Maine, it was resolved that "resistance to a le[g]al enforcement" of the Fugitive Slave Law "would call for the indignant frown of every true friend of this country. . . ."[24]

In New York City, at a Union meeting called by prominent merchants, ten thousand names were signed to a resolution cordially approving the compromise measures. The Fugitive Slave Law's constitutionality was defended, and a promise was made to support its enforcement.[25] The staid and conservative *Journal of Commerce* commented that it could see "no severity in the new law" beyond what was necessary to fulfill the constitutional obligations to return fugitive slaves.[26] Inspired by the meeting in New York, a similar meeting in Philadelphia, attended by some six or seven thousand people, passed resolutions much like those adopted in New York.[27]

The general responses to passage of the Fugitive Slave Law in other northern states were similar. An enthusiastic crowd at Dayton, Ohio, addressed by Clement L. Vallandigham, declared in a series of resolutions that the compromise measures were the "best attainable" and that "the Union, the Constitution, and the laws must and shall be maintained." According to a correspondent from Cincinnati, there was minimal sympathy in his city for further antislavery agitation, and in New Lisbon one citizen contended that while the population of his state as a whole was opposed to slavery, "not one in twenty," was an abolitionist. "All right thinking men," he said, "agree that under the compromises of the constitution, owners of fugitive slaves are entitled to some efficient remedy. . . ." Further-

23. *Boston Advertiser*, November 26, 20, 1850.
24. *National Intelligencer*, November 16, December 21, 1850.
25. *New York Tribune*, October 30, 1850.
26. *Boston Liberator*, October 25, 1850.
27. *New York Tribune*, November 21, 1850.

more, no one "who understands these compromises, and does not erroneously rest upon what he claims as a higher law in regard to slavery, can think otherwise." In his inaugural address, Ohio's Governor Reuben Wood vindicated the constitutionality of the Fugitive Slave Law and warned the people of his state "to beware how they followed the lead of the people of South Carolina in resisting laws of Congress." [28]

Although majority opinion in northern Ohio was avidly antislavery, the prevailing opinion in the southern part of the state was quiescent on the slavery question. Of the pioneers who settled in southern Ohio, David Carl Schilling has estimated that nearly one half were of southern birth. Most of these settlers came from Virginia, Kentucky, Maryland, and North Carolina. As late as 1845, says Schilling, nearly 20 per cent of the state legislators had been born in the South.[29] As might be expected, there was little sympathy for fugitive slaves in southern Ohio. Just across the Ohio River, the *Maysville Eagle* noted that, after the escape of some thirty slaves into Ohio, those who pursued and captured the fugitives "were not obstructed or ill-treated in any way. . . . though their business was perfectly known . . . they experienced from the people of Ohio . . . every aid they desired, many citizens of that State volunteering their personal Assistance and extending the kindest hospitality. . . ." [30] The high percentage of first and second generation Southerners helps explain the considerable support in that area for enforcement of the Fugitive Slave Law.

Opinion in Michigan was also divided. Excitement was extensive in the state after passage of the Fugitive Slave Law. Antislavery organizations, such as the Friends of Freedom with Sherman Booth as one of its vice presidents, remonstrated against the law and called for its repeal. In Detroit, money was raised by subscription to free arrested fugitive slaves.[31] On the other hand, Senator Lewis Cass, justifying the position he had taken in support of the compromise

28. *National Intelligencer*, October 26, December 17, 1850.
29. David Carl Schilling, "Relation of Southern Ohio to the South During the Decade Preceding the Civil War," *Quarterly Publication of the Historical and Philosophical Society of Ohio* 8 (January 1913): 4.
30. *National Intelligencer*, November 4, 1852, quoting the *Maysville* (Kentucky) *Eagle*.
31. *New York Weekly Tribune*, October 19, 1850.

measures, said: "I would have voted for twenty Fugitive Slave Laws, if I had believed the safety of the Union depended upon my doing so." Now that the law was in force, it would "never be touched, or altered, or shaken, or repealed," by any vote of his.[32] In the state elections of 1851, the Whig and Democratic parties wrote planks into their platforms in support of the compromise measures.[33]

In Indiana, newspaper comments and other studies of the problem indicate that general support was given to the compromise measures. Union sentiment was strong in the state, and public opinion was opposed to anything that might offend neighboring slave states.[34] At a meeting in Greencastle, a small town southwest of Indianapolis, it was resolved: "That we regard all sectional agitation as prejudicial to our interest and dangerous to the perpetuation of our free institutions and we therefore appeal to the north as well as the south to respect the prejudices and feelings of each and cultivate feelings of mutual forbearance and respect for the interests and rights of all, and to abandon now and forever all agitation and interference by the citizens of one state with the institutions of another and hush the cry of disunion and the thought of treason from the halls of congress." [35] The response of the grand jury of the United States District Court in its report on November 30, 1850 was indicative of public opinion in Indiana toward enforcement of the Fugitive Slave Law. The grand jury, comprising a cross section of opinion within the state, unanimously reported:

No overt act has been brought to the notice of the jury upon which to frame an indictment for violations of this law; but acts of public notoriety, breathing strong disaffection and opposition to this law, have been committed by small bodies of persons in some several instances within this district. It is, however, well ascertained that the number of those expressing their opposition to enforcement of the law amounts to a very small portion of our population, and it is believed that no serious

32. *Congressional Globe,* 32nd Cong., 1st sess., Appendix, p. 1124.
33. *New York Weekly Tribune,* September 20, October 4, 1851.
34. Emma Lou Thornbrough, *The Negro in Indiana: A Study of a Minority* (Indianapolis: Indiana Historical Bureau, 1957), p. 109 (hereafter cited as Thornbrough, *Negro in Indiana*).
35. Charles H. Money, "The Fugitive Slave Law of 1850 in Indiana," *Indiana Magazine of History* 17 (June 1921): 169–70, quoting *Indianapolis Indiana State Sentinel,* October 12, 1850 (hereafter cited as Money, "Fugitive Slave Law in Indiana").

resistance of this . . . law of Congress is to be apprehended in this State.[36]

Public sentiment toward the Negro often provided the basis upon which attitudes about enforcement of the Fugitive Slave Law were established. Racial prejudice toward the Negro in Indiana was illustrated by an editorial in the *Indiana State Sentinel.* Commenting upon an Ohio meeting of Negroes who had gathered to protest the law, the editor wrote: "They speak in trumpet tones to the orderly, law abiding people of the country. They tell the danger of encouraging a distinct and inferior race to abide in the same community with us. They are aliens and enemies, and some mode should be adopted to rid the country of their presence, or at least of preventing their further emigration." [37] Such anti-Negro feeling found fruition in the adoption of the new state constitution in 1851. Article 8 prohibited the settlement of Negroes and mulattoes in the state. In the constitutional convention, this article was passed by a vote of 93 to 40. Most of the opponents of the measure were Quakers who represented counties in the eastern and northern part of the state. Article 8 was submitted for ratification separately from the rest of the document and was adopted by a vote larger than that given the main body of the constitution. As a result of increasing hostility of the white population to the settlement of Negroes in Indiana, the adoption of the exclusionary clause in the new constitution, and enforcement of the Fugitive Slave Law, the Negro population in the southern counties declined absolutely between 1850 and 1860.[38]

A majority of the people in Illinois were favorably disposed toward the compromise measures in general and the Fugitive Slave Law in particular. On November 22, 1850, the *Alton Telegraph & Democrat Review* accurately expressed Whig opinion when the editor observed: "The law in question may be defective—it may, in some particulars, be unnecessarily severe—its operation may, in a few cases, prove oppressive, perhaps, unjust. But, so long as it shall remain on the Statute book of the United States, it will be the

36. *National Intelligencer,* December 12, 1850.

37. Thornbrough, *Negro in Indiana,* p. 65, note 15, quoting the *Indianapolis Indiana Sentinel,* November 2, 1850.

38. Ibid., pp. 53–54, 67–68. See also Wilson, *Rise and Fall of the Slave Power,* 2:183–86.

bounden duty of every good citizen to interpose no resistance to its execution." [39] In a letter published in Washington repudiating a request for the "unconditional repeal" of the Fugitive Slave Law, Congressman Thomas Langrell Harris from Petersburg stated the Democratic position. He said: "My opinion is, that the law referred to is a law necessary to enforce one of the guaranties of the Constitution of the United States. I am opposed to its repeal, because its repeal would be unjust; and in the present state of public feeling at the South, it would be followed by evil discord, in its most disastrous form." [40] Indiana was not the only northern state that manifested hostility to the Negro. Negrophobia abounded in Illinois.

With the exception of the area north and west of the Illinois River, the state of Illinois was enemy territory for fugitive slaves. Generally speaking, in the southern half of the state, any person who openly aided a fugitive slave felt quickly the brunt of public animosity. For many years prior to 1850, the Negro had been denied suffrage. He had no standing in the courts, could not act as a witness against a white person, could not serve in the state militia, and, in order to reside in the state, he had to present a certificate of freedom to a county court and give a one-thousand-dollar bond to insure that he would not become a charge of the county. No Negro could hold public office; educational and employment opportunities were extremely limited. To prevent the Negro from achieving social status, intermarriage with the white population was forbidden, and custom forbade him to own property.[41] Therefore, freedom for the Negro was extremely illusive in Illinois unless he were fortunate enough to settle in the northern part of the state.

Although the people of Chicago were generally opposed to the Fugitive Slave Law and sympathetic to the plight of fugitive slaves, even there the Negro found that he could not escape intolerance and bigotry. In her *History of Chicago*, Bessie Louise Pierce noted that

39. Ameda Ruth King, "The Last Years of the Whig Party in Illinois, 1847–1856," *Transactions of the Illinois State Historical Society*, no. 32 (1925): 138, quoting the *Alton Telegraph and Democrat Review*.

40. Thomas Langrell Harris, *Letter of Hon. Thos. L. Harris, of Illinois, Upon the Repeal of the Fugitive Slave Law* (Washington: J. T. Towers, 1851), pp. 3–4.

41. N. Dwight Harris, *The History of Negro Servitude in Illinois and of the Slavery Agitation in That State 1719–1864* (Chicago: A. C. McClurg & Co., 1904), pp. 226–36 (hereafter cited as Harris, *Negro Servitude in Illinois*).

"these protectors of fugitive slaves raised no objection to the exclusion of Negro testimony against a white person," nor did they seem to see "inconsistencies in providing a separate section in the theaters for Negroes, and in segregating the races in the common schools." [42]

By 1847, public opinion was strongly in favor of prohibiting free Negroes from settling in the state. At the constitutional convention, which convened in June, a petition was read requesting action against the immigration of free Negroes into Illinois. Such a proposal was introduced and passed, and the question was then submitted to a popular referendum. Article 14 of the new constitution, which empowered the legislature to enact laws which would "prohibit free persons of color from immigrating to and settling in" the state of Illinois, was adopted by a large and significant majority. The new constitution, which also denied the Negro suffrage and the right to serve in the state militia, was approved by an even larger majority. [43]

A bill to exclude Negroes from settling in the state was introduced in the Illinois legislature in January, 1853. The so-called Black Law passed both houses without difficulty and was signed by the governor on February 12, 1853. [44] This law provided that anyone aiding a Negro to settle in Illinois was subject to a fine of not less than one hundred dollars, nor more than five hundred dollars and imprisonment in the county jail for not more than one year. If any Negro remained in the state for ten days with the intention of continuing his residence, he was subject to a fine of fifty dollars. If the fine was not paid, the Negro was arrested, advertised for ten days by the sheriff, and sold to the person who would pay the fine and costs for the shortest term of service. During this period, the Negro could be worked at his benefactor's pleasure. To encourage compliance with the law, prosecuting witnesses received half the fine. [45] Although the

42. Bessie Louise Pierce, *A History of Chicago*, 3 vols. (New York: Alfred A. Knopf, 1959), 2:12 (hereafter cited as Pierce, *History of Chicago*).

43. Harris, *Negro Servitude in Illinois*, p. 235. The majority for Article 14 was 28,182, for the new constitution, 44,028.

44. Mason McCloud Fishback, "Illinois Legislation on Slavery and Free Negroes, 1818–1865," *Transactions of the Illinois State Historical Society*, no. 9 (1904): 428–29 (hereafter cited as Fishback, "Illinois Legislation on Slavery").

45. *General Laws of the State of Illinois Passed By the Eighteenth General Assembly, Convened January 3, 1853* (Springfield: Lamphier & Walker, 1853), pp. 57–60. See also Harris, *Negro Servitude in Illinois*, pp. 235–36, and Fishback, "Illinois Legislation on Slavery," pp. 428–29.

law was obviously designed to keep Negroes from settling in the state, it had the further purpose of conciliating southern critics. The law provided owners of slaves with the right to "claim, prove, and take back" their fugitive slaves simply by paying the costs.[46] Fugitive slaves in Illinois could therefore be returned to their owners without recourse to federal jurisdiction and the Fugitive Slave Law.

Another indication of public opinion in the North toward enforcement of the Fugitive Slave Law was the effect of the law's passage on Negroes residing in the northern states. With the enactment of the law, the freedom of every Negro living in the free states was placed in jeopardy. Negro communities, particularly along the northern border, reacted accordingly. Nearly all the waiters in the Pittsburgh hotels fled to Canada. An estimated 300 had taken flight from the city only ten days after the president signed the bill. "They went in large bodies, armed with pistols and bowie knives, determined to die rather than be captured." Negro churches along the Canadian border lost many of their members. Of the 114 members of the Negro Baptist church in Rochester, New York, all but 2 left the country rather than face the possibility of being captured and returned to slavery.[47] The pastor of the Negro Baptist church in Buffalo, New York reported that 130 of his members moved across the line into Canada because they feared arrest as fugitive slaves. The Negro Methodist church in Buffalo also reported heavy losses from its membership for the same reason.[48] Wilbur H. Siebert asserted that the number of passengers on the Underground Railroad in Vermont "reached its peak" during the months immediately following passage of the new law for reclaiming fugitive slaves.[49] In Indiana, the Negro population had a net increase of only 160 person between 1850 and 1860. "The principal reason appears to have been the alarm aroused by the Fugitive Slave Act. . . ."[50] According to Fred Landon, in his

46. Harris, *Negro Servitude in Illinois*, p. 236.

47. *Boston Liberator*, October 4, 1850; February 14, 1851. See also Foner, *Frederick Douglass* 2:545.

48. American and Foreign Anti-Slavery Society, *The Annual Report of the American and Foreign Anti-Slavery Society, Presented at New York, May 6, 1851* (New York: William Harned, 1851), p. 31 (hereafter cited as American and Foreign Anti-Slavery Society, *Annual Report* [1851]).

49. Wilbur H. Siebert, *Vermont's Anti-Slavery and Underground Railroad Record* (Columbus, Ohio: Spahr and Glenn Co., 1937), p. 101.

50. Thornbrough, *Negro in Indiana*, p. 53.

study of Negro migration to Canada, an estimated 3,000 fugitive slaves crossed the border into Canada within three months after the Fugitive Slave Law was signed.[51]

In some northern communities, the Negro population organized to prevent the capture of fugitive slaves. Negroes in Chicago were frequently successful in thwarting the efforts of slave catchers and officers of the law.[52] In Oswego, New York, the Negroes organized and armed themselves. According to William Lloyd Garrison, they were "determined to resist to the last any attempt on their liberties." [53] The *Rochester Advertiser* warned the white community that Negroes were "pricing and buying fire arms . . . with the avowed intention of using them against the ministers of the law, and our orderly citizens, should they be called upon to aid in executing the fugitive law in our city." [54]

Negroes residing in northern communities had little reason to believe that public opinion would protect them. Feeling that they could not remain safely in their homes and go about their daily tasks without fear of arrest, they either armed themselves or sought safety beyond the jurisdiction of the federal marshals.

By midsummer 1851, most of the agitation over passage of the Fugitive Slave Law had subsided, and a peaceful calm seemed to settle over the land. Despite efforts of extremists to arouse public opinion against the compromise measures, "popular sentiment," said the *Boston Courier*, "has settled down into general and hearty acquiescence in them. . . . They have come to be regarded . . . as a final settlement." [55] In a letter to Richard Henry Dana, Jr., Josiah Quincy expressed the consternation of many abolitionists. He wrote: "When the [Fugitive Slave] law was passed, I did think the moral sense of the community would not enforce it; I said that it never

51. Fred Landon, "The Negro Migration to Canada After the Passing of the Fugitive Slave Act," *Journal of Negro History* 5 (January 1920): 26–27. See also Wendell Phillips Garrison, *William Lloyd Garrison, 1805–1879: The Story of His Life Told By His Children*, 4 vols. (Boston: Houghton, Mifflin and Company, 1894), 3:302 (hereafter cited as Garrison, *William Lloyd Garrison*).

52. Cooley, "Illinois and the Underground Railroad," p. 81.

53. *Boston Liberator*, October 4, 1850.

54. Foner, *Frederick Douglass*, 2:164, quoting *Rochester Advertiser*.

55. *National Intelligencer*, July 31, 1851, quoting Richard Henry Dana, Jr. See also *New York Weekly Tribune*, July 31, 1852, and Nevins, *Ordeal of Union*, 1:399.

would be. But now I find that my fellow-citizens are not only *submissive* to, but that they are earnestly active for, its enforcement. The Boston of 1851 is not the Boston of 1775. Boston has now become a mere shop—a place for buying and selling goods; and I suppose, of *buying and selling men*." [56] There were those who admitted that the compromise measures were being complied with even in the South. William S. Pettigrew, a well-to-do planter in Tyrrell County, North Carolina, said: "The South has . . . gained a great triumph" in the Fugitive Slave Law. The "constitution, at least on the subject of the recapture of slaves, is now more faithfully complied with than it has been for many years." [57] Henry Clay, in an open letter to the citizens of New York, wrote: "Everywhere, north, south, east and west, an immense majority of the people are satisfied with, or acquiesce in, the Compromise." Opposition to the Fugitive Slave Law, he continued, "is constantly abating, and the patriotic obligations of obeying the Constitution and the laws, made directly or indirectly by the people themselves, is now almost universally recognized and admitted." [58] From Massachusetts in the East to Iowa in the West, Union sentiment was prevailing. The compromise measures were generally being accepted as a satisfactory settlement. Abolitionists came to be regarded in Boston "as agitators, wicked and wanton." [59] In Indiana, abolitionists were deplored as fanatics. Urging that the compromise measures be carried out in good faith, Governor Joseph Wright said: "Above all, Indiana recognizes the imperative duty, by every good citizen, of obedience to the laws of the land. . . . Indiana takes her stand in the ranks, not of *Southern destiny*, nor yet of NORTHERN DESTINY. She plants herself on the basis of the Constitution; and takes her stand in the ranks of

56. Garrison, *William Lloyd Garrison*, 3:328.

57. Pettigrew to James C. Johnston, February 27, 1851, Pettigrew Papers, Southern Historical Collection, University of North Carolina, Chapel Hill, N.C.

58. *New York Weekly Tribune*, October 25, 1851.

59. Charles Francis Adams, *Richard Henry Dana, A Biography*, rev. ed., 2 vols. (Boston: Houghton, Mifflin and Company, 1891), 1:165–66 (hereafter cited as Adams, *Richard Henry Dana*). See also David Herbert Donald, *Charles Sumner and the Coming of the Civil War* (New York: Alfred A. Knopf, 1960), p. 132 (hereafter cited as Donald, *Charles Sumner*), and David D. Van Tassel, "Gentlemen of Property and Standing: Compromise Sentiment in Boston in 1850," *New England Quarterly* 23 (September 1950): 317.

AMERICAN DESTINY." [60] Some of the citizens of Chicago began also to have second thoughts. If the Union was dissolved, many of the markets of which Chicagoans dreamed would be lost. Preservation of the Union "would inevitably accelerate the much desired commercial achievements." In the local elections, therefore, those who supported the compromise were most often successful.[61]

The actions of political conventions and state legislatures further attest to the acceptance of the compromise measures as a satisfactory settlement. Although the Free Soilers and Independents in their respective conventions in Wisconsin remained "irreconcilably opposed" to the Fugitive Slave Law, the Whig party, in its platform, gave conditional support to the law. Wisconsin Whigs did reserve the right to seek amendments or repeal of the unpopular statute.[62] Democratic conventions in Illinois and Michigan gave unconditional support to the Compromise. Democrats in Illinois resolved: "That the Compromise measures, passed at the last session of Congress, by the United exertions of the patriots of both parties, prove that our Government is founded in justice, and on such principles, that all honest men can cordially unite in its support and defense." [63] In the fall of 1851, perhaps the most important elections were held in New York and Pennsylvania. In both states, Democrats who had pledged their support of the compromise were victorious.[64]

The legislatures of Delaware, Illinois, Iowa, and New Hampshire in 1851, and New Jersey and Connecticut in 1852, adopted resolutions approving all the compromise measures. The resolutions of New Jersey and Connecticut were typical. The legislators in New Jersey cordially approved the compromise and declared that "every patriot, in every part of our widely extended country, has cause to rejoice in the adoption of said measures, as a triumph of constitutional rights

60. Emma Lou Thornbrough, "Indiana and Fugitive Slave Legislation," *Indiana Magazine of History* 50 (September 1954) : 223 (hereafter cited as Thornbrough, "Indiana and Fugitive Slave Legislation"), quoting *Indiana House Journal* (1850–51), pp. 40–42. See also Money, "Fugitive Slave Law in Indiana," p. 172.

61. Pierce, *History of Chicago*, 2:198–99.

62. Mason, "Fugitive Slave Law in Wisconsin," pp. 120–21. See also *New York Weekly Tribune*, September 20, October 11, 1851.

63. *New York Weekly Tribune*, October 4, 1851.

64. Nevins, *Ordeal of Union*, 1:399.

over a spirit of wild and disorganized fanaticism." [65] The Connecticut legislature resolved that the Fugitive Slave Law was "in accordance with the provisions of the constitution, containing merely provisions in detail necessary to carry into effect the provisions of that instrument. . . ." The duty to sustain enforcement of the law "by all lawful and proper means" was also proclaimed.[66]

That the tide had turned against radicalism which threatened to tear the nation asunder was perhaps best illustrated by the fate of the Free Soil party. By the end of 1851, outside New England, Ohio, and Wisconsin the party was dead. Nearly all of its newspapers in the Northwest had gone under. "When Congress met at the end of 1851," said Nevins, "it was with even fewer animosities and more kindliness than in the previous session. Since in both chambers the Democrats had an overwhelming majority to checkmate the Administration, partisan legislation was impossible." [67]

There is little doubt that majority opinion in the North favored the compromise measures and that by mid-1851 there was little sympathy for abolitionist agitation. An explanation for the decline of opposition to enforcement of the Fugitive Slave Law and the increase in Union sentiment is not difficult to find. The three major groups which exerted the greatest influence upon public opinion had done their work well. American clergymen, businessmen and industrialists in the large cities, and politicians in Congress had cooperated effectively in an effort to put down antislavery agitation. They worked diligently to convince the public that opposition to enforcement of the Fugitive Slave Law would result in disruption of the Union. Because of the efforts of these three groups, the compromise was hopefully accepted by a large majority as final settlement of the slavery crisis.

In the period before the Civil War, the clergy was one of the most influential segments of American society. For the most part, minis-

65. Herman V. Ames, ed., *State Documents on Federal Relations: The States and the United States* (Philadelphia: The Department of History, University of Pennsylvania, 1900), pp. 37, 39 (hereafter cited as Ames, *State Documents*). See also *New York Weekly Tribune*, July 12, 1851, and Robert Field Stockton, *Remarks of Hon. R. F. Stockton, of New Jersey, on the Presentation of the Legislature Upon the Compromise Measures* (Washington: Jno. T. Towers, 1852), p. 4.

66. *House Miscellaneous No. 65*, 32nd Cong., 1st sess.

67. Nevins, *Ordeal of Union*, 1:401.

ters of the gospel either supported the institution of slavery or were strangely silent on the subject. When John Quincy Adams had presented his carefully planned proposal for the gradual abolition of slavery, he expected to receive the support and cooperation of the religious community. He received little or no support. William Goodell, in *Slavery and Anti-Slavery*, indignantly observed: "Not a sermon, not a clerical letter, not an ecclesiastical resolution, not a paragraph of a religious editor, not a correspondent of a religious periodical . . . commended the measure." In Goodell's opinion, this "one fact" decided "the position of the leading churches and ministry of the North on the slave question." [68] Albert Barnes, in *The Church and Slavery*, concluded that it would have been difficult to sustain slavery in America if it had not been for the "countenance, direct and indirect, of the churches. . . ." "It cannot be doubted," he said, "that the views entertained and expressed by Christian ministers, and by others connected with the Christian Church . . . do much to sustain slave-holders in their own views." [69] According to the American and Foreign Anti-Slavery Society, an estimated 16,346 ministers of the Methodist, Presbyterian, Baptist, and Episcopal faiths owned slaves.[70] On August 18, 1851, Lewis Tappan, in a letter to the *British and Foreign Anti-Slavery Reporter*, said that "a large portion" of the American clergy acted "as if they were indifferent or hostile to the cause of freedom." Tappan's explanation for this was probably correct. With regard to ministers in the North, he said: "Their ecclesiastical connections with southern ministers, their deference to political men high in office, their aversion to the Garrison school of abolitionists, their unwillingness to offend rich parishioners in trade with the south or associated in political parties with southern men, are the reasons why many are silent, equivocal or opposed to the cause of abolition." [71]

68. William Goodell, *Slavery and Anti-Slavery; A History of the Great Struggle in Both Hemispheres; With a View of the Slavery Question in the United States* (New York: William Goodell, 1853), p. 219.

69. Albert Barnes, *The Church and Slavery* (Philadelphia: Parry & McMillan, 1857), pp. 28–30.

70. American and Foreign Anti-Slavery Society, *Annual Report* (1851), p. 56. See also American Anti-Slavery Society, *Annual Report of the American Anti-Slavery Society, By the Executive Committee, For the Year Ending May 1, 1859* (New York: Prentiss & Deland, 1860), p. 285 (hereafter cited as American Anti-Slavery Society, *Annual Report*).

71. Tappan to the editor of the *British and Foreign Anti-Slavery Reporter*,

The policies of the American Tract Society and the American Bible Society further attest to the lack of ministerial support given the anti-slavery crusade. The American Tract Society published hundreds of thousands of books and tracts condemning every sin imaginable, except slavery. As the society's most generous donor, Arthur Tappan used all his influence to correct this inconsistency. Because he was the only abolitionist officer in the society, his efforts were futile. The attempts of abolitionists to take over the executive committee of the society also failed. The society continued its conservative attitude toward slavery by electing to the executive committee only those with conservative views.[72] No more successful were the attempts of abolitionists to control policies of the American Bible Society. Despite abolitionist pressure to change the policy, the managers of this society were opposed to sending Bibles to slaves against the wishes of their owners. In 1854, Lewis Tappan, sourly recalling twenty years of failure, said that the American Bible Society was a "pro-slavery institution, managed by men who take no interest in the anti-slavery movement."[73]

"The most serious obstacle to the progress of the anti-slavery cause," said Samuel Joseph May, Unitarian minister and abolitionist of the Garrison school, "was the conduct of the clergy and churches. . . ." May believed that this was the result of submission by ministers to popular opinion within the churches. It was "only too obvious," he said, "that . . . the shepherds were driven by the sheep." Of an estimated thirty thousand ministers in the United States, May asserted that "not one in a hundred" openly condemned slavery or "lifted a finger" to protect a fugitive slave.[74]

August 18, 1851, in Annie Heloise Abel and Frank J. Klingberg, eds., *A Side-Light on Anglo-American Relations, 1839–1858* (Lancaster, Pennsylvania: The Association for the Study of Negro Life and History, Incorporated, 1927), p. 271 (hereafter cited as Abel and Klingberg, *Side-Light on Anglo-American Relations*).

72. Clifford S. Griffin, "The Abolitionists and the Benevolent Societies, 1831–1861," *Journal of Negro History* 44 (July 1959): 210.

73. Abel and Klingberg, *Side-Light on Anglo-American Relations*, pp. 342–44.

74. Samuel Joseph May, *Some Recollections of Our Antislavery Conflict* (Boston: Fields, Osgood & Co., 1869), pp. 329–32, 365 (hereafter cited as May, *Recollections of Our Antislavery Conflict*). See also Samuel Joseph May, *Speech of Rev. Samuel J. May, To the Convention of Citizens, of Onandaga County, in Syracuse, On the 14th of October, 1851, Called "To Consider the*

As regards enforcement of the Fugitive Slave Law, Wendell Phillips accused the clergy of "longing to endorse that law. . . ." Furthermore, he said: "The great sects, the leading theological newspapers, the leading divines . . . of the country, were all for the law." [75] On those occasions when a preacher did speak out against the Fugitive Slave Law, chances were that he would suffer not only loss of support from his congregation but loss of esteem from fellow ministers as well. In Newburyport, Massachusetts, for example, proslavery sentiment was strong. In the parish of Thomas Wentworth Higginson, there were several sea captains who saw nothing wrong with returning fugitive slaves to their owners. Higginson's abolitionist sympathies aroused such opposition among influential members of his congregation that he was forced to resign.[76] With regard to sermons preaching disobedience to the Fugitive Slave Law, the Reverend John Mason Peck, in an address to the General Assembly of Illinois, had this to say: "I cannot conceive of more demoralizing doctrines, or more wicked principles, than are here uttered by men who profess to be ministers of Christ. They are in rapid progress, in qualification, either for the penitentiary, or the lunatic asylum." [77] The threat of resistance to the Fugitive Slave Law was regarded by Reverend George F. Kettell, in a sermon published in New York "as wicked and abominable, answering no end but to exhibit the ferocity and madness of those who make it, and exposing them to the just indignation of all good citizens." [78]

Many sermons that supported enforcement of the Fugitive Slave Law were warmly accepted by conservatives. Several were printed

Principles of the American Government, and the Extent to Which They are Trampled Under Foot By the Fugitive Slave Law," Occasioned by an Attempt to Enslave An Inhabitant of Syracuse* (Syracuse: Agan & Summers, 1851), pp. 8–9.

75. American Anti-Slavery Society, *Proceedings of the American Anti-Slavery Society, At Its Second Decade, Held in the City of Philadelphia, Dec. 3d, 4th and 5th, 1853* (New York: American Anti-Slavery Society, 1854), p. 113.

76. Mary Thacher Higginson, *Thomas Wentworth Higginson: The Story of His Life* (Boston: Houghton Mifflin Company, 1914), pp. 103–4 (hereafter cited as Higginson, *Thomas Wentworth Higginson*).

77. John Mason Peck, *The Duties of American Citizens: A Discourse, Preached in the State-House, Springfield, Illinois, January 26, 1851* (St. Louis: T. W. Ustick, 1851), pp. 10–11.

78. George F. Kettell, *A Sermon on the Duty of Citizens, With Respect to the Fugitive Slave Law* (White Plains, New York: Eastern State Journal, 1851), pp. 10–11.

and given wide circulation. In the arguments developed in most of these sermons, the duty of the citizen to obey the law rested upon two points. First, the disobedience of one law could lead to the disrespect for all law. If one law could be resisted with impunity just because it did not square with an individual's concept of a higher law, the freedom of all people was placed in jeopardy. Even if the law were unjust, and a few fugitive slaves lost their freedom, "law without liberty was only despotism, liberty without law was license." [79] A highly popular subject of debate, the higher law doctrine was severely criticized by conservative ministers. One of the more critical sermons was delivered in the Central Presbyterian Church in New York by the Reverend John Chase Lord. His sermon was published and distributed widely. No statute could be enforced, said Lord, on a principle that "would leave every man to do what seemed right in his own eyes, under the plea of a higher law and a delicate conscience." Furthermore, he said:

to allege that there is a higher law, which makes slavery, *per se*, sinful, and that all legislation that protects the rights of masters, and enjoins the redelivery of the slave, is necessarily void and without authority, and may be conscientiously resisted by arms and violence, is an infidel position, which is contradicted by both Testaments; . . . [it] may be taught in the gospel of Jean Jacques Rousseau . . . a gospel whose baptism was blood, a revelation whose sacrament was crime; but it cannot be found in the Gospel of Jesus Christ, or in the revelation of God's will to men.[80]

Second, most ministers were convinced that the preservation of the Union depended upon enforcement of the Fugitive Slave Law. "When the slave asks me to stand between him and his master," said Reverend W. M. Rogers in Boston, "what does he ask? He asks me to *murder a nation's life*; and I will not do it because I have a conscience—because there is a God." [81] As regards disruption of the Union, Reverend Joshua Thomas Tucker, in Holliston, Massachu-

79. Weiss, *Theodore Parker*, 2:113–14.

80. John Chase Lord, *"The Higher Law" In Its Application to the Fugitive Slave Bill. A Sermon on the Duties Men Owe to God and to Governments. Delivered at the Central Presbyterian Church on Thanksgiving Day* (New York: Union Safety Committee, 1851), pp. 9–10.

81. American and Foreign Anti-Slavery Society, *Annual Report* (1851), p. 33–38. This report lists a series of sermons that supported enforcement of the Fugitive Slave Law.

setts, said that if, "under our solemnly reiterated protests against slavery, we have consented to dwell legally in this league of States thus long," there was no logic or justification for over-throwing the Union because of what he called the "adventitious aggravations of this special Bill." [82] Even the Quaker press, deploring the existence of slavery in any part of the Union, counseled an "unresisting submission" to the laws provided for the reclamation of fugitive slaves. The editor of *Friend's Review* said, "The unresisting delivery of actual fugitives from labour, when clearly proved to be such, is all the concession to the slaveholding policy that can be claimed at our hands." [83]

Clergymen were tremendously influential in shaping an acquiescent posture toward the Fugitive Slave Law, but their efforts might have amounted to little without the support and cooperation of economic interests in the large cities of the North. Businessmen in Boston, New York, Philadelphia, Baltimore, Pittsburgh, Cincinnati, and Chicago used their influence to quell agitation over the slavery controversy. For three decades merchants had been haunted by the fear that the abolitionist movement would result in the secession of the southern states from the Union. If the present crisis were not settled satisfactorily, that fear might now become reality.

Daniel Webster's call for concessions to the demands of the South as the "sole means of preserving the Union" won immediate approval

82. Joshua Thomas Tucker, *The Citizen and the Commonwealth. A discourse Delivered in the First Congregational Church in Holliston, Mass., on the Day of the Annual State Fast, April 10, 1851* (Holliston: Parker & Plimpton, 1851), p. 11. Other representative sermons which supported enforcement of the Fugitive Slave Law were the following: Orville Dewey, *The Laws of Human Progress and Modern Reforms. A Lecture Delivered Before the Mercantile Library Association of the City of New York* (New York: C. S. Francis & Company, 1852); John Michael Krebs, *The American Citizen. A Discourse on the Nature and Extent of Our Religious Subjection to the Government Under Which We Live: Including an Inquiry into the Scriptural Authority of that Provision of the Constitution of the United States, Which Requires the Surrender of Fugitive Slaves. Delivered in the Rutgers Street Presbyterian Church, In the City of New York, December 12, 1850* (New York: C. Scribner, 1851); Abel McEwen, *A Sermon Preached in the First Congregational Church, New London, Conn., on the Day of Thanksgiving, November 28, 1850* (New London: Daniels & Bacon, 1851); Samuel Thayer Spear, *The Law-Abiding Conscience, and the Higher Law Conscience; With Remarks on the Fugitive Slave Question. A Sermon, Preached in the South Presbyterian Church, Brooklyn, December 12, 1850* (New York: Lambert & Lane, 1850).

83. *Friend's Review: A Religious, Literary, and Miscellaneous Journal*, 48 vols. (Philadelphia: n.p., 1847–1894), 3:617; 4:106, 249.

from a large majority of businessmen.[84] In a conversation with Samuel J. May, one merchant expressed the prevailing attitude of the economic interests in the North. To May the merchant said:

. . . we are not such fools as not to know that slavery is a great evil, a great wrong. But a great portion of the property of the Southerners is invested under its sanction; and the business of the North, as well as of the South, has become adjusted to it. There are millions upon millions of dollars due from Southerners to the merchants and mechanics alone, the payment of which would be jeopardized by any rupture between the North and the South. We cannot afford, sir, to let you and your associates endeavor to overthrow slavery. It is not a matter of principles with us. It is a matter of business necessity. . . . We mean, sir, to put you abolitionists down, by fair means if we can, by foul means if we must.[85]

For good reasons, therefore, business interests were concerned about the rising tide of opposition to the compromise measures.

After passage of the compromise measures, conventions were called in many of the southern states to consider whether the compromise should be accepted. In general the response was favorable, but there were some reservations. In December, 1850, a convention was called in Georgia. Representative of opinion in the state, over seventy-one thousand voters, or three fourths of the qualified electorate, turned out to elect the delegates.[86] The delegates decided to abide by the compromise as a "permanent adjustment of the sectional controversy," but resolved:

. . . That the State of Georgia, in the judgment of this Convention, will and ought to resist, even (as a last resort) to a disruption of every tie which binds her to the Union, any action of Congress, upon the subject of slavery in the District of Columbia, or in places subject to the jurisdiction of Congress, incompatible with the safety, domestic tranquility, the rights and the honor of the slave-holding States . . . or any act repealing or materially modifying the laws now in force for the recovery of fugitive slaves.

More to the point, it was also resolved ". . . That it is the deliberate opinion of this Convention that upon the faithful execution of the Fugitive Slave Law by the proper authorities depends the preservation of our much loved Union." [87] The contention was well reasoned.

84. Philip Sheldon Foner, *Business and Slavery: The New York Merchants and the Irrepressible Conflict* (Chapel Hill: University of North Carolina Press, 1941), p. 26 (hereafter cited as Foner, *Business and Slavery*).
85. May, *Recollections of Our Antislavery Conflict*, pp. 127–28.
86. *National Intelligencer*, December 14, 1850.
87. Ames, *State Documents*, pp. 31–32.

A move was already underway to create a favorable climate of opinion for enforcement of the law.

As a result of dissatisfaction among New York merchants with increasing sectional animosity, a special committee was appointed on October 11 at a meeting of Whig merchants. The committee was asked to confer with leading representatives of Democratic business-men. After meeting several times and consulting Webster, the mer-chants of both parties agreed to sponsor a mass Union meeting. A joint committee of Whig and Democratic merchants, putting aside partisan politics for the moment, issued a call to the businessmen of New York for a mass assembly to promote good feelings between the North and South on the basis of the finality of the compromise.[88] Within a week, ten thousand merchants and business firms had already endorsed the call for a meeting. Of all the business firms on Broad Street, Pearl Street, Wall Street, and Exchange Place, said Philip Foner, "only eight refused to sign the call." [89]

On October 23, 1850, a mass meeting was held in Castle Garden in New York City. The compromise measures were discussed at length by various speakers. Feeling that "the entire economic and social structure of the country would collapse" if the abolitionists had their way, most of the speakers emphasized the necessity of supporting the compromise as the only means of safeguarding the Union.[90]

Because of their dislike of certain clauses in the Fugitive Slave Law, some of the merchants were reluctant to give wholehearted support to the compromise. Quite certain that the timidity arose over a misconception of the law, five outstanding lawyers devoted much time to trying to convince the more hesitant merchants that their fears were unwarranted. To the statement that the law required northern free men to become slave catchers, the answer was: "How, and in what way, are you required to become so? Officers, empow-ered by law, are the parties to perform that duty. It is only when a law is *resisted*, that the citizen may be called on to lend his aid in

---

88. *New York Tribune*, October 30, 1850. See also Foner, *Business* and Slavery, p. 42; Roy Franklin Nichols, *The Democratic Machine, 1850–1854* (New York: Columbia University, 1923), pp. 26–27 (hereafter cited as Nichols, *Democratic Machine*).
89. Foner, *Business and Slavery*, p. 43.
90. Ibid., p. 46.

support of magisterial authority. Resistance to any law of the land is a wrong against society and good order—and any citizen may be required to assist, if his assistance should become necessary, in upholding the supremacy of law." It was suggested by some of the doubters that only individual citizens were opposed to the Fugitive Slave Law. John T. Brady, in his speech at Castle Garden, admitted that the government was "not responsible for the acts of citizens," but it was his belief "that our constitution and Union are a mockery, and our professions here a silly dillusion, if we do not feel ourselves required to demand, that, in the efficient and thorough execution of the Fugitive Slave Law, the entire power of the federal government be so exercised, that no effort of an individual or a mob shall possibly prevail against it. Unless this be done, our pretended Union is not worthy of a moment's regard. . . ." [91] By the time the merchants were ready to vote on resolutions, there seemed to be general approval of the compromise measures.

Unanimously adopted by the several thousand merchants present in Castle Garden, the resolutions emphasized the principles advocated by the speakers at the convention. The compromise was a "fair one," and the Fugitive Slave Law was deemed necessary; every effort should be exerted to enforce it. Further agitation of the slavery question was "fraught with incalculable danger to our Union" and should be halted at all costs. Finally, it was resolved to form a Union Safety Committee. The committee would be "charged with the duty, by correspondence and otherwise, of carrying out the objects of this meeting, which are hereby declared to be . . . to revive and foster among the whole people of the United States, the spirit in which the Union was formed and the Constitution was adopted; and to resist every attempt to alienate any portion of our country from the rest or to enfeeble the sacred ties which now link together the various parts." [92]

The Union Safety Committee was composed of one hundred of the

91. Union Safety Committee, *Selections from the Speeches and Writings of Prominent Men in the United States on the Subject of Abolition and Agitation, and Addressed to the People of the State of New York* (New York: Union Safety Committee, 1854), pp. 6, 19–20 (hereafter cited as Union Safety Committee, *Selections from Speeches on Abolition and Agitation*).

92. Union Safety Committee, *Proceedings of the Union Safety Meeting Held at Castle Garden, October 23, 1850* (New York: Union Safety Committee, 1850), pp. 37–38.

most prominent businessmen in the city. To the duty assigned them, they gave extensive time, effort, and money. A Committee of Correspondence began immediately to solicit the aid of influential men from all over the country. Special attention was given to the task of obtaining sermons and letters from clergymen in defense of the Fugitive Slave Law. The response was greater than the committee expected. Letters praising the work of the committee poured in from every corner of the nation. Sermons denouncing the higher law doctrine and advising acquiescence in the Fugitive Slave Law came in great abundance. In New York, December 12, 1850 was set aside as a special day which was devoted to sermons on the compromise measures. The publication and distribution of sermons, letters, and speeches was expensive, but a special committee had no difficulty in subscribing twenty-five thousand dollars. Summarizing the work of the Union Safety Committee, the *Journal of Commerce* said: "Thousands and thousands of speeches, letters and sermons . . . have been distributed in different parts of the State. All this costs money, and a good deal of it. But men are found among us, with their hearts and purses open, ready to give liberally for an object so dear to their patriotic hearts, and odious to "wooly heads" and rebels." [93] The meeting at Castle Garden was only the beginning. For two years merchants in New York, Boston, and Philadelphia, and men with economic interests in other large cities, strove to consolidate the Union movement throughout the country. If a Union victory could be achieved in the presidential election of 1852, perhaps the slavery issue would disappear from the political scene and the Compromise of 1850 would become a finality.

In the spring and summer preceding the presidential election of 1852, politicians in Congress devoted their talents, time, and energy to making the compromise a final settlement of the slavery issue. When the Thirty-second Congress assembled in December, 1851, Senator Henry Stuart Foote, hoping to consolidate Union sentiment in Mississippi, offered a resolution, later amended by Senator George Edmund Badger of North Carolina, that the " 'Compromise Acts,' are, in the judgement of this body . . . a final settlement . . . and ought to be adhered to by Congress until time and experience shall

93. Foner, *Business and Slavery*, p. 58, quoting the *Journal of Commerce*, March 13, 1851.

demonstrate the necessity of further legislation to guard against evasion or abuse." [94] A long and rambling debate ensued, but the resolution was never brought to a vote. Opposition to Foote's resolution was led by Senators James Murray Mason and Robert Mercer Taliaferro Hunter of Virginia, Andrew Pickens Butler of South Carolina, and David Rice Atchison of Missouri. The Senate Democrats, divided between hunkers and state rights sympathizers, held only by a slim majority in the Thirty-second Congress. The hunker senators, led by Lewis Cass of Michigan, Stephen Arnold Douglas of Illinois, Jesse David Bright of Indiana, James Ware Bradbury of Maine, William Rufus de Vane King of Alabama, and Thomas Jefferson Rusk of Texas, were determined to unite the party on the principle of the compromise as a final settlement. They agreed that union on such a principle would "drive the distracting question from politics, remove an easy issue from the reach of any who might wish to revolt, make unnecessary a third or Compromise party and bring victory—and spoils in 1852." [95]

In the House of Representatives, unionists were more successful. On April 5, 1852, a nonpartisan coalition of Whigs and Democrats adopted a resolution which declared ". . . the series of acts passed during the first session of the Thirty-first Congress, known as the compromise, are regarded as a final adjustment and a permanent settlement of the questions therein embraced, and should be maintained and executed as such." [96] According to the *Washington Union*, 67 percent of the Democrats in the House, including a majority from both sections of the country, voted for the resolution. [97]

By June, 1852, when the national conventions of both parties met in Baltimore, the Union Democrats had gained control of the party. In answer to a circular letter, almost every prominent candidate replied that "he would maintain and enforce all the measures in the Compromise of 1850, including the Fugitive Slave Law." [98] The Whig party was still split. Those who supported Webster and Fill-

94. *Congressional Globe*, 32nd Cong., 1st sess., 24:125.
95. Nichols, *Democratic Machine*, p. 31.
96. *Congressional Globe*, 32nd Cong., 1st sess., 24:983.
97. Nichols, *Democratic Machine*, p. 40, quoting the *Washington Union*, April 30, 1852.
98. Claude M. Fuess, *The Life of Caleb Cushing*, 2 vols. (New York: Harcourt, Brace and Company, 1923), 2:119–20 (hereafter cited as Fuess, *Cushing*).

more accepted the compromise without reservations, but the supporters of General Winfield Scott could not give their whole-hearted
support to the hated Fugitive Slave Law.[99]

At the national conventions in Baltimore, the Democratic and
Whig parties adopted platforms which endorsed the finality of the
compromise. The Democrats pledged that they would "abide by, and
adhere to, a faithful execution of the acts known as the Compromise
measures settled by the last Congress—the act for reclaiming fugitives from service or labor included: which act, being designed to
carry out an express provision of the Constitution, cannot with
fidelity thereto be repealed, nor so changed as to destroy or impair
its efficiency." After the resolution endorsing the Fugitive Slave Law
was read, said the *Tribune*, "the applause became tremendous. So
extreme was the delight of the great mass of the Convention with this
platform, that they had it read over twice, each time breaking out in
new plaudits." [100] Endorsing the compromise, but not so enthusiastically, the Whigs declared:

the series of measures known as the Compromise, including the Fugitive
Slave Law, are received and acquiesced in by the Whig party . . . as a
settlement in principle and substance—a final settlement of the dangerous and exciting subjects which they embrace, and so far as the Fugitive
Slave Law is concerned, we will maintain the same and insist on its enforcement until time and experience shall demonstrate the necessity of
further legislation against evasion or abuses . . . and will maintain this
system of measures as a policy essential to the nationality of the Whig
party and the integrity of the Union.[101]

The resolutions of the Whig platform were adopted unanimously,
with the exception of the plank endorsing the Fugitive Slave Law.
The latter resolution carried by a vote of 212 to 70. The supporters
of General Scott voted against it. Only in the delegations from New
York and Ohio was a majority opposed to endorsing the Fugitive
Slave Law.[102] Horace Greeley was exasperated. He said that any

99. Rhodes, *History of the United States*, 1:207.

100. *New York Weekly Tribune*, June 12, 1852.

101. Ibid., June 19, 1852.

102. Horace Greeley and John F. Cleveland, comps., *A Political Text-Book
For 1860: Comprising a Brief View of Presidential Nominations and Elections:
Including All the National Platforms Ever Yet Adopted: Also, A History of the
Struggle Respecting Slavery in the Territories, And of the Action of Congress
as to the Freedom of the Public Lands, With the Most Notable Speeches of
Messrs. Lincoln, Bell, Cass, Seward, Everett, Breckinridge, H. V. Johnson, etc.,*

resolution that represented the Whigs as "satisfied" with the Fugitive Slave Law, and that committed them "to its maintenance unmodified," would be false, "binding no one and discrediting none but its utterers." Greeley, who spoke for a significant number of Whigs, thought that a few voters would be won to the Whig standard by such a ruse. Its only purpose, he said, was "to divide, disorganize and weaken the Whig party, in order to degrade, humble, and, if possible, alienate a hated portion of its members." [103]

On August 11, 1852, the Free Soil party held its national convention in Pittsburgh, Pennsylvania. All the free states were represented. Remaining adamant in their opposition to the Fugitive Slave Law, they exclaimed once again that the law was "repugnant to the Constitution, to the principles of common law, to the spirit of Christianity, and to the sentiments of the civilized world. We therefore deny its binding force upon the American people, and demand its immediate repeal." The Free Soilers hopefully nominated John Parker Hale of New Hampshire for president and George Washington Julian of Indiana as his running mate. For the Free Soil candidates, the election returns were disastrous. Hale received only 155,825 votes in a turnout at the polls of over 3,100,000 people.[104] Only five Free Soil candidates were elected to the House and two to the Senate. In the Senate of 1853, Charles Sumner and Salmon Portland Chase were the only Free Soil members. So "hopeless was their position," commented David Donald, "that rumors of Sumner's impending resignation were widely circulated." [105] Apparently tired of the ceaseless agitation aroused by the slavery controversy, and wanting to insure the integrity of the Union, the people elected to public office men who had pledged support to the Compromise of 1850.

For the two major parties, the picture was much less clear. While Democrat Franklin Pierce, a dark horse candidate who had been nominated on the forty-ninth ballot, received 214,694 more popular votes than Winfield Scott, the Whig candidate, the electoral college

---

etc., Touching the Questions of the Day: and Returns of All Presidential Elections Since 1836 (New York: The Tribune Association, 1860), p. 19 (hereafter cited as Greeley, *Political Text-Book*).

103. *New York Weekly Tribune*, June 12, 1852.

104. Greeley, *Political Textbook*, pp. 21, 239.

105. Donald, *Charles Sumner*, p. 249. See also Greeley, *Political Text-Book*, p. 239.

vote was more sweeping. Pierce received 254 electoral votes to Scott's 42. In the free states, Scott carried only Massachusetts and Vermont. Only 86 Whigs were returned to the House and 24 to the Senate. The Democrats now had a 56 vote majority in the House and a 10 vote majority in the Senate.[106] The Democratic majority bolstered by southern Whigs could now easily prevent any attempt to modify or repeal the Fugitive Slave Law. There no longer seemed to be any point in continuing the agitation against slavery. "There is no probability," said Horace Greeley, "that . . . the Fugitive Slave Law . . . will be altered by Congress during the present generation. . . . There will be no need of menacing the Dissolution of the Union—the law may be upheld a great deal cheaper than that."[107] The slavery issue was not dead; it had merely been placed in a state of suspended animation. Those who had hated the law for reclaiming fugitive slaves still hated it, but the "irresistible public opinion" which Charles Sumner predicted would make the Fugitive Slave Law a dead letter did not materialize.

Between 1852 and 1854, there were occasional outbursts against the law in some communities. For the most part, however, the law was enforced quietly and without fanfare. Indeed, along the border between the slave and the free states, runaway slaves were frequently returned without due process of law. When a slave was returned quietly by his owner, or when federal marshals enforced the law without violence, the press paid little attention.

In 1854, the tide began to turn. The passage of the Kansas-Nebraska Act, the widely publicized return of Anthony Burns from Boston, and the Dred Scott decision convinced many people living in the North that the Compromise of 1850 had settled nothing finally. The same old sectional issues still faced the nation. Many citizens no longer felt any restraint in their criticism of the Fugitive Slave Law. In this atmosphere the abolitionists were able to exploit the deep-seated hatred for slavery in their efforts to nullify the law or make its enforcement impossible.

106. Greeley, *Political Text-Book*, p. 239.
107. *New York Weekly Tribune*, June 26, 1852.

Chapter IV

The Fugitive Slave Law
and
Public Opinion,
1854–1860

Confronted with the possibility of disunion as a result of anti-slavery agitation and opposition to enforcement of the Fugitive Slave Law, both great political parties had closed ranks. With businessmen and churchmen they had worked overtime in an effort to sustain the Union, and, after three years of turmoil, the country seemed to be at peace. President Franklin Pierce had assured the country that the public calm would "suffer no shock" during his administration. It was his hope that the slavery question had been put to rest and that "no sectional or ambitious or fanatical excitement" would again "threaten the durability of our institutions or obscure the light of our prosperity."[1] On this thin veneer of domestic tranquility, however, tiny cracks began to appear. In some communities in the northern states, a small turbulence, a paroxysm of anger, an outburst of public

1. James D. Richardson, ed., *A Compilation of the Messages and Papers of the Presidents 1789–1897*, 10 vols. (Washington: Government Printing Office, 1896–1899), 5:202 (hereafter cited as Richardson, *Messages and Papers*).

indignation indicated the existence of strong but latent antislavery sentiment. Frequently roused by some particularly harsh and brutal example of the enforcement of the Fugitive Slave Law, these public outbursts added fuel to the fires of abolitionist discontent. This deceptively calm but potentially dangerous state of affairs persisted until 1854.

During the second year of President Pierce's administration, three events occurred which convulsed the nation in even greater turmoil than before. In Washington, the nation's capital, Congress passed and the president signed the Kansas-Nebraska Act, thus reopening the question of whether slavery could be extended to the Northwest Territory. In Racine, Wisconsin, a Negro laborer named Joshua Glover was arrested and incarcerated in a Milwaukee jail as a fugitive slave. The following day Glover was rescued by a sympathetic crowd and sent to Canada. In Boston, another Negro named Anthony Burns was captured and, after a highly publicized trial, was remanded to slavery at the expense of the national government. It was thus demonstrated that even in the Old Bay State the Fugitive Slave Law could be enforced. Because the Kansas-Nebraska Act abrogated the long-standing Missouri Compromise, many citizens in the North who had given their support to the Compromise of 1850 no longer felt any compunction to honor the more recent adjustment. The rescue of Joshua Glover and subsequent arrest of Sherman M. Booth for aiding and abetting the escape embroiled the state of Wisconsin in a bitter jurisdictional dispute with the federal courts that did not end until 1860. The return of Anthony Burns from Boston to his owner was exploited by abolitionists in their efforts to create animosity toward slavery and encumber enforcement of the Fugitive Slave Law. Largely as a result of these three events, public opinion, once acquiescent toward enforcement of the Fugitive Slave Law, now became increasingly hostile. In many communities, enforcement of the law became increasingly difficult.

This chapter will be concerned primarily with reopening the sectional dispute over slavery and its effect upon public opinion in the North toward the Fugitive Slave Law.[2]

On December 14, 1853, Senator Augustus Caesar Dodge of Iowa

2. The rescue of Joshua Glover and the return of Anthony Burns will be treated in the chapter on enforcement of the Fugitive Slave Law.

introduced a bill to organize the Nebraska Territory, and it was referred to the Senate Committee on Territories.[3] Having been amended twice, the bill was reported to the Senate in its final form on January 23, 1854 by the committee chairman, Senator Douglas. Originally, the bill had simply provided for the organization of the Nebraska Territory. Unfortunately, the bill had contained an ambiguous statement regarding slavery. With regard to the peculiar institution, one of the clauses read: "And when admitted as a State or States, the said Territory, or any portion of the same, shall be received into the Union, with or without slavery, as their constitution may prescribe at the time of their admission." On January 10, as a result of pressure from Missouri's Senator David Rice Atchison, Douglas added another section which said that "all questions pertaining to slavery in the Territories, and in the new States to be formed therefrom, are to be left to the people residing therein, through their appropriate representatives." In other words, the principle of popular sovereignty was incorporated into the new version of the bill. This was interpreted to mean that the Missouri Compromise restriction upon slavery was no longer in effect.[4] Still not satisfied, Senators Atchison, Archibald Dixon, and Philip Phillips pressed for a definite repeal of the Missouri Compromise line. The version of the bill reported on January 23 explicitly repealed the compromise that had stood since 1820.

For three months, with a great deal of rancour, acrimony, and bitterness, the bill was debated in the Senate. The bill's advocates argued that repeal of the Missouri Compromise was a mere incident of no great importance when compared with the opening of new territory into which thousands of emigrants were pouring every year. Just as vehemently the opposition charged that passage of such a law would be an act of bad faith. Senator Douglas's assertion that the Missouri Compromise had already been abrogated by the Compromise of 1850 was considered as preposterous, and the Little Giant's efforts to marshal evidence in support of his position were equivocal and unconvincing. Finally, after an all-night session on March 3 and

3. *Congressional Globe*, 33rd Cong., 1st sess., 37:175, 221–22. See also Avery Craven, *The Coming of the Civil War* (Chicago: University of Chicago Press, Phoenix Books, 1966), pp. 325–26.

4. Nevins, *Ordeal of Union*, 2:95.

4, Douglas triumphed, and the bill came to a vote. Despite an obviously hostile public opinion, party discipline was magnificent, and the bill was passed 37 to 14.[5]

In the House of Representatives, debate on the Nebraska bill did not begin until May 8. Before that date it had been buried on the bottom of the calendar in the Committeee of the Whole. Debate in the House was frequently interrupted by the violent invective and abuse heaped upon one another by members of opposing factions. Finally pushed through the House by an adroit maneuver of Alexander H. Stephens, the bill was passed on May 22 by a majority of thirteen votes. Of the eighty-six northern Democrats, forty-four had voted for the bill. Only two of fifty-nine southern Democrats had voted no. Of the sixty-four Whigs in the House, all forty-five northern and seven southern Whigs had voted against the bill.[6] Because members of the House were closer to their constituents, the House vote more accurately reflected public opinion than did the vote in the Senate.

With the passage of the Kansas-Nebraska Act, the attitude toward antislavery agitation changed perceptively. The gauntlet had been thrown down and antislavery leaders were quick to pick it up. "What had been radical opinion in the North," said Nevins, "now became general opinion; Douglas had converted more men to intransigent freesoil doctrine in two months than Garrison and Phillips had converted to abolitionism in twenty years." [7]

With a great deal of reluctance, Horace Greeley had grudgingly accepted the Compromise of 1850. However, with the introduction of the Nebraska bill, Greeley was incensed and thereafter became an indomitable and unremitting opponent of both slavery and its extension into the free territories. On January 28, in an editorial revealing more optimism than the circumstances justified, Greeley said: "Our faith in the intelligence and sense of justice among the people is such, that on the momentous question of a Repeal of the Missouri Compromise, we believe the Free States will rise as one man and crush the repudiating and traitorous dough faces who dare to counsel it. . . . We believe the proposition will be put down by acclamation." [8] An

5. Ibid., p. 144.
6. Ibid., pp. 156–57.
7. Ibid., pp. 153–54.
8. *New York Weekly Tribune*, January 28, 1854.

important and influential editor, Greeley was only one among legions of critics of Douglas's proposal.

As in 1850, but more widespread, public meetings were held in several cities in every northern state. The *Tribune* noted sixty-four such meetings between January 17 and February 24. In New York City, a great meeting in opposition to the overthrow of the Missouri Compromise was held in the Tabernacle. Present at the meeting was a large number of the Union Safety Committee. These men had labored long and hard in support of the compromise measures in 1850 but now felt as though they had been sold out.[9] Fearing that the Nebraska bill might set a precedent for the recognition of slave property in the free states, a great many of the Boston merchants who had supported the compromise felt cheated. They now were obliged, said Dana in a letter to Sumner, "to talk Free Soil . . . with a sheepish feeling that they had been *sold*." [10] On March 14, at a Whig convention in Harrisburg, Pennsylvania, resolutions were adopted which declared: ". . . the provisions of the Nebraska bill, now before Congress, are a deliberate breach of plighted faith and public compact—a high-handed attempt to force Slavery into a vast Territory now free from it by law—a reckless renewing of a quieted agitation, and therefore, meets the stern, indignant and unanimous condemnation of the Whig party of Pennsylvania." Feeling that repeal of the Missouri Compromise demonstrated that the compromise measures had been held sacred only by the "Slavery propagandists," citizens in Albany, New York pledged to unite in an effort to "modify the odious features" of the Fugitive Slave Law and "to regain for Freedom its lost territory. . . ." At an anti-Nebraska convention in Jackson, Michigan, it was resolved: "That after this gross breach of faith and wanton affront to us as northern men, we hold ourselves absolved from all *"compromises"* except those expressed in the Constitution for the protection of Slavery and slaveowners; that we now demand measures of protection and immunity for ourselves, and among them we demand the REPEAL OF THE FUGITIVE SLAVE LAW, and an act to abolish Slavery in the District of

9. *New York Weekly Tribune*, February 18, 25, and 4, 1854.
10. Samuel Shapiro, "The Rendition of Anthony Burns," *Journal of Negro History* 44 (January 1959) : 48 (hereafter cited as Shapiro, "Rendition of Anthony Burns"), quoting Richard Henry Dana, Jr.

Columbia." At an anti-Nebraska union meeting in Vermont, a group of citizens proclaimed that all "compromises with slavery" were at an end. They vowed also to seek the repeal of the Fugitive Slave Law.[11]

Among New England clergymen, passage of the Kansas–Nebraska Act and the rendition of Anthony Burns created great turmoil. Several clergymen who had strongly supported the compromise measures now denounced the "Nebraska villainy" and the Fugitive Slave Law.[12] So great was the reaction that Harriet Beecher Stowe used part of her royalties from *Uncle Tom's Cabin* to finance the collection of the *"united clerical protest of New England"* against the Kansas-Nebraska bill. The petition, forming a scroll some two hundred feet long and signed by three thousand clergymen, was presented in Congress on March 14 by the reluctant Senator Edward Everett of Massachusetts.[13] These clergymen protested the act "as a great moral wrong, as a breach of faith eminently injurious to the moral principles of the community, and subversive of all confidence in national engagements. . . ."[14]

In the Northwest, the churchmen of Chicago met to protest the repeal of the Missouri Compromise and the extension of slavery into Kansas and Nebraska. Despite the vigorous attack by Senator Douglas "on men of the cloth who participated in political discussions," clerical criticism continued. "The political vane of Kansas determined editorial lines of Baptist, Methodist, and Congregational organs, just as it came to be the theme of pastoral descant on these exciting Sundays."[15] In a letter to the secretary of the British and Foreign Anti-Slavery Society, Lewis Tappan noted that "a vast change has taken place in public sentiment." In his opinion, the recent enforcement of the Fugitive Slave Law in Boston and passage of the Kansas–Nebraska Act had finally "opened the eyes of the clergy and laity in the free States. . . ."[16]

In his diary on February 19, 1854, Richard Henry Dana confided that the most important event of the week in Boston had been the

<hr />

11. *New York Weekly Tribune*, March 18, July 29, 15, 29, 1854.
12. Ibid., June 24, 1854.
13. Donald, *Charles Sumner*, pp. 259–60.
14. *New York Weekly Tribune*, March 18, 1854.
15. Pierce, *History of Chicago*, 2:383–4.
16. Tappan to L. A. Chamerovzow, October 29, 1854, in Abel and Klingberg, *Side-Light on Anglo-American Relations*, p. 347.

anti-Nebraska meeting in Faneuil Hall. With regard to sentiments
expressed at the meeting, Dana said: "All men agree that the audience were far ahead of the speakers. All attempts to get up applause
for the measures and men of 1850 failed, and even Webster's great
name fell dead, while every sentiment hostile to the Compromise
measures of 1850, and everything of a Free Soil character, went off
with rapturous applause. . . . The Compromise men feel themselves
sold." [17] On August 16, the venerable Josiah Quincy, at the age of
eighty-three, responded to a call to speak in the Music Hall at Boston.
"From such an individual," he said, "and under such circumstances,
you have a right to expect the words of truth, of duty, and of
soberness." Offering what came to be the most prevalent rationale for
the changing sentiment which followed repeal of the Missouri Compromise, Quincy said: "When the fundamental relations of things,
which were the basis of a political contract, have been changed by
the art and artifice of one of the contracting parties, the moral
obligations resulting from that contract, upon the other party, are
also materially changed." Thinking it futile to criticize the Fugitive
Slave Law, he turned his ire upon the provision in the Constitution
which required the return of fugitive slaves. Angrily he exclaimed:
"There is not a Negro in the South that can be compelled, even by
his master, to cut the throat or blow out the brains of his brother
Negro. Yet, so long as the fugitive-slave obligation remains in the
Constitution, there is not a militia-man in Massachusetts who may
not be compelled to-morrow to cut the throat or blow out the brains
of a fellow-citizen, at the will of the basest Southern slaveholder." [18]

The Kansas–Nebraska Act was excoriated not only by public
assemblies but also by several state legislatures. In the two years
immediately following the introduction of the Nebraska bill in Congress, seven state legislatures adopted resolutions condemning the
repeal of the Missouri Compromise, and some of them now demanded the repeal of the Fugitive Slave Law. The Connecticut
resolves declared that, since the compromise on slavery had been
"repudiated and deprived of [its] moral force and authority," the

17. Adams, *Richard Henry Dana*, 1:257–58.
18. Josiah Quincy, *Speech Delivered . . . Before the State Whig Convention,
Assembled at the Music Hall, Boston, Aug. 16, 1854* (Boston: J. Wilson & Son,
1854), pp. 3, 7.

state of Connecticut would "return to the original policy of the government, founded upon the Constitution of the United States." Rather than cooperate in the enforcement of the Fugitive Slave Law, Connecticut would return to the policy established by the Supreme Court in the Prigg decision. Henceforth, it would be the responsibility of federal officers to capture fugitive slaves in Connecticut. Rhode Island's resolution was similar, and, moreover, it expressed opposition to further acquisition of territory. Both sets of resolutions called for amendment or repeal of the Fugitive Slave Law. The legislatures in Maine, Massachusetts, Michigan, and New York called for the "immediate and unconditional repeal" of both the Fugitive Slave Law and the Kansas–Nebraska Act. In April, 1856, the General Assembly of Ohio declared that the Fugitive Slave Law was "inconsistent with and unwarranted by the Constitution." Her representatives were requested and her senators were instructed to work for early repeal of the law.[19]

Further action, by northern state legislatures, which indicated that opposition to enforcement of the Fugitive Slave Law was gaining wider support was the passage of the so-called personal liberty laws. Despite a popular misconception, with the exception of a law in Vermont, the personal liberty laws were not passed until after 1854. Enacted in 1850, Vermont's personal liberty law was the only statute of its type which can be attributed largely to reaction against the Fugitive Slave Law. The personal liberty laws enacted in the other northern states between 1855 and 1859 were the result not only of hostility to the Fugitive Slave Law but to animosity generated by repeal of the Missouri Compromise and the extension of slavery into the free territories.

Between 1855 and 1859, personal liberty laws were enacted in Connecticut, Rhode Island, Massachusetts, Michigan, Maine, Ohio, and Wisconsin. The two-fold object of these laws was to encumber enforcement of the Fugitive Slave Law to discourage slave owners from pursuing their slaves and to prevent the kidnapping of free Negroes. In general, these statutes provided three things: (1) that

19. *Senate Miscellaneous Document Nos. 70, 71, 22, 24, 28*, 33rd Cong., 1st sess.; *Senate Miscellaneous Document No. 11*, 33rd Cong., 2nd sess.; *Senate Miscellaneous Document Nos. 11, 18*, 34th Cong., 1st sess.; *House of Representatives Miscellaneous Document Nos. 16, 20, 23, 77, 94, 96*, 33rd Cong., 1st sess.; *Senate Miscellaneous Document No. 54*, 34th Cong., 1st sess.

certain state legal officers should act as counsel for anyone arrested as a fugitive slave; (2) that Negroes arrested and held as fugitive slaves were entitled to the writ of habeas corpus and trial by jury; and (3) that the kidnapping of free Negroes was punishable by heavy fine and imprisonment. Some of the laws contained provisions which prohibited the use of state jails for holding federal prisoners.

Although these laws were unfriendly in their motives, and some of them steered very close to nullification, most of the statutes conformed to the specifications in the Prigg decision. That decision relieved the states from responsibility in the enforcement of the Fugitive Slave Law.[20] In 1857, Ohio passed a law to prevent kidnapping of free Negroes and a law to prevent fugitive slaves from being held in Ohio jails. Both laws were repealed the following year. Pennsylvania enacted no legislation contrary to the Fugitive Slave Law; New Jersey gave official sanction to the rendition of fugitive slaves, and no personal liberty laws whatever were passed in Illinois, Indiana, and Minnesota.

After passage of the Kansas–Nebraska Act, Horace Greeley, exaggerating in good abolitionist fashion, predicted that the Fugitive Slave Law would now be enforced only in "exceptional cases." In some communities it was already virtually impossible to capture a fugitive slave. In Greeley's opinion, those places would multiply rapidly. "Towns will be followed by counties," he said, "and counties by states." The "forcible annulment" of the statute would then become general.[21] Greeley's prediction bears little resemblance to the facts.

Repeal of the Missouri Compromise and extension of slavery into the territories created extensive hostility in the northern states, but such hostility did not become general with regard to the Fugitive Slave Law. In other words, the Fugitive Slave Law did not become a dead letter in every state in the North. Antislavery sentiment was intensified in those states in the North which bordered on the slave states, but seldom did this result in open resistance to enforcement of the law. In most cases, a distinction was made between opposition to

---

20. The acts of only four states, namely, Vermont, Massachusetts, Michigan, and Wisconsin, actually provided for interference with the exercise of powers conferred by Congress on the commissioners of the fugitive slave tribunals.

21. *New York Weekly Tribune*, June 3, 1854.

the institution of slavery on the one hand and resistance to enforcement of law on the other. In the states of Pennsylvania, Ohio, Indiana, and Illinois, where the fugitive slave problem was greatest, the abolitionists picked up considerable support. But a majority of the people in those states still favored enforcement of the Fugitive Slave Law over disunion.

In Illinois, public opinion toward the Fugitive Slave Law was consistent throughout the decade preceding the Civil War. According to John Reynolds, former governor of Illinois, opposition to the law was confined to Chicago. "So far as I know," he said, ". . . in that disaffected district the act was a dead letter. . . ." [22] When Senator Douglas returned to Chicago after Congress had adjourned, his reception was quiet despite the uneasy mood of Chicago's residents. Douglas announced with characteristic boldness that on the evening of September 1 he would speak in the public square. On the afternoon of his scheduled appearance, the flags in the harbor were lowered to half-mast, and an hour before he was to speak the church bells began to toll. An estimated ten thousand people gathered to hear the Little Giant speak. Greeted at first with an uneasy silence, a "storm of hisses and groans" increased in intensity until the speaker's voice was drowned out. Attempting to defend his position before the unruly crowd, Douglas stubbornly stood his ground. At midnight, finally out of patience, Douglas screamed at his hecklers: "Abolitionists of Chicago! It is now Sunday morning. I'll go to church and you may go to Hell." [23]

Such hostility was not as evident in the area south of Chicago. The resolutions adopted in the state legislature expressed the desire for peace, maintenance of the Union, and the suppression of all slavery agitation. After studying the debates in the Illinois legislature, Mason M. Fishback concluded that, in the years just prior to the Civil War, a majority of the people in the state were loyal to the Union. A majority in both houses of the legislature consistently endorsed popular sovereignty, denounced slavery agitation, and recommended nonintervention with slavery in the states. [24] Remaining

22. Wilbur H. Siebert, *The Underground Railroad From Slavery to Freedom* (New York: The Macmillan Company, 1898), p. 333.
23. Pierce, *History of Chicago*, 2:208–9.
24. Fishback, "Illinois Legislation on Slavery," pp. 429–31.

constant in their dislike of the Negro, the people of Illinois, with the exception of the area around Chicago, offered little resistance to enforcement of the Fugitive Slave Law. In fact, Negroes were returned to their owners from the southern part of the state with hardly any notice from the press.

The people of Indiana continued to acquiesce in the principles laid down in the Prigg decision. Antislavery groups in Indiana were apparently ignored by the legislature and the courts. The legislature made no attempt to nullify the Fugitive Slave Law, and Indiana courts made no effort to test the supremacy of national law. With few exceptions, the Fugitive Slave Law was quietly enforced in Indiana.[25]

After passage of the Kansas–Nebraska Act, resistance to enforcement of the Fugitive Slave Law in Ohio became more widespread. In Cincinnati, for example, the mayor discharged two policemen in 1856 for aiding in the capture of fugitive slaves. The *Cincinnati Plain Dealer* quoted the mayor as saying that the city police had no responsibility for capturing runaway slaves "unless called upon by the United States officers to aid them. . . ." The mayor maintained that any man who would "neglect his regular business and assist in hunting up runaway slaves, without authority of law, and for the sole purpose of obtaining a reward, is unfit to be a city policeman." [26] Indicative of changing sentiment in the state, a correspondent from Circleville, a small town in the southern part of Ohio, commented: "Since the passage of the Nebraska bill, we propose to let the southern gentlemen catch their own niggers." [27]

By no means did southern Ohio become a haven for fugitive slaves, however. The great antipathy toward Negroes in southern Ohio was illustrated by the experience of a former slave named John Stewart. Having been arrested for stealing clothing, Stewart pleaded guilty at his trial. In his defense, he said that he was out of funds and had no food; there seemed to be no other way to provide the necessities of life. He told the court that he was sorry that he had ever left North Carolina. Upon hearing that he would receive wonderful treatment at the hands of abolitionists in the North, he had

25. Thornbrough, "Indiana and Fugitive Slave Legislation," pp. 224–25, 228.

26. *National Intelligencer,* February 22, 1856, quoting the *Cincinnati Plain Dealer.*

27. *Boston Liberator,* August 18, 1854.

purchased his freedom at a cost of nine hundred dollars and had come to Ohio. "Since I came here," he continued, "I have been kicked about and abused by all classes of white men; can't get work from no one, and to borrow money to get bread with, that is out of the question." He declared that when he got out of prison he would "go South and become a slave again." [28]

The strongest opposition to the Fugitive Slave Law in Ohio continued to manifest itself in the northern part of the state. Negroes were received more kindly in the Western Reserve. Between 1850 and 1860, the Negro population in the reserve increased by 100 percent. This bears eloquent testimony to the complaint of a southern slave catcher who said, "Never see so many niggers and abolitionists in one place in my life. . . . Might as well try to hunt the *devil* there as hunt a nigger." [29] Few slaves were ever returned from northern Ohio, but this did not mean that the Fugitive Slave Law had become a dead letter because of the increasing hostility toward slavery. A great public clamor usually followed the more widely publicized cases, but for the most part such exhibitions were transitory.

On April 25, 1860, Ohio's Senator Thomas Corwin made a two-hour speech in Washington which centered on the Fugitive Slave Law. In his speech, Corwin accused the northern radicals of "unreasonableness" in their efforts to defy the law. This same conservative had been elected to the Senate by an overwhelming majority in 1858.[30] Corwin's victory and subsequent popularity was incongruous if a majority of Ohio's electorate was opposed to enforcement of the Fugitive Slave Law.

In Pennsylvania, division of opinion was not as sharp as in Ohio. For the most part, Pennsylvania's citizens were conservative and gave little encouragement to abolitionists. While the other northern states became inflamed over passage of the Kansas–Nebraska Act, the people in Pennsylvania were "chiefly alarmed over the power wielded by the Roman Catholics and immigrants," and they seemed to be more concerned about the liquor traffic than they were in the anti-

---

28. *National Intelligencer*, November 23, 1854.

29. Land, "John Brown," pp. 36–37.

30. Daryl Pendergraft, "Thomas Corwin and the Conservative Republican Reaction, 1858–1861," *Ohio State Archaeological and Historical Quarterly* 57 (January 1948): 18–19.

slavery movement.[31] The Pennsylvania legislature had declined to pass a resolution condemning the Kansas–Nebraska Act, and prior to the gubernatorial election of 1854 the efforts of national administration forces to get the Democratic convention in Pennsylvania to endorse the principles of the Nebraska bill ended in failure. The Democratic candidate William Bigler and his principal adviser, Jeremiah Black, were not "pulling anybody's chestnuts out of the fire." [32] "So moderate was Pennsylvania on the slavery question," concluded one student, "that, up to 1858, the Republicans shared the anti-Democratic vote with the 'Americans,' who still insisted that the Catholics and foreign born, not the slaveholders, were the nation's most evil forces." [33] As regards the Fugitive Slave Law, the legislature had repealed the law which forbade the use of state jails for holding fugitive slaves, and subsequent efforts to pass personal liberty laws failed. Numerous elements in the state were antagonized by the harshness of the Fugitive Slave Law, but enforcement of the law in Pennsylvania was little encumbered by hostile public opinion.

In the northeastern part of the United States, where the fugitive slave problem was not nearly as urgent as it was in the border states, public opinion toward the Fugitive Slave Law after 1854 was much more unfriendly. In upstate New York, abolitionist elements were gaining in influence. Even Gerrit Smith, an ultra-abolitionist, had been elected to Congress in 1852 from the twenty-second congressional district. Never a member of the inner councils, Smith found no satisfaction in his work as a congressman and, despite repeated appeals to stay on, resigned on August 7, 1854.[34] For the years following the passage of the Kansas–Nebraska Act, antislavery opinion in New York was summed up by the *Tribune*. "It now appears," said Greeley, "that the slave power keeps no truce, no plighted faith with Freedom, and that the Compromise, on which some people leaned, was only an audacious juggle." [35] Despite the growing senti-

31. Reinhard H. Luthin, "Pennsylvania and Lincoln's Rise to the Presidency," *Pennsylvania Magazine of History and Biography* 67 (January 1943): 61–62 (hereafter cited as Luthin, "Pennsylvania and Lincoln's Rise").

32. Nevins, *Ordeal of Union*, 2:146–47.

33. Luthin, "Pennsylvania and Lincoln's Rise," p. 62.

34. Ralph Volney Harlow, *Gerrit Smith, Philanthropist and Reformer* (New York: Henry Holt and Company, 1939), pp. 312, 331 (hereafter cited as Harlow, *Gerrit Smith*).

35. *New York Weekly Tribune*, July 29, 1854.

ment against slavery, however, the abolitionists never gained a majority in the state legislature.

Although New York City merchants were opposed to the Kansas–Nebraska Act, they were even more opposed to antislavery agitation. By antagonizing the South, the sectional conflict would be deepened. Continued agitation of the slavery issue could result in dissolution of the Union. In an appeal to the Whig voters in the state, the New York merchants pointed out that Southerners had the right under the Constitution to own slaves. Any Whig who believed in the Constitution, reasoned the merchants, would "never be a party to any attempt to deprive them of those rights." [36] Largely because of the influence of business interests, little difficulty was experienced in returning fugitive slaves from New York City.

In Boston, the *Daily Advertiser* noted the exasperation that many people felt because of the repeal of the Missouri Compromise. "Many persons who have hitherto used their utmost exertions and hazarded their influence in carrying into effect the compromise measures . . . are entirely disgusted and disheartened in finding themselves placed in the unexpected position of being held to a compromise which is binding on but one side." [37] Richard Henry Dana also noted the changing sentiment. He said, "I do not know how many who hardly spoke to me from 1850 to 1853, and whom I heard of in all quarters as speaking against me bitterly, come up to me with the freedom and warmth of old friends, and talk as though there had never been any difference between us." [38] Not only did the Massachusetts legislature pass a series of resolutions declaring the Fugitive Slave Law unconstitutional, but after the return of Anthony Burns there was a concerted effort to remove Edward Greeley Loring from his office as Judge of Probate. As United States commissioner, Judge Loring had been responsible for returning Burns to his owner.

During the governorship of Henry J. Gardiner, the legislature was unsuccessful in its attempt to remove Loring from office, but, in 1857, Nathaniel P. Banks was elected governor, and the question of removal was renewed. Under the leadership of John A. Andrew, the motion for the removal of Loring was again introduced, and this

36. Ibid., October 25, 1855.
37. *National Intelligencer*, June 2, 1854, quoting the *Boston Daily Advertiser*.
38. Adams, *Richard Henry Dana*, 1:285.

time it was passed. Judge Loring was removed from office. President Buchanan then appointed him to the United State Court of Claims where he served until his resignation in December, 1877.[39]

There seems to have been little objection from the press to Loring's removal, but the editor of the *Monthly Law Reporter* felt that the attempt to remove Loring was unjust. Extremists in Massachusetts who sought Loring's removal argued that in remanding Anthony Burns to slavery the judge had been guilty of a moral violation of the so-called Latimer law of 1843. That law had prohibited state officers from cooperating in the enforcement of the Fugitive Slave Law of 1793. After reviewing the case, the *Monthly Law Reporter* concluded that the charge was "so vague . . . so manifestly the product of mere party excitement . . . and is so utterly untrue in fact, that we may safely say that it is merely used as a veil to cover the moral nakedness which would be disclosed by an avowal of the real motive. . . ." In the editor's opinion, the real motive was "no other than an attempt to exercise a power reserved by the constitution, in an arbitrary manner for the purpose of gratifying the *odium politicum* of a party, at the expense of a most unoffending and upright magistrate." [40]

The turning point in the attitudes toward the Fugitive Slave Law in the North was the repeal of the Missouri Compromise. The subsequent events in the conflict over slavery, such as "bleeding Kansas," and the Dred Scott decision only intensified the hostility and won new converts to the abolitionist cause.

In New England, the prevailing opinion was that the Fugitive Slave Law should not be enforced. After the return of Anthony Burns, no runaway slaves were remanded to slavery from fugitive slave tribunals in New England. Because of the personal liberty laws and hostile public opinion, few slave owners could or would go to the trouble and expense of pursuing a slave into the states in the northeastern part of the United States. The same thing was true for Wisconsin and Michigan. Aside from the danger and expense in-

39. Garrison, *William Lloyd Garrison*, 3:415–16. See also Adams, *Richard Henry Dana*, 1:347.
40. "The Removal of Judge Loring," *Monthly Law Reporter*, 8, New Series (1856) : 8.

volved, it was just too simple a process for the fugitive to move across the border into Canada.

Many citizens in the northern states did not really perceive the danger of interferring with enforcement of the Fugitive Slave Law until South Carolina withdrew from the Union, and the secession of the other states in the Deep South seemed imminent. While there were a few extremists such as Theodore Parker who were glad to see the slave states secede, this was certainly not the prevailing opinion. Finally realizing the danger, a concerted effort was begun in December, 1860 by several northern governors to seek repeal or modification of the personal liberty laws. The governors of Maine, Massachusetts, New York, Rhode Island, and Pennsylvania agreed to recommend the "unconditional and early repeal of the Personal Liberty Bills passed by their respective States." [41] During the four months preceding the outbreak of the Civil War, Rhode Island and Maine repealed their personal liberty laws. The personal liberty laws of Massachusetts and Vermont were modified, and the legislature of Wisconsin passed a resolution which recommended the revision of her personal liberty laws.[42] There is little reason to doubt that, if the legislatures in the other northern states had believed it possible to hold the Union together by repealing or revising their personal liberty laws, public opinion in those states would have supported such a move. A majority of the northern states now exerted every effort to prevent the personal liberty laws and opposition to enforcement of the Fugitive Slave Law from being used as a pretext for secession. They were too late.

41. Rhodes, *History of the United States*, 3:252–53.
42. *National Intelligencer*, December 11, 1860, February 18, March 14, 1861; *Acts and Resolves of Massachusetts* (1861), pp. 398–99; and *Laws of Rhode Island* (1859–61), p. 115.

Chapter V

Executive Policy
and the
Fugitive Slave Law

Effective law enforcement requires not only a favorable climate of public opinion, but also a strong desire on the part of law enforcement agencies to see the law enforced. Because of the furor caused by passage of the Fugitive Slave Law in some northern communities, it would not have been difficult for the administrations of Presidents Fillmore, Pierce, and Buchanan to rationalize a soft policy toward enforcement of the law. But such was not the case. After the statute to reclaim runaway slaves was signed into law, President Millard Fillmore adopted a policy that was politically dangerous but which sternly demanded that the agencies responsible for the law's enforcement do their duty. This policy was followed consistently by the administrations of Franklin Pierce and James Buchanan.

Having supported the provisions of the Compromise of 1850, Fillmore had signed the bills as they were presented to him. With regard to the Fugitive Slave Law, he was hesitant. Because the question of whether the act suspended habeas corpus proceedings had arisen, Fillmore asked his attorney general, John J. Crittenden, for his opinion on the constitutionality of the law. When Crittenden replied that the act did not "in any manner" conflict with the Constitution,[1] Fillmore affixed his signature, and the bill became law. Since it was possible for free Negroes to be arrested and remanded to slavery under the new law, Fillmore was not at first opposed to modification of the law. Shortly after he had signed the bill, Fillmore wrote to Daniel Webster:

It seems to me . . . that the . . . true ground for our friends to take is this: that the law hav'g passed, must be executed. That so far as it provides for the surrender of fugitives from labor it is according to the requirements of the constitution and should be sustained against all attempts at repeal, but if there be any provision in it endangering the liberty of those who are free, it should be modified as to secure the free blacks from such an abuse of the object of the law, and that done we at the North have no just cause of complaint.[2]

On the contrary, Thurlow Weed and William H. Seward had adopted "immediate modification" as the symbol of their unity and of their resistance to the administration. The president had no desire to see his position on the law "become the sounding board for Weed's sectionalism—got up for political effect," and he changed his view.[3]

Soon after the Fugitive Slave Law was enacted, antislavery men in the North, both black and white, challenged the national government to enforce it. Because of the state of public opinion, and instances of overt interference with the law's execution, Judges Robert C. Grier and John K. Kane petitioned the president for authority to use federal troops in cases of emergency.[4] Not wishing to act without consulting Webster, Fillmore wrote to his secretary of state informing him of the request. He said:

This you perceive presents a very grave and delicate question. . . . These judges ask for a general order authorizing the employment of . . . troops . . . and I am disposed to exert whatever power I possess under the Constitution and laws, in enforcing this observance. I have sworn to support the Constitution. I know no higher law that conflicts with it. . . . I mean at every sacrifice and at every hazard to perform my duty. The

1. Hall, *Opinions of the Attorneys General,* 5:258–59.
2. *Publications of the Buffalo Historical Society, Millard Fillmore Papers,* 11 vols. Edited by Frank H. Severance (Buffalo: Buffalo Historical Society, 1907), 1:334–35 (hereafter cited as *Fillmore Papers*).
3. Robert J. Rayback, *Millard Fillmore: Biography of a President* (Buffalo: Buffalo Historical Society, 1959), pp. 277–78 (hereafter cited as Rayback, *Fillmore*).
4. *Fillmore Papers,* 1:333–35.

Union must and shall be preserved, and this can only be done, by a faithful and impartial administration of the laws. . . . Nullification can not and will not be tolerated.[5]

With Crittenden and Webster absent from Washington, Fillmore called two cabinet meetings and laid the question of the propriety of using federal troops in the enforcement of the Fugitive Slave Law before it. On October 28, Fillmore wrote to Webster again and informed him of his decision. After conferring with his advisers, the president had decided to give such authority to United States marshals and their special deputies when a judge of the District Court or a justice of the Supreme Court "should certify that in his opinion it was necessary." Feeling that it would be bad policy to antagonize the states north of Mason and Dixon's line any further, he had authorized the use of federal troops "only in the last resort. . . ." But "if necessary," he said, "I shall not hesitate to give greater power, and finally to bring the whole force of the government to sustain the law. . . ."[6]

In his first annual message, Fillmore noted that "mutual concession in the nature of a compromise must necessarily be unwelcome to men of extreme opinions." Yet, in his opinion, the compromise had been absolutely necessary if the Union were to be maintained. About the compromise, he said:

I believe those measures to have been required by the circumstances and condition of the country. I believe they were necessary to allay asperities and animosities that were rapidly alienating one section of the country from another and destroying those fraternal sentiments which are the strongest supports of the Constitution. . . .
The series of measures to which I have alluded are regarded by me as a settlement in principle and substance—a final settlement of the dangerous and exciting subjects which they embraced.[7]

Although public opinion opposed to enforcement of the Fugitive Slave Law had begun to subside in the spring and summer of 1851, three rescues and one attempted rescue occurred during that period which tested the will of the administration to enforce the law. They were the Shadrach rescue and the attempted rescue of Thomas Sims

5. Fillmore to Webster, October 23, 1850, ibid., 1:334.
6. Fillmore to Webster, October 28, 1850, ibid., 1:335–36. See also Rayback, *Fillmore*, pp. 270–71.
7. Richardson, *Messages and Papers*, 5:92–93.

in Boston, the Christiana riot in Pennsylvania, and the Jerry rescue in Syracuse, New York.

Arrested on February 15, a fugitive slave called Shadrach was taken to the courthouse in Boston for a hearing before United States Commissioner George Ticknor Curtis. During the course of the hearing, a group of Negroes burst into the courtroom, rescued the fugitive, and sent him on to Canada.[8] Fillmore's response to this outrage against federal law was to issue a proclamation calling upon all well-disposed citizens to aid in quelling any further riots and in capturing the rescued prisoner.[9] The United States attorney in Boston was ordered to prosecute to the fullest extent of the law all persons who had participated in the rescue. Furthermore, Fillmore responded to a demand by Henry Clay for an investigation into the affair by reporting to the Senate the following statement:

I use this occasion to repeat the assurance that so far as depends on me the laws shall be faithfully executed and all forcible opposition to them suppressed; and to this end I am prepared to exercise, whenever it may become necessary, the power constitutionally vested in me to the fullest extent. I am fully persuaded that the great majority of the people of this country are warmly and strongly attached to the Constitution, and the preservation of the Union, the just support of the Government, and the maintenance of the authority of law.[10]

United States troops in Boston were placed at the disposal of the federal marshal.[11] Although eight persons were indicted in the case, none was convicted because of hung juries.

The tables were turned in the Thomas Sims case in April, and the administration demonstrated that it could and would enforce the Fugitive Slave Law, even in Massachusetts. Thomas Sims, a fugitive slave who had escaped from Chatham County, Georgia, was arrested and presented for a hearing before Commissioner Curtis. The hearing proceeded according to schedule, and Thomas Sims was remanded to his owner. Plans to rescue the fugitive had failed. The slave was placed aboard a ship and delivered to Savannah, Georgia. On April 16, Fillmore wrote to Webster: ". . . I congratulate you and the country upon a triumph of law in Boston. She has done

---

8. For the details of the case, see Chapter VII.
9. Richardson, *Messages and Papers*, 5:109–10.
10. Ibid., pp. 5:105–6.
11. *National Intelligencer*, March 1, 1851.

nobly. She has wiped out the stain of the former rescue and freed herself from the reproach of nullification." In the same letter, the president stated his hope that "some satisfactory arrangement" could be made for the trial of those who attempted to rescue Sims. "It is very important," he said, "that these criminals should be punished. Their crime is contagious, and they must not escape with impunity." [12]

As regards enforcement of the Fugitive Slave Law, the year 1851 was frustrating for the president, but the news was not all bad. Fillmore could take comfort from the fact that public opinion was swinging from opposition to enforcement of the law to a posture of acquiescence. For example, the Reverend John Chase Lord preached a sermon *"The Higher Law" in its Application to the Fugitive Slave Bill*. Such sentiments for the maintenance of law and order and the preservation of the Union were appreciated by Fillmore, and he took time to write Lord and thank him. He wrote: "You have rendered the nation a great and valuable service, and I am highly gratified to learn, that thousands and tens of thousands have been reprinted in New York, and sent here, and are now being distributed under the franks of members of Congress. It cannot fail to do good. It reaches a class of people of excellent intentions, but somewhat bigoted prejudices, who could be reached in no other way." [13] Fillmore also rejoiced to learn that Pennsylvania had repealed her law which had refused the use of her jails to house fugitive slaves. [14] The situation seemed to be improving, antislavery agitation seemed to be waning, but two other rescues were to shock the nation and to inspire law enforcement agencies to greater diligence than before.

On September 11, 1851, the most violent episode in the history of the Fugitive Slave Law's enforcement occurred. A riot broke out between whites and Negroes in Christiana, Pennsylvania following an attempt by federal officers to capture a group of fugitive slaves. In a pitched battle, the owner of the slaves was killed, his son badly wounded, and three Negroes slain. Public reaction was one of shock, relations between the states of Maryland and Pennsylvania deteriorated, and the national government was embarrassed. [15] In his efforts

12. Fillmore to Webster, April 16, 1851, *Fillmore Papers*, 1:341, 342.
13. Fillmore to Lord, January 13, 1851, ibid., 2:306–7.
14. Fillmore to Webster, April 16, 1851, ibid., 1:342.
15. See Chapter VII.

to arrest and prosecute the rioters, United States Attorney George W. Ashmead was given full support of the administration.[16] Although forty-five persons were indicted for treason against the United States, Ashmead was unable to get convictions. Judge Grier ruled that the charge of treason had not been sustained by the evidence, and Castner Hanaway, who had been tried as a test case, was released. Ashmead entered *nolle prosequis* in the remaining cases. The failure to get convictions, however, can not be charged to a lack of diligence on the part of the administration. Wanting to make examples of the rioters in the Christiana affair, Ashmead may not have used sound judgment in trying to get convictions for treason, but this was the policy that he chose to implement, and the administration supported him.[17]

Another test of the administration's will to enforce the law in the face of fierce opposition occurred in Syracuse, New York in October, 1851. A fugitive slave named Jerry was arrested by United States Marshal Henry W. Allen at a most inappropriate time. The Liberty party convention was being held in Syracuse, and the city was also crowded with visitors to the Onandaga County Fair. News of the arrest spread rapidly, and before the day was over, Jerry had been rescued and sent to Canada. Implicated in the rescue were some of the most influential citizens of Syracuse, including Gerrit Smith. Despite the best efforts of the United States attorney, only one man was convicted. Southerners were incensed, and the administration was embarrassed. There is no evidence however, to support the contention that those responsible for enforcing the law lacked diligence.[18]

In his second annual message to the Congress on December 2, 1851, the president reviewed the administration's policy toward the Fugitive Slave Law. He acknowledged that federal officers had been openly resisted by "lawless and violent mobs . . . ," but, said he, "I have regarded it as my duty in these cases to give all aid legally in my power to the enforcement of the laws, and I shall continue to do so wherever and whenever their execution may be resisted." [19] Al-

16. Alexander H. H. Stuart to Ashmead, November 6, 14, 1851, Department of the Interior, Letter Book, Judiciary No. 1, 1849–1853, National Archives, Justice and Executive Branch, Washington, D.C.

17. Stuart to Ashmead, November 14, 1851, ibid.

18. See Chapter VII for details of the case.

19. Richardson, *Messages and Papers*, 5:137.

though there had been great opposition to enforcement of the law, Fillmore was pleased to note that resistance was crumbling. As regards the changing attitudes toward the compromise measures, he said:

. . . I congratulate you and the country upon the general acquiescence in these measures of peace which has been exhibited in all parts of the Republic. And not only is there this general acquiescence in these measures, but the spirit of concilliation which has been manifested in regard to them in all parts of the country has removed doubts and uncertainties in the minds of thousands of good men concerning the durability of our popular institutions and given renewed assurance that our liberty and our Union may subsist together for the benefit of this and all succeeding generations.[20]

By midsummer 1851, public acquiescence toward the Fugitive Slave Law was in fact becoming general, and, following the elections of 1852, the compromise measures were accepted by the vast majority as a final settlement of the slavery question.

When President Fillmore left office in March, 1853, he had demonstrated that the power of the national government supported law enforcement agencies in their efforts to enforce the unpopular law. In view of the public turmoil aroused by passage of the law, Fillmore is to be commended for the courage with which he faced an unpleasant duty. The policy established by his administration, moreover, was followed throughout the remainder of the decade with the same sense of duty and responsibility.

In his inaugural address to the nation, President Franklin Pierce indicated his intent to follow the policy of his predecessor by holding that the compromise measures were constitutional and would be "unhesitatingly carried into effect." Furthermore, it was Pierce's conviction that "the constituted authorities of this Republic are bound to regard the rights of the South in this respect as they would view any other legal and constitutional right, and that the laws to enforce them should be respected and obeyed, not with a reluctance encouraged by abstract opinions as to their propriety in a different state of society, but cheerfully and according to the decisions of the tribunal to which their exposition belongs." [21] In fact, Louis Filler, in

20. Ibid., pp. 138–39.
21. Ibid., 5:202.

his *Crusade Against Slavery*, concludes that Pierce was "determined, more forcefully than Fillmore had been, that the Fugitive Slave Law must operate." [22]

As pointed out by Roy Franklin Nichols, in his biography of Pierce, the new president had decided early to support the compromise measures. After the death of Zachary Taylor, the chances of electing a Democrat in 1852 were considerably enhanced. Pierce's advisers thought that "it would be better not to antagonize the South further." In any case, a decision was made by the New Hampshire leaders to support the compromise, and, after it was adopted, they began an active campaign for "popular endorsement even of the unpopular fugitive slave law." [23] Taking into consideration the Baltimore platform, which accepted the compromise as a final settlement of the slavery issue, it was not surprising that Pierce's administration should take a strong stand on enforcement of the Fugitive Slave Law.

After the new administration had taken office, the person more responsible than any other for carrying out the stern policy toward enforcement of the Fugitive Slave Law was Pierce's attorney general, Caleb Cushing. Indeed, Cushing soon made it clear that the entire power of the government, including the army and navy, would be used in forcing compliance with the law. According to Nichols, Cushing was the "most extraordinary member" of the cabinet. A former Whig turned Democrat, Cushing had served as first envoy to China and was a brigadier general in the Mexican War. After serving on the Massachusetts Supreme Court, he was called to Pierce's cabinet. Cushing was a brilliant lawyer, and "no better attorney-general could have been found as far as his legal duties were concerned." But as a politician the New England lawyer left much to be desired. "Confident in the knowledge of his accomplishments," said Nichols, "he had never found it necessary to acquire a fund of political common sense." If Cushing had been a better politician, he "might have been a great man rather than a millstone around Pierce's neck." Nonetheless, he was closer to the president than any

22. Louis Filler, *The Crusade Against Slavery* (New York: Harper & Brothers, 1960), p. 213.

23. Roy Franklin Nichols, *Franklin Pierce: Young Hickory of the Granite Hills* (Philadelphia: University of Pennsylvania Press, 1931), pp. 180–81 (hereafter cited as Nichols, *Pierce*).

of the cabinet members, and "his influence seems to have been greatest." [24]

Before becoming attorney general, he had formed certain clear-cut convictions about the slavery issue. Having prepared the report of the Democratic Central Committee of Massachusetts in 1851, his views largely influenced those of the Democratic party in the state toward the slavery question. Cushing believed in having nothing to do with abolitionists. At the Democratic state convention, the "National Democrats," with whom he identified himself, were able to push through a series of resolutions against Free Soil opposition which advocated "non-intervention" in state affairs, opposed all antislavery agitation, and approved the compromise measures including the Fugitive Slave Law. [25]

The views of the administration were stated forcefully in a letter to the editor of the *Boston Post* on September 29, 1853. As regards antislavery agitation, Cushing wrote:

The President entertains immovable convictions on this point, as I have had occasion to express to you heretofore, and all of us whom he has called to the public service here, most heartily and zealously sustain his views on this subject as being the only ones consistent with personal honor, the integrity of the Constitution, or the permanency of the Union. If there be any purpose more fixed than another in the mind of the President and those with whom he is accustomed to consult, it is that the dangerous element of Abolitionism, under whatever guise or form it may present itself, shall be crushed out, so far as his administration is concerned. This the President declared in his Inaugural,—this he has declared ever since, at all times, and in all places, where he has had occasion to speak on the subject. [26]

Believing that the Union could be preserved in no other way, President Pierce looked upon the constitutional rights of the states "as the cornerstone of the Union." [27] The return of fugitive slaves was a constitutional right of the southern states. The Fugitive Slave Law had been enacted to effect that right, and the administration meant to see it executed.

Under President Pierce, according to Cushing's biographer Claude Fuess, the office of attorney general became more important than at

24. Ibid., p. 248–49.
25. Fuess, *Cushing*, 2:107–8.
26. Ibid., pp. 139–40, quoting *Boston Post*, September 29, 1853.
27. Ibid., p. 140.

any time in its history. Giving scope to Cushing's great talents, William L. Marcy, secretary of state, advised the president to transfer to the attorney general many new duties. Henceforth, pardons, legal appointments, cases arising under the extradition laws, and judicial appointments were placed under Cushing's jurisdiction. Because of his new duties and his influence upon the president, Cushing "had a part in nearly every matter of significance arising during the next four years in Washington." [28]

Convinced that the Union must be maintained and, believing that in order to maintain the Union the compromise measures must be adhered to, the attorney general was particularly interested in seeing the Fugitive Slave Law enforced. In a letter to President Pierce on November 14, 1853, Cushing argued that in cases where suits were brought against United States marshals resulting from their efforts to enforce the Fugitive Slave Law the cost of defense counsel should be borne by the United States. The president agreed, and the law thus became easier to enforce. On February 18, 1854, Cushing extended his policy. Thereafter, any citizen of the United States had the right to recover fugitive slaves, and this right extended to the unorganized territorial possessions as well as the states and organized territories. In those territories where there was no United States commissioner, fugitive slaves could be captured without due process of law. The policy was broadened still further on May 27 when a United States marshal was given the authority to "summon the entire ablebodied force of his precinct, as a *posse commitatus*," when opposed in his efforts to capture a fugitive slave. Marshals were also given the right to call upon "any and all organized force, whether militia of the state, or officers, sailors, soldiers, and marines of the United States." Finally, Cushing ruled that no person who had been arrested "on a warrant of a competent judicial authority of the United States," could be legally discharged on a writ of habeas corpus by the state courts.[29] These policies called for no more than was provided for in the Fugitive Slave Law, but the definite statement of policy was designed to ensure enforcement of the law in spite of opposition by the states.

Perhaps the best example of the administration's determination to

28. Ibid., pp. 134–36.
29. Ibid., pp. 144–45.

enforce the Fugitive Slave Law was the Anthony Burns case in Boston in 1854. No slave had been returned from Boston since Thomas Sims had been remanded in 1851. Public opinion was so aroused by Burns's arrest that the United States marshal was compelled to call for federal troops to help maintain order. An attempt was made to rescue the fugitive from the courthouse, and, during the melee, one of the marshal's deputies was killed. In reply to his report, President Pierce wired the marshal: "Your conduct is approved. The law must be enforced." [30] At the same time the United States attorney was informed that he might "Incur any expense deemed necessary . . . to insure execution of the law. . . ." Finally, the adjutant general of the United States was sent to Boston to supervise the federal troops. When Burns was ultimately remanded to his owner, the president made a revenue cutter available for transporting the fugitive back to Virginia.[31]

Reviewing Cushing's policies editorially in December, 1857, Horace Greeley indicated the consternation of the abolitionists with the national government's determination to enforce the Fugitive Slave Law. In general, pointing out Cushing's white supremist attitudes as a rationale for his policies, Greeley said: "He is a Democrat and he therefore supports an aristocracy founded upon the color of his fellow-creatures' skin. In his Utopia there would be none but white folks." Moreover, he continued: "Mr. Caleb Cushing is about the hardest cushion ever pressed down by the weight of public opinion. He is rhinoscerously tough as to his outside, and inside he is like the apples of Sodom, full of ashes not very finely sifted. We do not say he is a bad man, but with our hat off and our best bow, we pronounce him to be a bold one." [32] Those opposed to slavery, and more specifically those who were opposed to enforcement of the Fugitive Slave Law, had good reason to be concerned. More slaves were returned from federal tribunals during Pierce's administration than at any other time during the decade preceding the Civil War, and, despite growing opposition, there were fewer rescues. The Pierce administration had adopted the policies of Millard Fillmore

30. *National Intelligencer*, May 29, 1854. See also Nichols, *Pierce*, p. 361.
31. Nichols, *Pierce*, p. 136; *National Intelligencer*, June 3, 1854. For the details of the case, see Chapter VI.
32. *New York Weekly Tribune*, December 5, 1857.

and strengthened them. President James Buchanan would do no less.

Like his two predecessors, James Buchanan entered the presidency with fixed convictions about the institution of slavery and the necessity of suppressing antislavery agitation if the Union were to be preserved. As early as November 19, 1850, in a speech before a Democratic meeting, Buchanan had said:

> Let us then resolve to put down agitation at the North on the slave question, by the force of enlightened public opinion, and faithfully execute the provisions of the Fugitive Slave Law. Should this be done, it will eventually extinguish those geographical parties—so dangerous to the Union . . . which have sprung into existence; it will ameliorate the condition of the slaves, by enabling the masters to remove the restrictions imposed upon them in self-defence, since the commencement of the present troubles, and will restore the natural and constitutional progress of emancipation which has, in several States, been arrested by the violence of the Abolitionists.[33]

An earnest advocate of the Compromise of 1850, Buchanan believed in the strict enforcement of the Fugitive Slave Law. The law had been enacted, he felt, to "carry into execution the plain, clear, and mandatory provision of the Constitution." [34] Since the Fugitive Slave Law was all the South had salvaged from the compromise, Buchanan hoped that public opinion in the North would support its faithful execution. In the election campaign of 1852, Buchanan had said, "I view the finality of the Compromise as necessary to peace and preservation of the Union. . . ." [35] That was the view he held at the time of his election to the presidency in 1856.

During the course of Buchanan's administration, enforcement of the Fugitive Slave Law was made more difficult and expensive by the continued passage of the personal liberty laws. But in spite of the growing opposition to slavery and the increasing hostility to the law for the reclamation of fugitive slaves, the law was enforced. In every

33. Union Safety Committee, *Selections from the Speeches or Abolition and Agitation*, p. 30.

34. James B. Ranack, "The Attitude of James Buchanan Towards Slavery," *Pennsylvania Magazine of History and Biography* 51 (January, 1927): 134, 137–38.

35. John Bassett Moore, ed., *The Works of James Buchanan*, 12 vols (Philadelphia: J. B. Lippincott Company, 1908–1911), 8:460–91 (hereafter cited as Moore, *Works of James Buchanan*). See also Philip Shriver Klein, *President James Buchanan: A Biography* (University Park: The Pennsylvania State University Press, 1962), pp. 214–16.

instance where the authority of the United States was challenged by the state courts, the administration remained firm and insisted upon maintenance of the supremacy of federal law. As was pointed out in the chapter on the constitutionality of the Fugitive Slave Law, Jeremiah S. Black defended successfully the validity of the law before the Supreme Court, and Wisconsin's attempt at nullifying federal law was overruled.[36]

Illustrative of the support given federal officers during Buchanan's administration is a letter written to United States Marshal Matthew Johnson, of the Northern District of Ohio, who was experiencing great difficulty with the state courts. The attorney general warned the marshal that he should be careful "not to give any just cause of offence to the state authorities. But it is necessary that you obey the Court whose officer you are." Furthermore, he said: "You will of course see to it that your prisoners are not rescued out of your custody either by the void process of Judges who have no jurisdiction or by open and undisguised violence. . . ." The attorney general went on to say that even though the Supreme Court of Ohio might issue a writ of habeas corpus, the marshal was to "respectfully decline to produce the bodies of the prisoners before the State Court" or let them be removed from his custody. Marshal Johnson was instructed further that, in fugitive slave cases, the federal courts had "exclusive jurisdiction," and no state court had authority to intervene. Black concluded by saying: "If the State authorities should disregard their duty to the Constitution and laws of the Union so entirely as to make an attack upon you, do not forget, nor let your assistants forget that they who defend the law are protected by the law. The assaulting party must take all the consequences upon their own heads. The moral as well as the physical power will be on your side."[37] On May 21, similar instructions were sent to United States Marshal Lewis N. Sifford and United States Attorney Stanley Matthews in Cincinnati, Ohio. Under no circumstances, said Black, should prisoners of the United States be surrendered. "In case of an attack upon you by State Officers, you must defend yourself, and

36. Ableman v. Booth, 21 Howard 506 (1859).

37. Jeremiah S. Black to Matthew Johnson, April 26, 1859, Letter Book, B/2, Attorney General's Office, 1859–1861, National Archives, Justice and Executive Branch, Washington, D.C.

maintain the rights of the United States, against all lawless aggressions." [38] Like Caleb Cushing before him, Jeremiah S. Black never wavered in his determination to use whatever means were necessary within the law to ensure enforcement of the Fugitive Slave Law.

In his fourth annual message on December 3, 1860, as the nation was on the brink of disaster, President Buchanan could truthfully say that, despite the "most palpable violations of constitutional duty which have yet been committed," the Fugitive Slave Law had been "carried into execution in every contested case since the commencement" of his administration. In fifty-seven cases presented before fugitive slave tribunals between 1857 and 1860, forty-five slaves were remanded to their owners, twenty of them at government expense. Even so, the law had been executed "with great loss and inconvenience to the master, and with considerable expense to the Government." [39] Buchanan feared for the Union if such practices persisted.

In December, 1850, the Georgia Platform had resolved that the preservation of the Union depended upon the "faithful execution of the *Fugitive Slave Law* by the proper authorities. . . ." [40] The "proper authorities" were the officers of the federal government, executive and judicial, who were charged by the Constitution with maintaining the supremacy of the laws of the United States. Since the Prigg decision in 1842, state officers had been exempted from responsibility in the enforcement of the Fugitive Slave Law. Following the adoption of the compromise measures, Millard Fillmore, Franklin Pierce, and James Buchanan exerted every effort within their power to enforce the law. The next two chapters will demonstrate that the judicial officers of the United States, supported by the national executives, did indeed enforce the Fugitive Slave Law.

38. Black to Sifford and Black to Matthews, May 21, 1859, ibid.
39. Richardson, *Messages and Papers*, 5:629–30; Moore, *Works of James Buchanan*, 12:103.
40. Ames, *State Documents*, pp. 31–32.

Chapter VI

Enforcement
of the
Fugitive Slave Law,
1850–1860

Many Southerners sincerely believed in 1860 that the Fugitive Slave Law, the one concession made to the South in the Compromise of 1850, had not been enforced. Non-enforcement and northern hostility to the law were frequently cited as justification for secession from the Union. Hostility toward the law as expressed in the passage of personal liberty laws was evidence enough for many Southerners that the institution of slavery stood in jeopardy. The widely publicized rescues of fugitive slaves convinced many others that the North had been faithless to its obligations under the Constitution and the provisions of the compromise measures. Well-known historians who have written on the fugitive slave problem have been generally critical of the enforcement of the Fugitive Slave Law. Following James Ford Rhodes and Allan Nevins, most historians have concluded that the law was never effectively enforced. Indeed, the concensus seems to be that by 1860 the law was for the most part unenforceable. Rhodes argued that after only one year it had become clear "that in most Northern communities" the law could not be enforced "without more trouble and expense than were worth the taking." [1] Writing in 1914, another student of the problem concluded: "Never did any law enacted by Congress more completely fail of its purpose than did the Fugitive Slave Law of 1850." [2] Textbook writers have generally accepted the thesis that because of hostile public opinion in the North the Fugitive Slave Law failed. Were the Southerners correct in their belief that the law was not enforced? Upon what kinds of evidence have historians concluded that the law was not enforced? What did enforcement of the law mean?

The views which hold that the Fugitive Slave Law was not enforced may have been based upon inconclusive research, and the criteria of measurement have not always been clear. Indeed, in most of the works dealing with enforcement of the Fugitive Slave Law there seems to have been no systematic method for treating the problem. Before concluding that the law was or was not enforced, the proper criteria by which to measure the law's effectiveness must be determined.

There are four criteria by which the effectiveness of the Fugitive Slave Law's enforcement can be measured: First, the annual decrease or increase in the number of fugitive slaves; second, the number of slaves returned to their owners compared with the number of fugitive slaves escaping annually; third, the number of fugitive slaves arrested and remanded to their owners compared with the number of claims made upon the fugitive slave tribunals; and finally, the number of convictions for harboring, concealing, or rescuing runaway slaves.

If measured by the first criterion, the law obviously failed. If the census reports are reliable, the number of slaves escaping each year remained relatively constant during the decade preceding the Civil War. Since there was no appreciable decrease in the number of fugitive slaves, the law evidently failed to act as a deterrent. But the first criterion is not adequate. The law was not designed to deter

1. Rhodes, *History of the United States*, 1:225. See also Allan Nevins, *Emergence of Lincoln*, 2 vols. (New York: Charles Scribner's Sons, 1950), 2:29, 115 (hereafter cited as Nevins, *Emergence of Lincoln*).
2. Daniel Wait Howe, *Political History of Secession to the Beginning of the American Civil War* (New York: G. P. Putnam's Sons, 1914), p. 220.

Negroes from running away, but it was expected that its new, more stringent provisions would facilitate the capture and return of fugitive slaves. The restrictive and punitive features of the law were not operant upon the slaves, but those who aided or abetted in the escape of fugitives from service were subject to prosecution.

The number of slaves captured and returned as compared with the number of slaves who absconded each year is virtually impossible to determine accurately. To ascertain what percentage escaped into the free states is not feasible. Nor is there any adequate means of arriving at the number of fugitive slaves captured by their owners and returned to slavery without recourse to the machinery provided by the Fugitive Slave Law. Senator Stephen A. Douglas asserted that "in nineteen cases out of twenty where a fugitive slave enters Illinois, he is arrested and returned without any judicial process whatever. Those portions of the State which border on the Kentucky and Missouri lines are in harmony with their neighbors on the other side, and a fugitive slave is returned as regularly as a stolen horse." [3] The same thing can be said about the other border states. Too many unknown variables make the second criterion unsatisfactory.

The only feasible means of measuring the effectiveness of the enforcement of the Fugitive Slave Law are, first, to compare the number of slaves arrested and returned under the auspices of the new law with the number of claims made upon the fugitive slave tribunals and, second, to determine the number of convictions for harboring, concealing, or rescuing fugitive slaves. But even these criteria are not wholly satisfactory. All too frequently the arrests of fugitive slaves were not reported in the press, and the records of many of the United States circuit courts have been destroyed. Hence, it would be extremely difficult to get an accurate count of the number of fugitive slaves arrested and returned to their owners. In some of the communities which were hostile to enforcement of the Fugitive Slave Law the press reported only the escapes, rescues, or attempted rescues. Such efforts to villify the law present a distorted picture of enforcement. In areas which were amenable to the return of fugitive slaves, the arrest of a runaway Negro was not considered newsworthy unless there was violence or the threat of it. While there is no way of obtaining a complete record of the claims made upon the fugitive slave tribunals, the cases reported in the press and other journals do provide an adequate basis for estimating the effectiveness of enforcement procedures.[4]

It has already been demonstrated that it was the policy of the national government during the administrations of Presidents Fillmore, Pierce, Buchanan, and Lincoln to enforce the law. If it can be demonstrated that in the known cases the fugitive slave tribunals remanded to their owners a significant majority of the Negroes brought before them who were proved to be slaves, then it must be concluded that, at least in those cases, the sections of the law which provided for the return of fugitive slaves were enforced by those responsible for enforcement. It must be emphasized at this point that the national government, not the northern state governments, was charged with the responsibility for executing the Fugitive Slave Law.

Since all the cases involving persons charged with aiding and abetting the escape of fugitive slaves may be found in the reports of the various courts, it is a relatively simple matter to determine the number of convictions for these infractions of the Fugitive Slave Law.

As one reviews enforcement procedures, it must be remembered that under the decision of the Supreme Court in the Prigg case the slaveholder or his agent was empowered to capture and return his fugitive slaves where he could do so without disturbing the peace. To recover a runaway slave under the Fugitive Slave Law of 1850, the owner had to go to a court of record in his own state and establish that his slave had escaped and that the slave owed service or labor to the claimant. Then he had to provide a general description of the fugitive. If the judge of the local court was satisfied that the first two

4. Because the complete official record is no longer extant, the problems involved in researching fugitive slave cases is difficult. In this study, the sources in the executive and judicial branches of the National Archives were exhausted. Other sources used were newspapers and contemporary accounts such as autobiographies and personal papers. Most of the important cases are well known and can be found in the secondary accounts. A great deal of research done at the local level has been published in state historical journals and has been extremely useful for this study. Further research would undoubtedly turn up more cases, but I doubt seriously that such research would change materially the results of this investigation.

points were correct, a record was made of the proceedings, and an official transcript was given to the claimant. The transcript, when presented to a fugitive slave commissioner in the district where the fugitive might be found, was to be received as conclusive evidence that the slave described in the transcript had escaped and owed service or labor to the claimant. The commissioner would then issue a warrant to the federal marshal for the fugitive's arrest. If the fugitive was arrested and brought before the commissioner, all that remained in the process was to ascertain whether the person arrested was the slave described in the transcript. If the commissioner was convinced that the person brought before him was the slave described in the transcript, the law required him to issue a certificate authorizing the removal of the fugitive back to the state from which he had escaped. If the slaveholder believed that the slave might be taken from him by an irate mob, the law permitted the commissioner to have the slave removed to the state from which he had escaped in the custody of a federal marshal at the expense of the national government. Without the transcript, the commissioner could not issue a warrant for the fugitive's arrest, and without a warrant no federal marshal had authority to arrest and hold a Negro as a fugitive slave. Therefore, as regards the recovery of fugitive slaves, the enforcement of the law depended in large part upon the initiative of the slave's owner and not upon federal officers. The central purpose of this chapter and the following chapter will be to show that, although relatively few fugitive slaves were returned in the decade before the Civil War, the national government cannot be charged with failure to enforce the law.

Within a few days after President Fillmore signed the new Fugitive Slave Law, southern slaveholders were filing claims for fugitive slaves in several of the northern states. In the ten years after enactment of the law, the great majority of fugitive slaves claimed in federal tribunals were remanded to their owners. These slaves were returned despite hostile public opinion. In some quarters, this hostility manifested itself in violent resistance to enforcement; in other quarters it was manifested in jurisdictional disputes between state and federal courts. In only a small minority of the cases were slaves rescued from federal custody. This would seem to call into question the assertion that the South could legitimately claim that the law was not enforced.

The first person arrested under the Fugitive Slave Law of 1850 was taken into custody in New York. Claimed by the agent of Mary Brown of Baltimore, Maryland, James Hamlet was brought before the fugitive slave commissioner. Evidence of the fugitive's identity was conclusive, and Hamlet was remanded to the custody of Marshal Henry E. Tallmadge who took him back to Baltimore.[5] An immediate effort was made by the citizens of New York to purchase Hamlet's freedom. The eight hundred dollars demanded by his mistress was quickly raised, and Hamlet was returned to New York a free man.[6]

On October 8, 1850, a Negro was claimed by his owner and was arrested in Detroit, Michigan. After his arrest, hundreds of armed Negroes gathered and threatened to rescue the prisoner. Federal troops were necessary to protect the captive as he was being transferred from the jail to the court for his hearing. Although no effort was made to rescue the Negro, the mob was angry, and several stones were thrown at the marshal's carriage. Before the excitement got out of hand, the freedom of the Negro was purchased for five hundred dollars. According to an account in the *National Intelligencer,* the subscription was headed by the son-in-law of General Lewis Cass, and "Not a real noisy abolitionist . . . subscribed a dollar." Having paid two hundred dollars in expenses, the owner pocketed three hundred dollars and returned home a poorer but wiser man.[7]

The first case in Indiana occurred in New Albany, just across the Ohio River from Louisville, Kentucky. Living in New Albany at that time was a Negro woman, her daughter, and grandson. Having moved from Kentucky, they had been living peacefully in the city for about four months. While the two women worked, the child attended the local school. One day late in November, 1850, Dennis Framell

5. The cost to the taxpayers was $152.50. Treasury Department, First Auditor's Certificate No. 108539, December 15, 1852, in Register of Audits, April 3, 1850 to July 18, 1853, vol. 6. Record Group 217, Records of the United States Accounting Office, National Archives, Fiscal Branch, Washington, D.C.

6. Samuel May, *The Fugitive Slave Law and Its Victims* (New York: American Anti-Slavery Society, 1861), p. 11 (hereafter cited as May, *Fugitive Slave Law and Its Victims*). See also *Boston Liberator,* October 4, 1850.

7. *New York Tribune,* October 5, 1850. See also May, *Fugitive Slave Law and Its Victims,* p. 11.

appeared with a warrant for the arrest of the three persons as fugitive slaves. They were taken into custody and held in the city jail. From all appearances, the alleged fugitives were white, and public opinion was suddenly aroused against the action of the claimant. At their trial the following day, the women testified that they had never been held as slaves. Their testimony was not acceptable as evidence before a fugitive slave tribunal, and the claimant was able to prove to the court's saisfaction that the women and child were his property. Remanded to the custody of the federal marshal, they were delivered to their claimant in Kentucky. Ironically, the three fugitives were rescued at Caseyville, Kentucky by a mob of slaveholders. Taken before a local court, the two women and the child were released as white persons. To protect them from further humiliation, however, the residents of New Albany subscribed the six hundred dollars which Framell asked for the three fugitives. A bill of sale was provided, and they were returned to Indiana.[8]

By the end of the year public hostility in many communities had begun to decline, and attempts to recover fugitive slaves were fraught with fewer hazards. As the danger subsided, more and more Southerners ventured into the free states in search of their lost slaves. The number of slaves arrested and returned under the auspices of the Fugitive Slave Law in 1851 was greater than any other year in the decade before the Civil War.

Attempting to demonstrate that the merchants of New York were sincere in their desire to put down antislavery agitation and to cooperate in the enforcement of the Fugitive Slave Law, the Union Safety Committee became involved in the case of Henry Long. Federal officers arrested Long in early January, and he was taken before the federal commissioner for a hearing. His case was moving along swiftly until the American Anti-Slavery Society supplied funds for Long's defense.[9] The expenses of the claimant began to rise sharply. The members of the Union Safey Committee were afraid

8. May, *Fugitive Slave Law and Its Victims*, p. 12; *New York Weekly Tribune*, December 21, 1850; Money, "Fugitive Slave Law in Indiana," pp. 270–71. In the period between September and December, 1850, thirteen fugitive slave cases were tried in the federal tribunals; eleven slaves were remanded to their owners, two were released from custody, and nine slaves were returned without due process of law. There were no escapes and no rescues reported. See Appendix I.

9. Foner, *Business and Slavery* pp. 60–61.

that should the claimant fail to recover his slave the failure would be interpreted in the South as an act of bad faith on the part of the citizens of New York. A fund of five hundred dollars was quickly established, and George Wood, prominent New York attorney and chairman of the Union Safety Committee, appeared in court on behalf of the slave's claimant.[10] After establishing Long's identity, the federal commissioner remanded the fugitive to the custody of a federal marshal who was ordered to deliver the slave to Alexandria, Virginia.[11]

Long was returned to Richmond and sold for $750. The expenses of the claimant for recovering his slave were $2,250. However, $800 of his costs had been paid by the Union Safety Committee.[12] An attempt by the Union Safety Committee to purchase Long's freedom failed. The slave's owner objected because he did not want other slaves in the South to learn that if they could get to New York their freedom would be purchased. The man to whom Long was sold was required to post a $3,000 bond that he would move the slave further South.[13] Henry Long was sold again in Atlanta, Georgia.[14]

The tide of public opinion in opposition to the Fugitive Slave Law had started to ebb when the determination of the government to enforce the law was tested in Boston. On April 3, 1851, a fugitive slave named Thomas Sims was arrested by city officials on a charge of theft. Sims had resisted the arrest and wounded one of the officers in the leg. The prisoner was hustled off to the courthouse where he was placed in the custody of the United States marshal, Charles Devens.[15]

Knowledge of the arrest spread rapidly over the city. Samuel E.

10. Ibid., p. 61.
11. *National Intelligencer*, January 9, 1851; *Boston Liberator*, January 17, 1851. The cost for removing Long from New York to Alexandria was $272. Treasury Department, First Auditor's Certificate No. 108539, December 15, 1852, in Register of Audits, April 3, 1850 to July 18, 1853, vol. 6, Record Group 217, Records of the United States Accounting Office, National Archives, Fiscal Branch, Washington, D.C.
12. Franklin Dexter, *A Letter to the Hon. Samuel A. Eliot, Representative in Congress from the City of Boston, in Reply to His Apology for Voting for the Fugitive Slave Bill* (Boston: W. Crosby & H. P. Nichols, 1851), p. 43.
13. *New York Weekly Tribune*, January 25, 1851; *Boston Liberator*, January 17, 1851. See also May, *Fugitive Slave Law and Its Victims*, pp. 12–13.
14. May *Fugitive Slave Law and Its Victims*, p. 13.
15. *National Intelligencer*, April 8, 1851. Thomas Sims's Case, 7 Cushing 286 (1851).

Sewall, a noted abolitionist, went immediately to the courthouse. On the front steps of the building, he met Deputy United States Marshal Patrick Riley and demanded to see the prisoner. When Riley refused, Sewall "became greatly excited, and, using violent language, was conducted to the watch-house. . . ." After he calmed down and promised to leave Court Square, he was released. Early the next morning, chains were placed around the courthouse to keep the crowd from the building. Police force was strengthened to maintain order and to limit courthouse entry to persons who had business there. The crowd which gathered in Court Square was composed of Negroes and the idly curious.[16]

Between nine and ten o'clock, Commissioner George Ticknor Curtis arrived at the courthouse for the hearing. Sims was claimed as the property of James Potter of Chatham County, Georgia. Acting for Potter were his agents John B. Bacon and M. S. D'Lyon. Seth J. Thomas appeared as counsel for the claimant. Sims was represented by Charles G. Loring, Robert Rantoul, Jr., and Samuel E. Sewall. After the preliminaries were over, the case was adjourned until the following day.[17] Sewall applied for a writ of habeas corpus before the Supreme Court of Massachusetts in order to bring Sims under the jurisdiction of the Massachusetts courts, but the petition was refused on the ground that, if the writ were issued and the petitioner brought before the Massachusetts court, it would have been the duty of the court to remand him to the custody of the United States marshal.[18]

A petition was also presented to the house of representatives of Massachusetts, then in session, by William A. White, Francis Jackson, Theodore Parker, Samuel G. Howe, Robert H. Morris, and twenty-three others requesting the use of the state house yard for a public meeting. By a vote of 147 to 113, the petition was tabled. That afternoon, Theodore Parker addressed a crowd on the common while Wendell Phillips and others were haranguing audiences in Tremont Temple. Phillips advised the friends of Sims to arm themselves, and,

16. *National Intelligencer*, April 8, 1851.
17. Ibid.
18. Thomas Sims's Case, 7 Cushing 285 (1851) ; Helen Turncliff Catterall, ed., *Judicial Cases Concerning American Slavery and the Negro*, 5 vols. (Washington: Carnegie Institution of Washington, 1926–37), 4:515–16 (hereafter cited as Catterall, *Judicial Cases*) ; *National Intelligencer*, April 8, 1851.

if no other way could be found to prevent Sims's rendition, to tear up the railroad rails.[19]

The crowd in Court Square in the meantime was increasing, but it was not particularly belligerent. The people "amused themselves in a good natured manner by cheering the Constitution, and groaning for some of the most noted Abolitionists." The mayor became anxious about preserving the peace and called out two companies of the state militia.[20]

While the case was proceeding before Commissioner Curtis, the Boston Vigilance Committee met to develop a plan to rescue Sims. Informed by Lewis Hayden, one of the leading Negroes in Boston, that few Negroes could be counted on to aid in the rescue because they had been scattered by prosecutions of the Shadrack case, the committee realized that the rescue force would be greatly diminished. Sims had been incarcerated on the third floor of the courthouse. While he was in the courtroom, two men sat on each side of the captive, and five men sat behind him. Only his counsel was permitted to approach him from the front. Hence, an assault in the courtroom was not practicable. Another method of rescue had to be determined. It was decided to communicate with Sims through a Negro clergyman who would encourage him to jump from his third story window into a pile of mattresses which would be placed below. A carriage would be held ready to take him away. Writing in the 1890's, Thomas Wentworth Higginson, one of the leaders in the rescue attempt, said: "We were not sure that Sims would have the courage to do this, rather than to go back to certain slavery. . . . At any rate the mattresses were got and placed in a lawyer's office in Court Square. Great pains were taken to keep the plan a secret and I well remember the sinking of the heart with which I saw, on walking through Court Square on the evening planned for the enterprise, that masons were at work putting iron bars in the window of Sims' cell. The whole plan was thus frustrated."[21] On April 11, all the evidence was in. Commissioner Curtis decided for the claimant, and Sims was

19. *National Intelligencer*, April 8, 1851.
20. Ibid.
21. Thomas Wentworth Higginson, *Cheerful Yesterdays* (Boston: Houghton, Mifflin and Company, 1899), pp. 140–43 (hereafter cited as Higginson, *Cheerful Yesterdays*); Higginson, *Thomas Wentworth Higginson*, p. 112.

remanded to his owner. The slave was taken from the courthouse, marched to the wharf surrounded by three hundred armed men, and placed on board the brig *Acorn* for delivery to Savannah, Georgia. The crowd in Court Square caused no disturbance.[22]

The *Acorn* remained at anchor in the outer harbor of Nantasket Roads for the remainder of the day. According to a report in the *Boston Telegraph,* an attempt was made to free Sims on a criminal warrant issued by Justice Richard Hildreth through Sheriff Eveleth, but the latter declined to act. The warrant was then placed in the hands of Constable Lawton of Boston and Deputy Sheriff Adams of Norfolk County. A steamer was chartered, and twenty men were hired to board the *Acorn.* The plan was to remove Sims from the custody of the federal marshal, by force if necessary. The scheme was abandoned, however, when it was discovered that the *Acorn* had already sailed.[23]

Sims was delivered to his owner in Savannah where he was confined to the city jail. After two months he was sent to the slave pens at Charleston, and from there he was sent to the auction block in New Orleans. Sims was sold to a brick mason in Vicksburg, Mississippi, from whom he escaped in 1863.[24] In 1877, Sims appeared in Washington and applied for a job. He was made a messenger in the Department of Justice through the efforts of Charles Devens, the marshal who had arrested him as a fugitive slave, who was now attorney general. According to Charles Francis Adams, Sims was still living in Washington in 1889, working as a bricklayer.[25]

Despite overt abolitionist hostility in Boston during the trial of Thomas Sims, reaction in the South was relatively mild. In fact, the *Savannah Republican* published an open letter to the citizens of Boston commending them for their support. Written by the agents of James Potter, the letter said:

> The undersigned received during their late visit to Boston, at the hands of the good people of that city, so much marked kindness, attention, courtesy, and aid, that they feel it to be their duty to make some formal

22. *National Intelligencer,* April 12, April 15, 1851.
23. Ibid., April 17, 1851.
24. Wilson, *Rise and Fall of Slave Power,* 2:335. See also Adams, *Richard Henry Dana,* 1:194.
25. Adams, *Richard Henry Dana,* 1:194.

and public acknowledgement of it. . . . we were most hospitably received, and were surrounded during our stay there by many hundreds of gentlemen who aided us by every means in their power. The merchants of the city in particular were conspicuous in their efforts to serve us. . . . From letters which can be seen, now in our possession, coming from merchants of high standing, we make no doubt that we could have obtained security (had it been required) to the amount of millions of dollars. Everything we saw and heard in Boston has left on our minds the strong and enduring impression that the respectable citizens of that place are a law-abiding people—determined to see the laws executed, and determined to do justice to the South. We venture to remark, in conclusion, that the recovery of another slave there would be attended with but little trouble or expense.[26]

The abolitionists did not dominate public opinion in Boston, and Thomas Sims was not the last slave to be recovered from the so-called cradle of liberty.[27]

Three 1853 cases, one in Ohio and two in Pennsylvania, are representative and worthy of note. George Washington McQuerry, the slave of Henry Miller, a resident of Washington County, Kentucky, escaped in 1849. He crossed the Ohio River and made his way to Miami County, Ohio where he settled and married a free Negro woman. Having learned that McQuerry was a fugitive slave, and making it a point to learn the name of his owner, a white man named John Russell wrote to Miller and informed him where his runaway slave could be found.[28] With four other Kentuckians, Miller crossed the river into Ohio hoping to recover his runaway property. McQuerry was arrested by federal marshals while working on a canal boat near Troy and was taken to Dayton. Deputy United States Marshal Trader took custody of the fugitive and moved him to Cincinnati.[29]

26. *National Intelligencer*, May 13, 1851, quoting the Savannah *Republican*.
27. For a discussion of the southern reaction to northern hostility to enforcement of the Fugitive Slave Law in the early 1850's, see Avery O. Craven, *The Growth of Southern Nationalism* (Baton Rouge: Louisiana State University Press, 1953), p. 152–53, 358. Craven, page 152, says: "The great mass of the people seemed indifferent. Northern resistance to the fugitive-slave act should, in light of earlier pronouncements, have reopened the whole sectional struggle. . . . The only result, however, was a few violent editorials in newspapers which brought little or no response from their readers."
28. Levi Coffin, *Reminiscences of Levi Coffin*, 3rd ed. (Cincinnati: The Robert Clarke Company, 1899), p. 542 (hereafter cited as Coffin, *Reminiscences*). See also Catterall, *Judicial Cases*, 4:15, and May, *Fugitive Slave Law and Its Victims*, p. 28.
29. Coffin, *Reminiscences*, p. 543.

The Negroes of Cincinnati began to congregate as the news spread that a fugitive slave had been arrested. Although these Negroes demonstrated their sympathy for McQuerry, the police were able to control the crowd.[30] Peter Clark, a prominent Cincinnati Negro, applied to Justice John McLean of the United States Circuit Court for a writ of habeas corpus. The writ was granted, and the hearing was set for ten o'clock the following morning. Meanwhile, Miller had appealed to United States Commissioner S. S. Carpenter for a hearing. Carpenter agreed to hear the case at seven o'clock the next morning, but when the commissioner learned that Justice McLean had agreed to hear the case he postponed further proceedings, preferring that the case be heard before the higher court. McQuerry remained in the custody of Deputy United States Marshal Trader.[31]

At the hearing before Justice McLean, Negroes and whites crowded the courtroom, and the mayor increased the number of police stationed around the courthouse. Messrs. John Jollife and James G. Birney represented the fugitive. T. C. Ware appeared for the claimant. After Jollife completed his argument, Birney requested that he be permitted to present his argument the next morning, and the court was adjourned until the following day. On the return of the prisoner to the jail, strongly guarded by the police, some demonstrations were made by crowds of Negroes, but violence was checked by the police.[32]

After Birney's presentation the next morning, Justice McLean gave his decision. He reviewed the evidence and, with regard to arguments that the Fugitive Slave Law was unconstitutional, asserted that

I can not here be governed by sympathy; I have to look to the law and be governed by the law. . . . The law has been enacted by the highest power—than none is higher is acknowledged by all men. Sooner or later a disregard for the law could bring chaos, anarchy and widespread ruin; the law must be enforced. Let those who think differently go to the people who make the laws. I can not turn aside from the sacred duties of my office to regard aught but the law. By the force of all the testimony and the law I am bound to remand the fugitive to his master.[33]

30. *National Intelligencer,* August 20, 1853.
31. Coffin, *Reminiscences,* pp. 543–44.
32. Coffin, *Reminiscences,* pp. 543–44.
33. Miller v. McQuerry, 5 McLean 469 (1853).

McQuerry was remanded to the custody of his owner and taken across the river to Covington.[34]

In 1845, two slaves had escaped from one Van Metre, their owner, in Virginia and fled to the state of Pennsylvania, not stopping until they had arrived in the town of Indiana. After the runaway slaves arrived in the town, a man named Mitchell sent the fugitives, with a letter of introduction, to his tenant farm about nine miles from the community, and they remained there about four months. Mitchell was aware of their being fugitive slaves.[35]

In 1853, Mitchell was tried in the United States Circuit Court in Philadelphia and charged with concealing and harboring fugitive slaves in violation of the Fugitive Slave Law. The owner of the slaves had never given Mitchell formal notice that the Negroes working on his farm were fugitive slaves. Mitchell argued that, since he had been given no notice that the Negroes were fugitives from labor, he could not be charged with harboring and concealing them. In his charge to the jury, however, Justice Grier said that "notice," as used in the Fugitive Slave Law, meant "knowledge." If the jury was convinced that the defendant had "afforded shelter . . . to the fugitive to further his escape," they should find for the plaintiff. The jury ruled in the plaintiff's favor, and Mitchell was fined five hundred dollars.[36]

One Mrs. Oliver returned to Williamsport, Maryland from Arkansas in May, 1847 with her children and the twelve slaves left them by their father who had died in Arkansas in 1846. On their trip home they had passed through the state of Pennsylvania. Five months later, the twelve slaves fled their masters and escaped into Pennsylvania. Although pursued by an agent of the owners, the slaves were not retaken. They were tracked into Cumberland County where all traces of the fugitives vanished. What actually happened was that, in Cumberland County, the fugitives had been hidden in the barn of

34. Miller v. McQuerry, 17 Federal Cases 335 (1853). See also Coffin, *Reminiscences*, pp. 542–47; American Anti-Slavery Society, *Annual Report* (1855), p. 41; Charles B. Galbreath, *History of Ohio*, 5 vols. (Chicago: American Historical Society, 1925), 2:239; *National Intelligencer*, August 20, 1853.

35. Van Metre v. Mitchell, 28 Federal Cases 1036 (1853). This report does not indicate whether Van Metre ever recovered his slaves.

36. Ibid.

Daniel Kauffman until Philip Breckbill and Stephen Weakley were able to move them.[37]

Kauffman, Weakley, and Breckbill were brought to trial in the United States Circuit Court in Philadelphia in October, 1853, and they were charged with harboring and concealing the slaves of the Oliver heirs. At the first trial, the jury was unable to reach a verdict. At the second trial, Kauffman was found guilty. The plaintiffs were awarded twenty-eight hundred dollars in damages; the other defendants were acquitted.[38] This case demonstrated at the very least that persons who aided fugitive slaves in Pennsylvania could not do so with impunity, for they could be convicted in court.

Perhaps the most notorious and highly publicized case in which a fugitive slave was returned despite an overtly hostile public opinion was that of Anthony Burns. Although the case is well known, it is treated here because it demonstrates the extent to which the national government was willing to go to enforce the Fugitive Slave Law. In a plan worked out in cooperation with the local police, Anthony Burns was arrested in Boston on the night of May 24, 1854. Charged with "breaking into and robbing a jewelry store," which justified arrest by city officers, Burns was surrounded by six or seven men, lifted bodily, and rushed down the center of the street to the courthouse where United States Marshal Watson Freeman was waiting. "Without pausing, or even allowing the prisoner's feet to touch the ground," said Richard H. Dana, "Burns was hurried up several flights of stairs to the jury room of the United States court, at the top of the building." The warrant for Burn's arrest had been issued on the claim of Charles F. Suttle of Alexandria, Virginia. Accompanied by William Brent, Suttle had come to Boston after hearing that Burns had found employment in the city. Burns had been working on the wharves in Richmond and, at the first opportunity, had secretly boarded a vessel tied at the wharf. In early March, the vessel had arrived in Boston, and Burns had slipped ashore unobserved. He had found employment in a clothing store owned by Coffin Pitts and was

37. Oliver *et al.* v. Kauffman, Weakley, and Breckbill, 18 Federal Cases 657 (1853).

38. Ibid.; American Law Register 142 (1853); Catterall, *Judicial Cases*, 4:306–8.

working there at the time of his apprehension.[39] He appeared before United States Commissioner Edward G. Loring on May 25 for the hearing, but the case was postponed until May 27 at the request of Richard H. Dana, Jr. and Charles Mayo Ellis who had offered to serve as counsel for the fugitive.[40]

On the grounds that Burns had been arrested illegally, a writ was issued by Seth Webb in a ten-thousand-dollar damage suit against Suttle and Brent. The suit was filed by Lewis Hayden, a Negro leader in Boston. The purpose, of course, was to harass the claimant of the fugitive slave and to make his trip to Boston as expensive as possible. The writ was served, and each of the two men put up five thousand dollars bail. Later in the day on which the hearing was scheduled, Chief Justice Wells issued a writ of *replevin* against Marshal Freeman, directing him to produce Burns before the Court of Common Pleas on June 7, 1854.[41]

A public meeting was called for Friday evening, May 26, in Faneuil Hall. In a letter to Thomas Wentworth Higginson, Samuel May appealed for help from Worcester. "Give all the notice you can," he said. "The friends here are wide awake and unanimous. . . . The country must back the city, and, if necessary, lead it. We shall summon all the country friends." [42] Wendell Phillips's wife wrote to Anne and Deborah Weston in Weymouth. "Do stir up Weymouth," she said, "for if this man is allowed to go back *there is no* anti-slavery in Massachusetts. We may as well disband at once if our meetings and papers are all talk and never are to do any *but* TALK." [43] The meeting was well publicized, and for good reason; it was to be used as a cover for rescuing Anthony Burns.

After hearing from May, Higginson contacted several people who might help, particularly Martin Stowell who had taken part in the

39. Adams, *Richard Henry Dana*, 1:262–65. See also Samuel May, Jr. to Thomas Wentworth Higginson, May 25, 1854, in "Trial of Anthony Burns, 1854," *Proceedings of the Massachusetts Historical Society* 44 (1910–11) : 323 (hereafter cited as "Trial of Anthony Burns, 1854") ; Higginson, *Cheerful Yesterdays*, p. 47; *National Intelligencer*, May 29, 1854.

40. *National Intelligencer*, May 29, 1854; Adams, *Richard Henry Dana*, 1:262.

41. *National Intelligencer*, May 29, 1854.

42. May to Higginson, May 25, 1854, in "Trial of Anthony Burns, 1854," p. 323.

43. Anne G. Phillips to Anne and Deborah Weston, May 25, 1854, ibid., p. 322.

Jerry rescue. On Friday morning, before the meeting in Faneuil Hall, Higginson went to Boston to meet with the Vigilance Committee. When he got there he was disgusted to find that no plan of action had been developed for rescuing Burns. The general committee adjourned without taking action, but those who were willing to "act personally in forcible resistance" remained behind. Twenty men pledged them- selves to organize and obey orders. An executive committee of seven was chosen, and the meeting adjourned until that afternoon.

Stowell arrived from Worcester on Friday evening. When Higgin- son met him and explained the situation, Stowell proposed that Burns would have to be taken from the courthouse. A frontal assault on the courthouse was not feasible. It was decided, therefore, to use the public meeting at Faneuil Hall as a cover. Rather than wait until the meeting was over, the plan was to remove Burns from the courthouse at the meeting's climax. A picked group of men would be held in readiness. At the proper moment, someone would rush to the gallery of Faneuil Hall and announce that a mob of Negroes was attacking the courthouse. It was hoped that the whole meeting would rush to the aid of the leaders and rescue Burns from the courtroom. As Higginson later said: ". . . it was one of the very best plots that ever failed." [44]

At the meeting in Faneuil Hall, highly inflammatory speeches were made by Samuel G. Howe, Wendell Phillips, Frances W. Bird, John L. Swift, and Theodore Parker. Excitement was mounting at a dangerous rate when a commotion was created at the door. Suddenly, a motion for adjournment was made from the floor because of a report that an attack was being made upon the courthouse by a mob of Negroes. The large crowd in the hall proved a great disadvantage. Because it was virtually impossible to communicate with the men on the speaker's platform, the leaders were not prepared when the signal came, but the meeting was adjourned immediately. [45]

There was a general rush toward the courthouse. The mob had already begun an assault on the doors of the east side of the courthouse, but to no avail. The attack was then shifted to the west side. Stones were thrown through the windows, and an attempt was

44. Higginson discussed the plan of rescue in great detail in his *Cheerful Yesterdays*, p. 150.
45. *National Intelligencer*, May 29, 1854.

made to batter down the doors. This having failed, two men came forward with axes and cut a hole through the door. The door was forced open, and several men rushed into the room. The marshal and his aides were able to repulse the attack, but during the melee James Batchelder, one of the guards, was killed.[46] The attempt to rescue Burns had failed.

Upon hearing what had taken place, the mayor issued an immediate call for two companies of artillery. At twelve o'clock, the Boston Artillery and the Columbian Artillery came to the aid of the civil authorities. Quiet was restored, and Court Square was soon deserted. One company of artillery was stationed in City Hall for the night, and the other company took up a position in the courthouse. At two o'clock in the morning a detachment of federal troops from Fort Independence and a company of marines from the navy yard arrived on the scene.[47]

Wishing to inform President Pierce of the situation, and desiring his support, Marshal Freeman sent him a message. He wrote:

In consequence of an attack upon the court-house last night, for the purpose of rescuing a fugitive slave under arrest, and in which one of my own guards was killed, I have availed myself of the resources of the United States, placed under my control by letter from the War and Navy Departments in 1851, and now have two companies of troops from Fort Independence stationed in the court-house. Everything is now quiet. The attack was repulsed by my own guard.[48]

The President's reply was telegraphed back immediately: *"Your conduct is approved; the law must be executed."* [49]

The fugitive slave hearing was resumed Saturday morning. As early as eight o'clock, several hundred persons had gathered in Court Square, and by ten o'clock the number had reached an estimated three thousand. Burns was brought into the courtroom under heavy guard. Commissioner Loring presided. Edward G. Parker and Seth J.

46. Ibid. For a more detailed account by one of the participants, see Higginson, *Cheerful Yesterdays*, pp. 153–54. For a contemporary account of the Burns case, see Charles Emery Stevens, *Anthony Burns A History* (Boston: John Jewett and Company, 1856).

47. *National Intelligencer,* May 29, 1854. See also the letter from Anne Warren Weston, Boston, May 30, 1854, in "Trial of Anthony Burns, 1854," p. 334, and R. H. Dana's diary entry, Friday, June 2, 1854, in Adams, *Richard Henry Dana,* 1:276.

48. *National Intelligencer,* May 29, 1854.

49. Ibid.

Thomas appeared as counsel for the claimant. Charles M. Ellis and Richard Henry Dana, Jr. represented the prisoner. As the arguments proceeded, counsel for the defense moved for postponement until Monday. Commissioner Loring, after hearing argument from both sides, decided to defer the case as requested.[50]

Excitement in the square was intense. Several persons were arrested for attempting to incite the crowd to acts of violence. The mayor, after addressing the crowd, issued a special proclamation "calling upon his fellow citizens generally to preserve the public peace and sustain the laws." The troops maintained their positions in City Hall and Court Square during Saturday night. Several hundred people continued to mill around in the square, but there was no further attack.[51]

Feeling remained high throughout Saturday and Sunday. Seeking additional support from the surrounding towns, the abolitionists circulated the following broadside:

To the yeomanry of New England!—Countrymen and brothers: The vigilance committee of Boston have to inform you that the mock trial of the poor fugitive slave has been further postponed to Monday next, at eleven o'clock A.M. You are requested, therefore, to come down and lend the moral weight of your presence and the aid of your counsel to the friends of justice and humanity in the city. Come down then, sons of Puritans, for even if the poor victim is to be carried off by the brute force of arms, and delivered over to slavery, you should at least be present to witness the sacrifice, and you should follow him in sad procession, with your tears and your prayers, and then go home and take such action as your manhood and your patriotism may suggest. Come, then, by the early trains on Monday, and rally in Court Square. Come with courage and resolution in your hearts, but this time with only such arms as God gave to you.[52]

Petitions in favor of repeal of the Fugitive Slave Law were circulated among the merchants. Sentiment against giving up the fugitive was growing stronger and deeper.

The case was continued on Monday and lasted all day. The court adjourned at six o'clock to be resumed the following day. The crowd around the courthouse at adjournment was estimated at ten thousand. On Tuesday the identity of Burns was clearly established, but the day was spent hearing the arguments of defense counsel. Joshua

50. Ibid.
51. Ibid.
52. Ibid.

R. Giddings, Wendell Phillips, and Theodore Parker were present as friends of the court. The hearing was concluded, but Commissioner Loring deferred his decision until Friday. The crowd in Court Square had increased since the day before, but some of the agitators from the country had gone home.[53]

The court convened at nine o'clock Friday morning, June 2, 1854. Guarded by six armed men, Burns was brought into the courtroom which was nearly filled with the marshal's guards. Wendell Phillips and Theodore Parker came in with the prisoner's counsel. Commissioner Loring then gave his decision. After analyzing the evidence, he discussed the constitutionality of the Fugitive Slave Law. In his opinion, the law was constitutional, and it was his duty to apply it. The facts concerning the escape and the slave's identity were all that the court had to consider. Commissioner Loring was satisfied that the claimant had fully established those facts. Suttle was therefore entitled to a certificate of his right to the fugitive.[54]

The delivery of Anthony Burns was a spectacle in itself. At an early hour on the day of his delivery, a company of United States infantry and a detachment of artillery were stationed to guard the main entrance of the courthouse. The crowd assembled rapidly and numbered several thousand by nine o'clock. Court Street, and every other street leading into the square, was thronged. After the commissioner's decision had been given, the troops were ordered to clear the square. Stores were closed, and several buildings facing the square were draped in black. A coffin was suspended from the building at the corner of Washington and State streets. No outbreak had occurred, but cannons were placed to sweep Court Square.[55]

Burns was to be taken to Central Wharf. A large body of police was stationed there, and an immense crowd had already assembled in anticipation of what might occur. At twelve o'clock, the entire brigade of Massachusetts militia left the square and marched down State Street, clearing the street as they went. They were greeted with hisses and cries of "shame" by the crowd. By half past twelve, a line of troops extended from Court Square to the wharf.[56]

The Negro pastor of the Baptist church and the defense counsel

53. Ibid., May 31, 1854.
54. Ibid., June 3, 1854.
55. Ibid.
56. Ibid.

had left Burns at twelve o'clock. He was "in good spirits," said the pastor. He laughed at the excitement and seemed glad to be on his way back to "Old Virginia." [57]

The throng in Court and State streets was estimated to be in the neighborhood of twenty thousand persons. An application was made to the mayor for permission to toll the bells, but the request was denied. William Jones, a witness at the trial, was arrested for "using exciting language" and was taken up State Street by the police. He was "enthusiastically cheered all the way whilst the police were greeted with groans and hisses." [58]

Burns was escorted from the courthouse that afternoon by a guard of two hundred men. They joined a military escort, and the fugitive was marched down to the wharf "amid the hisses and groans of the populace." Burns was placed aboard a steamer and conveyed out to the revenue cutter *Morris* which sailed directly for Norfolk, Virginia.[59] In Norfolk, Burns was kept in jail for a short time and was then transferred to Richmond. After four months confinement in the slave pen, he was bought by a North Carolina speculator for $905. In February, 1855, the Negro community of Boston purchased Burns's freedom, and he went to Cincinnati to study for the ministry. Later he moved to St. Catherines, Ontario where he became the pastor of a Baptist church. He died in 1862 at the age of twenty-eight.[60]

The national government had demonstrated again that a fugitive slave could be arrested and returned from Boston, even at a time when antislavery feeling was high because of the Kansas-Nebraska bill. The cost to the government for the rendition of Burns has been a matter of considerable speculation. Estimates run from as little as $27,000 to as much as $100,000.[61] The amount actually paid by the national government was $14,165.78—expenses of the United States courts were $6,872.28, and $7,293.50 was paid to the city of Boston.[62]

57. Ibid.
58. Ibid.
59. Ibid.
60. For a full account of the Burns case, see Shapiro, "Rendition of Anthony Burns," pp. 34–51.
61. *National Intelligencer*, October 26, 1854; Nevins, *Ordeal of Union*, 2:152.
62. Treasury Department, Treasury Interior Pay Warrant No. 8498, December 4, 1854, Record Group 39, Records of the Bureau of Accounts, National

Although Burns had been returned, the rioters were still to be prosecuted. The grand jury indicted Walter Bishop, Thomas Jackson, Martin Stowell, John Morrison, Samuel Proudman, Walter Phenix, John Wesley, and Thomas Wentworth Higginson. Bishop, Jackson, Stowell, and Morrison were arraigned on this indictment. They pleaded not guilty. Theodore Parker was arraigned November 29, and Wendell Phillips on December 15, 1854.[63]

April 3, 1855, the defendants in the Burns rescue attempt were brought to trial, Judges Curtis and Sprague presiding. By special agreement, it was decided that Martin Stowell would be tried first. Benjamin F. Hallet, United States district attorney, prosecuted for the national government. Stowell was defended by Henry F. Durant, one of the most competent lawyers in the country. The defense moved immediately to quash the indictment.[64] Judge Curtis delivered the decision of the court on April 12. The indictment was quashed on the ground that it failed properly to describe the power of the commissioner to issue the warrant to arrest Burns. Stowell and all the other defendants were acquitted.[65]

Further attempts to secure convictions proved futile. To test whether those under indictment could escape on a mere technical omission in the indictment, Hallet petitioned the court to call in the same grand jury that had issued the indictments so that the omission might be corrected. The court refused to call the same grand jury because it had been summoned by the United States marshal, "who was not an indifferent person." The court did not refuse to take such action, but it pointed out that by so doing two grand juries would be sitting at the same time. The real difficulty was disclosed in meetings with the two judges.

Hallet was informed that there "were grave difficulties behind the

Archives, Fiscal Branch, Washington, D.C. See also Secretary of the Treasury, Warrant Division, Treasury Appropriation Ledger, No. 15, p. 346, and No. 16, p. 561, Record Group 39, Records of the Bureau of Accounts, National Archives, Fiscal Branch, Washington, D.C.'
  63. *National Intelligencer*, July 17; November 30; December 16, 1854.
  64. United States v. Stowell, 27 Federal Cases 1350 (1854).
  65. *National Intelligencer*, April 4, 13, 1855. See also the letters of Hallet to Caleb Cushing and President Pierce, April 13, 1855, in Attorney General's Papers, Letters Received, Massachusetts, 1842–1861, National Archives, Justice and Executive Branch, Washington, D.C. (hereafter cited as Attorney General's Papers).

Indictments which in all probability no new Indictment could cure. . . ." In a letter to President Pierce, Hallet explained the problem. The judges had informed him that

. . . the defect was in the warrant issued by the Commissioner, & that it would not be held to be legal process because it did not describe the authority of the Commissioner either in the Complaint or Warrant. Had the Indictment therefore enlarged this description it would have been of no avail. The difficulty therefore is inherent, and the result is that no Indictment could be sustained, under the view held by Judges Curtis and Sprague who concur, for resisting the process under which Marshal Freeman held Anthony Burns.[66]

Although the marshal might have been justified in holding Burns, and an attempt to rescue him might have been a violation of the Fugitive Slave Law, in this case there was no actual attempt to rescue the fugitive. None of the would-be rescuers had even gotten close to Burns. The defendants could be charged only with "resistance to and obstruction of the officers of the law in serving legal process," which constituted a misdemeanor, not a felony. Hallet felt, therefore, that further prosecution would be fruitless. He said that "it is better that the prosecuting officer should be supposed to have made a technical omission in the form of the Indictment than that the issue should be pressed to a decision establishing the invalidity of the legal process on the part of the Commissioner." [67] In other words, Hallet did not want the authority of a United States commissioner challenged.

In the second half of the decade before the Civil War, enforcement of the Fugitive Slave Law was encumbered by an even more antagonistic public opinion. Passage of the Kansas-Nebraska Act, the return of Anthony Burns, and the Sherman M. Booth case in Wisconsin caused a ground swell of public reaction against the inhumanity of the law for reclaiming runaway slaves. Despite this fact, when called upon to enforce the law, federal officers did a more than adequate job.

On November 26, 1857, the agents of Dr. Austin W. Vallandigham of Frankfort, Kentucky captured a fugitive slave named West at Naples, Illinois. Apparently the arrest was made without a warrant,

66. Hallet to Pierce, June 9, 1855, in Attorney General's Papers.
67. Hallet to Pierce, June 9, 1855, in Attorney General's Papers. On the back of Hallet's letter, President Pierce wrote: "I deem it quite evident that the course suggested by Mr. Hallett is the only one to be pursued—I[t] may become necessary to make public the true ground of difficulty."

and the captors had no certificate of removal. When the party reached Indianapolis, Indiana, a writ of habeas corpus was served on them. West was taken into custody and was presented before the court of common pleas. The court discharged the fugitive. Having anticipated the fugitive's release, West's claimant had the fugitive arrested again by a deputy United States marshal under Section 10 of the Fugitive Slave Law and taken before the United States commissioner. After five days of taking testimony and listening to the arguments of both sides, the commissioner remanded West to the custody of the claimant. While the trial was in progress, however, George W. Julian and John Coburn, counsel for the fugitive, had had the claimants charged with kidnapping. They were arrested and taken before the court of common pleas, the same court that had earlier discharged the fugitive slave, but they were never tried. The charges were dropped when the United States commissioner ordered the slave returned to Kentucky under the protection of federal officers.[68]

The Fugitive Slave Law was opposed but not as frequently as most Southerners supposed. On December 18, 1857, a fugitive slave named Jacob Dupen, the property of William M. Edelin of Baltimore, Maryland, was taken before Judge Kane of the United States District Court in Philadelphia. Dupen had been arrested earlier in the week by deputy United States marshals about four miles from Harrisburg. He was in the field plowing at the time and made no resistance to arrest. After the hearing, Judge Kane remanded the fugitive to his owner. According to the *Philadelphia Bulletin,* there was no excitement about the courtroom; in fact, the only people present were the officers and parties involved in the hearing.[69]

A case in 1858 illustrates a degree of cooperation between the claimants of fugitive slaves and federal officers. Two runaway slaves, the property of Robert W. Ingraham of Mason County, Kentucky, had absconded to Canada. Not content with having secured their own

68. Treasury Department, Treasury Interior Pay Warrant No. 5927, February 18, 1858. Record Group 39, Records of the Bureau of Accounts, National Archives, Fiscal Branch, Washington, D.C.; *Boston Liberator,* December 11, 25, 1857; May, *Fugitive Slave Law and Its Victims,* pp. 88–89. See also Thornbrough, "Indiana and Fugitive Slave Legislation," pp. 225–27.

69. *Boston Liberator,* December 25, 1857; May, *Fugitive Slave Law and Its Victims,* pp. 91–92.

freedom, by correspondence they made arrangements in Mason County to aid other slaves in escaping. One of the letters detailing their plans was intercepted, and the information was given to Ingraham. The two fugitives came to Cincinnati in August, unaware that their plans were known. Informed by a Negro man of the fugitive's arrival, Ingraham came to Cincinnati, obtained a warrant from United States Commissioner Edward R. Newhall, and, with the aid of deputy marshals B. P. Churchill and William L. Manson, prepared for making the arrest. The deputy marshal apprehended the two runaways as they were getting ready to leave Cincinnati for Richmond, Virginia. They were taken to the marshal's office in the Customs House, and Commissioner Newhall was summoned. Although the commissioner objected to an examination of the fugitive at ten o'clock at night, Ingraham insisted upon his rights under the Fugitive Slave Law and was given a hearing. After examining the witnesses, Newhall remanded the slaves to the custody of their owner, and at midnight they were taken without incident to the Covington ferry and across the river to Kentucky. They were lodged in the Covington jail until preparations were completed to return them to Mason County.[70]

On May 3, 1859, a fugitive slave named Jackson, who had escaped from Clarksburg, Virginia, was arrested at Zanesville, Ohio. Having been decoyed into the city from Belmont County by another Negro, Jackson was betrayed and placed in the custody of Deputy United States Marshal Cox. The fugitive was taken to the office of United States Commissioner Cochran, who heard the case behind locked doors. Jackson was remanded to his owner and committed to the local jail. While Jackson awaited removal to Virginia, a writ of habeas corpus was served on the sheriff who was ordered to bring the fugitive before the local court. Judge Marsh decided that Jackson was being held illegally and discharged him. Immediately after his release, federal officers re-arrested Jackson and took him to the train depot. On the way, a "desperate effort was made by the negroes to rescue him, and during the excitement clubs and pistols were freely used, and several persons were badly injured." The attempt to rescue the fugitive failed. Marshal Cox and his posse retained custody of the

70. *Boston Liberator*, September 3, 10, 1858; May, *Fugitive Slave Law and Its Victims*, p. 102.

slave until the next morning when he was placed on a train to be delivered to his owner in Virginia.[71] Illustrative of the hardening attitudes in Ohio toward enforcement of the Fugitive Slave Law, Marshal Cox was "excommunicated" from the Zanesville Baptist Church for his part in the case.[72]

Further evidence that the Fugitive Slave Law would be enforced in spite of public hostility is found in the case of Henry Seaton. In late November, 1859, United States Deputy Marshal William L. Manson penetrated the very heart of the Western Reserve and arrested Seaton in the city of Cleveland. Without "encountering Sharp's rifles or Sheriff's writs," Deputy Manson transported the fugitive to Cincinnati for a hearing before the United States commissioner. John Seaton, the claimant, his attorney L. D. Ross, and R. M. Robb, all of Greenupsburg, Kentucky, identified the fugitive, and he was remanded to his claimant. The captive slave was returned to Kentucky without trouble.[73] George Hartman, the man responsible for betraying the Negro into the hands of federal officers, did not fare so well. According to the *Cleveland Leader*, Hartman was forced to take refuge in the city jail to escape retribution at the hands of members of the Negro community in Cleveland. The following day, closely followed by incensed Negroes, he was barely able to make his way back to his room. Having attained the safety of his quarters, he armed himself and "suffered no further molestation." [74]

Animosity toward slavery in general and the Fugitive Slave Law in particular had made enforcement of the law difficult in some areas, but slaves were returned throughout the decade from communities both sensitive and insensitive to the plight of runaway Negroes. Two final cases illustrated that, in areas as far apart as New York City and Sandusky, Ohio, slaves were returned in 1860 with no difficulty.

On April 30, 1860, Josiah Hay and Allen Graff, claimed as fugitive slaves by Absolom Cline and Charles Augustus Lawrence of Frederick County, Maryland were taken before United States Commissioner

71. *New York Weekly Tribune*, May 7, 1859; *Boston Liberator*, May 6, 13, 1859.

72. American Anti-Slavery Society, *Annual Report* (1860), p. 56.

73. *Boston Liberator*, December 2, 1859.

74. May, *Fugitive Slave Law and Its Victims*, p. 125, quoting the *Cleveland Leader*.

Betts in New York City. With little ceremony the commissioner remanded the two Negroes to their owners. The proceedings were conducted so quietly that no person connected with the city knew anything about the case until the next morning, after the fugitives had been returned to their owners, and were already on their way South.[75] Questioning how anything so cruel and unjust could happen in New York City, the editor of the *National Anti-Slavery Standard* said: "What must be the public sentiment in this great city, where two human beings can be thus consigned to life-long bondage, with less excitement than is caused by sending a common thief to the penitentiary, and where, of all the pulpits existing therein, there are not, probably three, if even so many, that will have courage to rebuke the outrage!"[76] Finally, in October, 1860, Deputy United States Marshal W. L. Manson, with a posse of seven men, went to Sandusky, Ohio. In one of the most sensitive areas in the country, they searched for two Negro families who had escaped from Mason County, Kentucky. About three miles south of town, on thirty acres of land which they had rented and had begun to clear and cultivate, the former slaves were found and arrested. The two men and their wives with two children, the latter born in Ohio, were put on a train and taken to Cincinnati where, after a summary hearing, they were remanded to slavery and returned to Kentucky at government expense. According to the *Sandusky Register*, a party of rescuers was alerted, but the marshal and his party could not be found.[77]

The number of slaves captured and returned without due process of law in the 1850's was almost as great as the number remanded by fugitive slave tribunals under the Fugitive Slave Law. These slaves were apprehended by their masters, or agents of the masters, and

75. *National Intelligencer*, May 3, 1860; *New York Weekly Tribune*, May 5, 1860; American Anti-Slavery Society, *Annual Report* (1860), p. 61.

76. American Anti-Slavery Society, *Annual Report* (1860), p. 61, quoting the *National Anti-Slavery Standard*.

77. May, *Fugitive Slave Law and Its Victims*, pp. 156–57, citing the *Sandusky Register*. The cases above were selective but demonstrate that, in spite of public hostility to enforcement of the Fugitive Slave Law in many northern communities, the law was enforced. Of 191 known cases tried before federal tribunals, 157 fugitive slaves were successfully remanded to their owners and delivered to the states from which they had fled. In only 68 of the cases was it necessary to remand the slaves to the custody of federal officers for delivery, and in only 11 of the cases had a mistaken arrest been made; these Negroes were released from custody. See Appendices I–XII.

returned from nine of the northern states, although the majority were recovered from Pennsylvania, Ohio, Indiana, and Illinois. The record would seem to support the assertion of Senator Stephen A. Douglas that many runaway slaves were returned like stolen horses, at least in the northern communities along the border between the slave and free states.[78] The great majority of these slaves were recovered with a minimum of difficulty, but when the slave owners in pursuit of their runaway slaves did encounter resistance, they were not without remedy in the courts.

On the evening of October 20, 1852, two Negro men and women with several children were arrested in Sandusky, Ohio on a power of attorney issued by a Kentucky court. The Negroes were removed from the steamboat *Arrow* just as it was getting ready to depart for Detroit. Having been seen by the claimant as they boarded the steamer, the claimant had sought the assistance of the city marshal who, with the aid of two other men, made the arrest. The fugitives were taken to the office of the mayor, F. M. Follette. When presented with the power of attorney authorizing the owner's agent to arrest the fugitives, Mayor Follette stated that he had no authority to act and said that he would refer the case to the federal magistrate.

Aroused by the confusion, a crowd quickly assembled. The mayor's office was filled by an anxious swarm of spectators, the majority of whom were Negroes. Members of the Negro community living in Sandusky retained Rush R. Sloane as counsel for the fugitives. When it became apparent that the mayor was not going to act, Sloane asked the city marshal if the alleged fugitives were in his custody. The answer was no. Sloane then asked if the alleged fugitives were in the custody of the federal marshal. Again the answer was no. Sloane demanded to see the warrants authorizing the arrest of the alleged fugitives. Informed that there were none, Sloane said to the agent that he should have had a warrant. The reply was that none was needed. Furthermore, if the slaves were taken from him, said the agent, he would hold Sloane responsible. At this point, according to the court record, Sloane turned to the crowd, took off his hat, waved

---

78. Nevins, *Emergence of Lincoln*, 2:31. Of the 332 fugitive slave cases the writer was able to find reported in various sources, 141 slaves, or 42.5 per cent, were captured and returned without due process of law. See Appendices I–XII.

it over his head, and said, "Colored friends, arise, and take those colored friends of yours out of the room. . . ." The crowd rushed forward, carried the slaves out of the room, and hurried them off. They were not retaken.[79]

The slave owner decided to prosecute, and, in October, 185., Sloane was tried in federal court and was charged with "having aided . . . in the escape of the . . . fugitives." After the evidence had been presented, the judge said in his charge to the jury that "authority is expressly given to the owner . . . or his agent or attorney, to arrest without a warrant. . . ." He said also that the power of attorney under which the agent had acted "was executed . . . according to the requirement of the act of congress." The verdict was for the plaintiff. Sloane was fined $3,950 and imprisoned for six months.[80]

On several occasions during the 1850's, state and federal courts engaged in legal warfare over jurisdiction in fugitive slave cases. Whenever abolitionists attempted to remove fugitive slaves from federal custody by writs of habeas corpus issued by state courts, federal officers frequently found themselves the victims of jurisdictional disputes. If the marshals refused to give up their prisoners, they were oftentimes held in contempt by the state courts. If they gave up their prisoners, and in the process the fugitives were released, the marshal was liable under the Fugitive Slave Law to a fine of one thousand dollars and a damage suit to the value of the slave. The only recourse open to the marshals was to seek release by habeas corpus in the federal courts.

United States Deputy Marshal G. M. Wynkoop arrested George Smith in Philadelphia in July, 1853. Smith was taken before the federal commissioner who decided that Smith was the slave claimed in the process, and he was remanded to slavery. In the meantime, a writ of habeas corpus had been issued requiring the marshal to present Smith before a state judge. Refusing to jeopardize his custody of the Negro, Marshal Wynkoop did not respond to the writ and was arrested by the sheriff for contempt of court. Having been placed

79. Catterall, *Judicial Cases*, 4:15–16.
80. Weimer v. Sloane, 29 Federal Cases 599 (1854) ; Catterall, *Judicial Cases*, 4:15–16; *Boston Liberator*, November 5, 1852; *New York Weekly Tribune*, February 10, 1855.

in jail, he was not released until he had made proper answer to the writ and had shown that Smith was in the custody of a federal officer performing his duty under the Fugitive Slave Law.[81]

On September 3, 1853, G. M. Wynkoop, John Jenkins, and James Crossin, United States deputy marshals, were issued a warrant for the arrest of William Thomas, a Negro waiter at the Phoenix Hotel in Wilkesbarre, Pennsylvania. Thomas was claimed as the slave of Isham Keith of Farquhar County, Virginia.[82] When the arrest was attempted, Thomas resisted violently and, after a great struggle, escaped. While pursuing the fugitive, the marshals fired several shots, one of which found its mark. Thomas, unable to elude his captors and covered with blood, plunged into a nearby river. When ordered to come out of the river, Thomas, standing in water up to his neck, refused; he would rather drown than be taken alive. Not wishing to cause the fugitive to commit suicide, the officers left the scene.[83] Aided by Negro friends, Thomas was helped from the river and was not heard from again in Wilkesbarre.[84]

On October 4, 1853, William C. Gildersleeve, an abolitionist, appeared before the justice of the peace of Luzerne County and charged the three deputy marshals with assault and battery with intent to kill. A warrant was issued for their arrest. They were taken into custody and placed in jail. Held under authority of the state of Pennsylvania, the prisoners applied for a writ of habeas corpus from the United States Circuit Court.[85]

At the hearing, United States District Attorney George Ashmead represented the deputy marshals. Counsel for the plaintiff asserted that the court had no authority to discharge the prisoners because they were held by a warrant from a state court for alleged offenses against the state of Pennsylvania. Justice Grier set another hearing for the following week, but warned:

81. *National Intelligencer*, July 26, 28, 1853.
82. *Ex parte* Jenkins et al., 13 Federal Cases 445 (1853).
83. Manuscript opinion of Justice Robert C. Grier, *Ex parte* Jenkins et al., in United States District Courts, Eastern District of Pennsylvania, *Circuit Court, Habeas Corpus Cases, 1848–1862*, National Archives, Judicial and Executive Branch, Washington, D.C.
84. May *Fugitive Slave Law and Its Victims*, p. 30.
85. Manuscript opinion of Justice Grier, *Ex parte* Jenkins et al., in United States District Courts, Eastern District of Pennsylvania, *Circuit Court, Habeas Corpus Cases, 1848–1862*.

If this man Gildersleeve fails to make out the facts set forth in the warrant of arrest, I will request the Prosecuting Attorney of Luzerne County to prosecute him for perjury. I know that the United States have a limited authority; but where they have it, it is clear, undoubted, and conclusive that theirs is the sovereign authority. If any two-penny magistrate or any unprincipled interloper can come in and cause to be arrested the officers of the United States whenever they please, it is a sad state of affairs. . . . If habeas corpuses, are to be taken out in that manner, I will have an indictment sent to the United States Grand Jury against the person who applies for the writ, or assists in getting it, the lawyer who defends it, and the sheriff who serves the writ, to see whether the United States' officers are to be arrested and harassed whenever they attempt to serve a process of the United States. . . . I will see that my officers are protected.[86]

On October 15, Justice Grier delivered his opinion in the case. To meet the objection of counsel for the plaintiff, as regards the power of the court to discharge the prisoners, District Attorney Ashmead had stated that the power to issue writs of habeas corpus in such cases had not been granted under the Judiciary Act of 1789, but it had been granted under special powers conferred by the Force Act of March 5, 1833. This act provided federal judges the power to discharge on habeas corpus when officers of the federal courts were held by process of the state. Justice Grier forced the release of his officers on the authority granted him by the Force Act.[87]

The abolitionists were not through yet. In February, 1854, suit was brought against the same officers in the Supreme Court of Pennsylvania. Sheriff Samuel Allen arrested the three deputy marshals and placed them in jail. Again the officers applied for a writ of habeas corpus, this time before the United States District Court. Because insufficient evidence was presented to sustain the charges of assault and battery with the intent to kill, and because the judge was satisfied that the deputy marshals were carrying out their duty, the three officers were discharged.[88]

Wynkoop, Jenkins, and Crossin had been free but a short time when they were arrested again. The grand jury had indicted them for "riot, assault and battery, and assault with intent to kill." At the habeas corpus hearing before Judge Kane, insufficient evidence was

86. *Monthly Law Reporter*, n.s., 4 (1854) : 468.

87. *Ex parte* Jenkins et al., 13 Federal Cases 447–48 (1853). See also *Monthly Law Reporter*, n.s., 4 (1854), 468–71.

88. Catterall, *Judicial Cases*, IV, 309; *National Intelligencer*, May 19, 1854.

found to sustain the charges against them. On the contrary, it was clear that they had acted in accordance with their duty under the Fugitive Slave Law. The deputy marshals were released, and the harassment finally stopped.[89]

While passing through the state of Ohio in March, 1855, one Dr. Miller, agent of the Reverend Henry M. Dennison, was stopped in Columbus. Dennison was the son-in-law of former President John Tyler. A slave girl named Rosetta Armstead had been given to Dennison's wife to serve as nurse for their child. Mrs. Dennison had died, and the girl was placed in the care of Dr. Miller. He was returning her to Virginia so that she could continue to act as the child's nurse. Under the impression that he could cross Ohio on the Little Miami Railroad without stopping, Dr. Miller had boarded the train with Rosetta. The train had stopped in Columbus, however, and, by writ of habeas corpus, the judge of the local probate court authorized the removal of the slave girl from Miller's custody. Since Rosetta had been brought into Ohio with the consent of her master, the court declared that she was free. Because she was a minor, the court appointed L. G. Van Slyke as her guardian.[90]

Under the provisions of the Fugitive Slave Law, Dennison appealed to the United States Commissioner at Cincinnati and had Rosetta arrested. United States Marshal H. H. Robinson made the arrest and, on March 24, produced the alleged fugitive slave before Commissioner John L. Pendery. Arguments were heard on both sides, and the commissioner, considering the importance of the case, deferred his decision until later. On March 29, while the case was still pending, Rosetta was released from custody by order of the Court of Common Pleas of Hamilton County. After Rosetta had been placed once again in the custody of her appointed guardian, Marshal Robinson arrested her on a warrant issued by Commissioner Pendery. In an attempt to reestablish state jurisdiction, Judge Parker, of the court of common pleas, issued a writ of habeas corpus. In his

89. Manuscript opinion of Judge Kane, *In re* James Crossin, John Jenkins and George Wynkoop v. Samuel Allen, Sheriff of Philadelphia, United States District Courts, Eastern District of Pennsylvania, *Circuit Court, Habeas Corpus Cases, 1848–1862.* See also Catterall, *Judicial Cases,* 4:309–10, and *National Intelligencer,* December 13, 1854.

90. *National Intelligencer,* April 7, 1855; *New York Weekly Tribune,* April 7, 1855. See also Coffin, *Reminiscences,* pp. 554–77, and May, *Fugitive Slave Law and Its Victims,* pp. 43–44.

answer to the writ, Marshal Robinson denied the jurisdiction of the court and refused to release the slave girl. At the order of Judge Parker, the sheriff of Hamilton County, with several deputies, removed the girl from the custody of Marshal Robinson and delivered her to her guardian, Van Slyke. In this legal tug of war, Dennison then had another warrant issued by Commissioner Pendery, and Rosetta was rearrested by Marshal Robinson. The following morning, Judge Parker required Dennison and Robinson to show cause why they should not be held in contempt of court. On the same day, Rosetta was presented before Commissioner Pendery. The case was argued at length, and the commissioner said that he would deliver his decision later.[91]

Because Rosetta had been delivered to her guardian and no contempt had actually been committed, Judge Parker dismissed the case of contempt against Dennison and Robinson. But the judge had issued another writ of habeas corpus directing Marshal Robinson to produce the girl. Marshal Robinson refused to comply with the order. He was fined fifty dollars and imprisoned until he complied with the order.[92]

To remove himself as a victim in the dispute between the two jurisdictions, Marshal Robinson petitioned Justice John McLean, of the United States Supreme Court, for a writ of habeas corpus. After hearing the arguments from both sides, Justice McLean ruled: "The marshal omitted to do the act ordered to be done by the Honorable Judge Parker, because it would be in express violation of his duty under an act of congress. . . ." Furthermore, he said, "A sense of duty compels me to say that the proceedings of the honorable judge were not only without the authority of law, but against law, and that the proceedings were void, and I am bound to treat them as a nullity." Marshal Robinson was discharged.[93] The supremacy of federal jurisdiction had been sustained, and Dennison retained the custody of Rosetta Armstead.

In July, 1855, John H. Wheeler, United States minister to Nicaragua, was about to embark from Philadelphia for New York. He was

---

91. *National Intelligencer*, April 7, 1855.
92. Ibid.; *New York Weekly Tribune*, April 7, 1855.
93. *Ex parte* Robinson, 20 Federal Cases 969 (1855). See also *National Intelligencer*, April 6, 1855.

accompanied by a Negro woman named Jane Johnson and her two children. After boarding the boat, Wheeler and his three servants retired to the hurricane deck. Passmore Williamson, secretary of Pennsylvania Antislavery Society, approached Wheeler and asked permission to speak to his servants. Wheeler refused, but Williamson pushed past him and asked Jane if she were a slave. Receiving an affirmative answer, Williamson informed her that, since she had been brought into free territory by her master, she could be freed. The ensuing argument caused considerable excitement. A group of Negroes who had accompanied Williamson picked up the woman and her two children and carried them off the boat. Two of the Negroes threatened Wheeler if he offered any resistance. The slaves were loaded into a waiting carriage and were carried away. Williamson had taken no part in removing the slaves from the deck of the boat, nor had he helped in loading them into the carriage. Wheeler sought help from a policeman standing on the pier, but the officer refused to have anything to do with the affair.[94]

Wheeler petitioned the United States District Court for a writ of habeas corpus in an attempt to force Williamson to produce the slaves before the court. Williamson answered that the slaves had never been in his custody or possession. Judge John K. Kane thought Williamson's answer evasive, charged him with contempt of court, and had him imprisoned. On July 31, Williamson petitioned the chief justice of the Supreme Court of Pennsylvania for a writ of habeas corpus, but he was refused. In August he petitioned the court again, now in recess, but to no avail. The court ruled that it had no jurisdiction in contempt cases.[95]

On October 3, Jane Johnson, who had escaped to Massachusetts after being taken from the boat, appeared before Judge Kane with her counsel, Joseph B. Townsend and John M. Read, and informed Kane that neither she nor her children had ever been in the custody of Williamson. In fact, she said that she had not seen Williamson since she left the boat. She requested that the writ of habeas corpus, which Wheeler had secured for her and her children's return, be quashed. At the same time, she asked that Williamson be released from prison. The court refused to enter the plea. Judge Kane held

94. United States *ex rel.* Wheeler v. Williamson, 28 Federal Cases 682 (1855).
95. Ibid. See also *National Intelligencer*, September 10, 1855.

that the Negro woman had "no status whatever" in the federal court. Judge Kane pointed out that Williamson was not being punished; he was "undergoing restraint" for contempt of court. Moreover, he ruled that the act of the slaveholder in bringing the slaves into the state of Pennsylvania did not free them from slavery.[96] Finally, on November 3, Williamson appeared in the United States District Court and testified that he had intended no contempt of court nor had he tried to evade the process of the court. He had not produced the slaves in court because it would have been impossible for him to have done so. The court accepted his statement and released him from the charge of contempt.[97] Jane Johnson and her children remained free, for Wheeler was no longer in the country to press the issue before the fugitive slave tribunals.

Perhaps the most poignant case involving a jurisdictional dispute was that of Margaret Garner. On January 27, 1856, eight slaves belonging to Archibald K. Gaines and James Marshall of Boone County, Kentucky escaped across the Ohio River into Cincinnati. The slave party, two men, two women, and four children, took refuge in the house of Elijah Kite near Mill Creek Bridge. Having traced the fugitives to their place of refuge, Gaines obtained a warrant for their arrest from United States Commissioner John L. Pendery. Deputy United States Marshall Ellis, with several assistants, proceeded to the place of hiding and asked the slaves to surrender quietly. They refused and, in fact, offered considerable resistance. The door of the house was finally broken down; in the melee that followed, one man was wounded, but the slaves were overpowered and seized.[98]

Margaret Garner, one of the slaves belonging to Gaines, decided that rather than see her children returned to slavery she would kill them. She managed to cut the throat of her little girl but was stopped before she could slay two of her small sons. A large crowd had gathered around the house, and it was only with great difficulty that the officers were able to remove the fugitives to the marshal's office. Commissioner Pendery placed the slaves in the custody of United

96. United States *ex rel.* Wheeler v. Williamson, 28 Federal Cases 691–95 (1855).

97. *National Intelligencer*, November 5, 1855; *New York Weekly Tribune*, November 10, 1855.

98. *Ex Parte* Robinson, 20 Federal Cases 965 (1856); May, *Fugitive Slave Law and Its Victims*, pp. 50–51.

States Marshal Hiram H. Robinson and deferred the case until the morning of January 29.[99]

On the afternoon of January 28, an application was made to Judge John Burgoyne, of the probate court, for a writ of habeas corpus. The writ was issued directing Deputy Sheriff Jeff Buckingham to secure the custody of the fugitives. After considerable haggling, the slaves were turned over to the state officers, and they were placed in the county jail. On the morning of January 29, Sheriff Gazoway Brashears was informed by certain lawyers that, based on Justice McLean's decision in the Rosetta Armstead case, Judge Burgoyne did not have the authority to release the slaves from federal custody. Thus, the custody of the slaves passed back to the federal officers. By agreement between state and federal officers, the fugitives were kept in the county jail. In the meantime, an Ohio grand jury had indicted Margaret Garner for the murder of her daughter.[100]

The examination before Commissioner Pendery was held January 30. The defense counsel asked for more time to prepare their case, and the commissioner agreed. Witnesses were examined until February 4, and the arguments of defense counsel did not end until three days later. With regard to the slaves of James Marshall, the case was closed February 8. The examination of Margaret Garner and her children was continued. Arguments in her case were heard until February 21, but the commissioner postponed his decision.[101]

Having issued a writ of habeas corpus, the court of common pleas insisted that Sheriff Brashears take custody of the fugitives. Because the slaves were being held in the county jail, the court would not accept the sheriff's answer that they were in the custody of federal officers. With no other alternative, the sheriff was forced to take possession of the prisoners on the indictment for murder.[102] The conflict between state and federal courts for jurisdiction of the case deepened.

On February 26, Commissioner Pendery rendered his decision. He decided that Gaine's claim was good and ordered Margaret Garner and her three children into custody. Fearful that his slaves would be

99. May, *Fugitive Slave Law and Its Victims*, p. 52.
100. Ibid., p. 53.
101. Ibid.
102. Ibid., p. 55.

taken from him by force, Gaines asked that his slaves be delivered to him in Kentucky. The commissioner agreed and ordered the marshal to deliver them as requested.[103]

Having been ordered by Judge Burgoyne not to remove the slaves from the jurisdiction of his court until the case was finally settled, the marshal appealed to Judge Humphrey H. Leavitt of the United States District Court. Basing his decision on Justice McLean's ruling in the Rosetta Armstead case, Judge Leavitt maintained that Judge Burgoyne did not have authority to release by habeas corpus a fugitive slave from the custody of a federal officer. The slaves were therefore in the legal custody of the United States marshal, and the marshal delivered the slaves to their owner in Kentucky as ordered.[104] Ruling that suspension of habeas corpus under the provisions of the Fugitive Slave Law was unconstitutional, Judge Burgoyne ordered the marshal to present the slaves before his court for a hearing. When Marshal Robinson was unable to do so, he was adjudged guilty of contempt of court, fined three hundred dollars, and committed to jail. To extricate himself, Marshal Robinson petitioned Judge Leavitt for a writ of habeas corpus which resulted in his release.[105]

The jurisdiction of the federal courts had won over the state courts once again, but the charge of murder against Margaret Garner was yet to be prosecuted. Governor Salmon P. Chase of Ohio requested Governor Charles S. Morehead of Kentucky to extradite the slave woman to face the charge of murder. Governor Morehead complied and issued the order but found that Margaret Garner and the rest of Gaines' slaves had been sent down the river to be sold in Arkansas. On the trip down the river the boat collided with another, causing the death of twenty-five persons, including the infant child of Margaret Garner. After the accident, Gaines changed his mind and brought the slave woman back to Covington to face extradition to Ohio. When the Ohio officers reached Covington, they found that Gaines had reconsidered and had shipped her to the New Orleans slave mar-

103. *Ex Parte* Robinson, 20 Federal Cases 965 (1856). See also *National Intelligencer*, February 29, 1856.

104. *Ex Parte* Robinson, 20 Federal Cases (1856); *National Intelligencer*, March 4, 1856; *New York Weekly Tribune*, March 8, 1856.

105. *Ex Parte* Robinson, 20 Federal Cases 968 (1856); *National Intelligencer*, April 26, 1856.

ket.[106] The Ohio courts were therefore frustrated, but the Fugitive Slave Law had been enforced.

The cases involving jurisdictional disputes were the occasion for considerable irony. The disputes resulted in the return of fugitive slaves, or the prosecution of violators of the Fugitive Slave Law, which was beneficial from the southern point of view. They also resulted in the maintenance of the supremacy of federal law, which must have afforded cold comfort to ardent state rights advocates in the South. Moreover, the Force Act of 1833, enacted to ensure the supremacy of federal law in South Carolina, was utilized to free federal officers from harassment by Pennsylvania courts in 1854.

In the great majority of cases which came before the fugitive slave tribunals, slaves were remanded to their owners or were returned to the South at goverment expense. This was not known to most Southerners in the 1850's, and perhaps it could not have been known. The majority of slaveholders apparently believed that the Fugitive Slave Law had failed.

106. May, *Fugitive Slave Law and Its Victims*, pp. 58–60. For a detailed account of the Garner case, see Julian Yanuck, "The Garner Fugitive Slave Case," *Mississippi Valley Historical Review* 40 (June 1953) : 47–66.

Chapter VII

Non-Enforcement
of the
Fugitive Slave Law:
Slave Rescues,
1850–1860

The record for capturing and returning fugitive slaves in the 1850's was obscured by the relatively few cases in which slaves were rescued from federal custody. The rescue cases prompted great outrage in the South, and, because of the wide publicity they received, many Southerners became convinced that the Fugitive Slave Law was not being enforced. Indeed, many Southerners felt that, as long as a majority in the North remained hostile to the institution of slavery and the recovery of fugitive slaves, the law was unenforceable. Compared with the number of slaves returned, the number of rescues was small, but three of the most notorious cases occurred in 1851 when opposition to enforcement of the Fugitive Slave Law was at its highest.

Frederick Jenkins, called Shadrack, was a waiter at the Cornhill Coffee House in Boston. He had escaped in May, 1850, from the service of John Debree of Norfolk, Virginia, a purser in the United

States Navy. Debree learned where Shadrack was, had an affidavit made out in the Virginia courts, and, in February, 1851, sent John Caphart to Boston to secure the rendition of his slave. A warrant was issued by Commissioner George Ticknor Curtis, and Shadrack was arrested on February 15 by Deputy United States Marshal Patrick Riley.[1]

Shadrack was taken directly to the courtroom for a hearing before Commissioner Curtis. Seth J. Thomas served as counsel for John Caphart. Samuel E. Sewall, Ellis Gray Loring, Charles List, Richard H. Dana, Jr., Charles G. Davis, and Robert H. Morris acted as counsel for the fugitive. Having had no opportunity to prepare their case, defense counsel asked the commissioner to delay the proceedings until February 18. The request was granted, and Shadrack was remanded to the custody of the deputy marshal.[2]

At the order to clear the courtroom, all left quietly except the marshals and Robert H. Morris, a Negro lawyer. Shadrack remained in his seat unshackled between two of the officers. There was a large crowd outside the courtroom, mostly Negroes who had been excluded from the court. At this point, the Negroes pushed open the door of the court, burst into the room, and "invited" Shadrack to accompany them. Richard Henry Dana, Jr. had just returned to his office from the courtroom when he heard a shout from the courthouse. He turned to see what the commotion was and saw "two huge negroes bearing the prisoner between them" down the steps. Shadrack's clothing was "half torn off," said Dana, and he appeared "so stupified by the sudden rescue and the violence of his dragging off that he sat almost dumb. . . ." The men who had seized the fugitive "hurried him through the square into Court Street, where he found the use of his feet, and they went off toward Cambridge, like a black squall, the crowd driving along with them and cheering as they went." According to Dana's account, none of the officers were hurt, "except by being crowded into corners and held fast. . . ." Adding insult to injury, the sword of justice which Patrick Riley displayed on his desk was stolen by one of the Negroes.[3]

---

1. *Boston Liberator,* February 21, 1851.
2. Ibid.
3. Adams, *Richard Henry Dana,* 1:182–83. See also Higginson, *Cheerful Yesterdays,* pp. 135–36.

Shadrack was taken to Canada beyond the reach of federal officers. Stopping finally in Montreal, he suffered the fate of many Negroes who had escaped into Canada—he was forced to ask for financial aid from his friends in Boston.[4] Shadrack's condition improved, however. The *Liberator* reported in September, 1853, that Shadrack was operating an "eating house" in Montreal, that he was married to an Irish woman, and that he had "added a subject to Her Majesty's dominion within the year." [5]

Reverberations from the Shadrack rescue were heard all the way from Boston to Washington. Supported by the aldermen, the mayor of Boston now ordered the city marshal, with "the whole police force under his control," to provide assistance to the federal marshal when it appeared that mob action would interfere with the performance of his duties.[6] Senator Henry Clay demanded an investigation of the case and called upon the president to lay before the Senate any information he had with regard to the Shadrack case.[7] On February 18, President Fillmore responded by issuing a proclamation calling upon "all well-disposed citizens to rally to the support of the laws of their country, and requiring and commanding all officers, civil and military, who shall be found within the vicinity of the outrage, to be aiding and assisting by all means in their power in quelling this and other such combinations. . . ." The president also ordered the district attorney and "all other persons concerned in the administration or execution of the laws of the United States" to prosecute all persons who had "aided, abetted, or assisted" in the escape of Shadrack.[8] The secretary of war and the secretary of the navy placed their forces in Boston at the disposal of the federal marshal.[9]

After an investigation, eight men were arrested for aiding in the rescue of Shadrack. Bail was set at three thousand dollars each. Four of the defendants were Negroes: Robert H. Morris, Lewis Hayden, James Scott, and John A. Coburn. The white defendants were Joseph K. Hayes, Elizur Wright, Charles G. Davis, and Thomas P. Smith. The grand jury indicted all of them. The trials began in the United

4. *National Intelligencer*, March 25, 1851.
5. *Boston Liberator*, September 30, 1853.
6. *National Intelligencer*, February 22, 1851.
7. *Congressional Globe*, 21, 31st Cong., 1st sess., p. 596.
8. Richardson, *Messages and Papers*, 5:109–10.
9. *National Intelligencer*, March 1, 1851.

States District Court before Judge Peleg Sprague on May 27 and lasted through June 18. The cases of Elizur Wright, James Scott, and Robert H. Morris were suspended because the juries could not agree. The other cases were dropped. No one was convicted for aiding in Shadrack's escape.[10]

The Shadrack rescue was the greatest defeat suffered by the national government in the enforcement of the Fugitive Slave Law. Not only was a fugitive slave snatched from a federal marshal in the Boston courthouse, but the district attorney was unable to secure a single conviction against those charged with aiding and abetting the escape. This caused great consternation in Washington, and moves were made to see that it never happened again.

One of the more interesting and least appreciated aspects of the Shadrack rescue was the role played by Negroes. The rescue was carried out with great skill and daring. Throughout the decade, Negroes would continue to play a prominent part in almost every instance where a fugitive slave was rescued or where attempts were made to effect a rescue. Sometimes led by white men, but often acting on their own initiative, members of the Negro communities in the North demonstrated by their action their desire to prevent the return of fellow Negroes to slavery. Many of the Negroes who participated in such activities were liable to capture themselves. Within a few days after Shadrack's rescue, for example, nearly one hundred Negroes fled the city of Boston to prevent their capture and prosecution as fugitive slaves.[11]

The most violent of the fugitive slave rescues occurred at Christiana, Pennsylvania on September 11, 1851. Edward Gorsuch, accompanied by his son, nephew, and other relatives, went to Christiana after two slaves who were reported to be hiding there. Deputy United States Marshal Henry W. Kline led the party to the home of William Parker, a Negro, where it was believed the fugitives were staying. A Negro named Williams had warned the fugitives early that morning that Gorsuch would be coming after them. As the party approached the Parker house, a bugle and several horns were blown as a signal

10. Ibid., March 1, 4, 29, April 24, May 29, June 7, 21, November 13, 1851, June 12, 1852; Adams, *Richard Henry Dana*, 1:195–96, 210–11; Catterall, *Judicial Cases*, 4:514–17.

11. Wendell Phillips to Elizabeth Pease, March 9, 1851, in Garrison, *William Lloyd Garrison*, 3:323–25. See also Higginson, *Cheerful Yesterdays*, p. 135.

that slave catchers were in the neighborhood. When they arrived, Gorsuch found the fugitives for whom he was looking. They were hiding with several others in the Parker house. Marshal Kline read the warrants and requested the two fugitives to come quietly, but the Negroes resisted arrest.

At this point, Castner Hanaway, a member of the Society of Friends and a neighbor of Parker's, arrived on the scene. Marshal Kline called upon him to assist in the arrest and to do what he could to prevent bloodshed, but Hanaway refused. He said that the Negroes had a right to defend themselves. Another Quaker, Elijah Lewis, arrived and asked for Kline's authority to be there. After reading the warrants, he refused also to assist in the arrest of the Negroes. In the meantime, several other Negroes had responded to the alarm and had hurried to the Parker residence. They were armed with guns and clubs. After conferring with Hanaway, "the negroes shouted, and immediately fired from every direction." Hanaway rode into the lane leading away from the house and watched the ensuing battle.

During the melee, Gorsuch was struck on the back of the head, and fell forward on his face. As he attempted to rise, he was shot, and, while he lay prostrate on the ground, he was "cut on the head with a corn cutter." His son rushed to his aid, but he too was shot. The remainder of the party escaped unharmed; the wounded were carried to houses in the vicinity. Gorsuch died, and his son had been severely wounded. Three Negroes had been killed in the affray.[12]

Excitement was high in Lancaster County, and statements in the national press expressed revulsion. Citizens from Baltimore County, Maryland, Gorsuch's home, were determined "to see the authors of the outrage brought to a strict accountability." An editorial in the *Boston Courier* stated that "this melancholy occurrence never would have taken place but for the instigations which have been applied to the ignorant and deluded blacks by the fanatics of the 'higher law' creed." In Philadelphia, the *United States Gazette* called the Christiana affair more than a "murderous riot." It was an "act of insurrection, . . . almost . . . a servile insurrection, if not, also, one of

12. Catterall, *Judicial Cases*, 4:301–4. See also W. U. Hensel, *The Christiana Riot and the Treason Trials of 1851: An Historical Sketch* (Lancaster, Pa.: New Era Printing Company, 1911), pp. 20–39 (hereafter cited as Hensel, *Christiana Riot*).

treason." The *New York Express* said that the "real murderers" were "the white Abolitionists who advised the negroes to arm and to resist the law. . . ." [13]

It was realized in Washington that if such a crime were permitted to go unpunished the chances for successfully enforcing the Fugitive Slave Law would be jeopardized. The Department of the Interior gave United States District Attorney George W. Ashmead full cooperation and support, for the government wanted convictions in these cases. In a letter to Ashmead on November 6, Secretary of the Interior Alexander H. H. Stuart wrote: "All . . . reasonable and proper expenses which you may have incurred or which [you] may deem it necessary to incur will be sanctioned and allowed by the Dept. if approved by both the Judges of the U. S. Circuit Court, as it is the wish of the Dept. to give you all necessary and proper aid in the management of these important cases. . . ." [14]

The grand jury of the United States Circuit Court at Philadelphia returned indictments for high treason against Jacob Townsend, George Williams, Castner Hanaway, Elijah Lewis, Joseph Scarlet, and forty others, all of whom had taken part in the riot at Christiana. [15] It was Ashmead's decision to charge the defendants in the Christiana riot with treason, and Judge John K. Kane seemed to concur. In his statement to the grand jury, Kane said: "It has been thought safe, to . . . instigate others to acts of forcible oppugnation to the provisions of a statute . . . to represent the constitution . . . as a compact of iniquity, which it were meritorious to violate . . . the mistake has been a grievous one; . . . successfully to instigate treason, is to commit it." [16] The possibility that the district attorney could get convictions for treason in a fugitive slave case before a Pennsylvania jury was remote from the beginning. If the defendants had been tried for violations of the Fugitive Slave Law, the chances for getting convictions would have been much better.

13. *National Intelligencer*, September 16, 1851, quoting *Baltimore American;* September 18, 1851, quoting *Boston Courier, United States Gazette,* and *New York Express.*
14. Alexander H. H. Stuart to George W. Ashmead, November 6, 1851, in Department of Interior, Letter Book, Judiciary No. 1, 1849–1853, National Archives, Justice and Executive Branch, Washington, D.C.
15. *National Intelligencer*, November 18, 1851; Hensel, *Christiana Riots,* pp. 40–45.
16. Catterall, *Judicial Cases,* 4:300–301.

As a test case, Ashmead decided to try Hanaway first. His trial began in Philadelphia before Justice Robert C. Grier on November 25. Hanaway pleaded not guilty to the charges in the indictment. Represented by John M. Read, Thaddeus Stevens, and Theodore Cuyler, Hanaway was ably defended. The escape of two principal witnesses, Peter Washington and John Clark, from the debtor's prison weakened the prosecution's case immeasureably. When the case went to the jury, Justice Grier charged that the treason charges had not been sustained by the evidence. Hanaway was acquitted December 12, and on December 17, District Attorney Ashmead entered *nolle prosequi* in all the indictments for treason which had not been tried.[17] Having failed to obtain a conviction for treason in Hanaway's case, the government dropped the charges in the remaining cases.

In late September, 1851, a large number of abilitionists had congregated in Syracuse, New York to attend the annual Liberty party convention. At the same time, the city was crowded with visitors to the Onandaga County Fair. Living in Syracuse was a fugitive slave named William Henry, popularly known as Jerry, who was working as a cooper. Jerry had escaped from the service of John McReynolds of Marion County, Missouri. Deputy United States Marshal Henry W. Allen arrested Jerry on October 1 on a warrant issued by Commissioner Joseph F. Sabine. When the arrest was made, Jerry was informed that he was being held for violation of state law, and he submitted quietly. Once the fugitive was in custody, however, Marshal Allen told him that he was being taken before Commissioner Sabine for a hearing to ascertain whether he was McReynold's slave.[18]

A manacled slave in Syracuse was a novelty and aroused great excitement. A large crowd gathered before the commissioner's office, church bells were tolled, and several men volunteered to serve as counsel for the fugitive. As the hearing proceeded, counsel raised

17. *National Intelligencer*, November 27, December 13, 16, 22, 1851; Catterall, *Judicial Cases*, 4:304. See also Hensel, *Christiana Riots*, pp. 61–90.

18. *Trial of Henry W. Allen, U. S. Deputy Marshal, For Kidnapping, With Arguments of Counsel & Charge of Justice Marvin, on the Constitutionality of the Fugitive Slave Law, in the Supreme Court of New York* (Syracuse: Daily Journal Office, 1852), p. 3 (hereafter cited as *Trial of Henry W. Allen*); *National Intelligencer*, October 7, 1851; *Boston Liberator*, October 10, 1851.

objections to the fact that the fugitive was forced to sit in irons. Although he had no authority to require it, Commissioner Sabine advised the marshal to remove the hand cuffs. Just as the commissioner was about to adjourn the hearing for lunch, the court was attacked by several men, both colored and white, and Jerry was rescued. But the fugitive was overtaken by city police and, with the aid of volunteers, was taken to the police station where the hearing resumed that afternoon. As evening approached, excitement continued to mount, and the crowd outside the police station increased. Because the mood of the crowd was becoming ugly, the hearing was adjourned until morning. Marshal Allen, assisted by the marshals of Auburn, Canadaigua, and Rochester, retained custody of the fugitive slave.[19]

Before the hearing that afternoon, a group of abolitionists had met at the office of Dr. Hiram Hoyt, a local physician, to plan a rescue. In the group were Gerrit Smith, Samuel Joseph May, C. A. Wheaton, and J. S. Loguen, a Negro minister. Believing that the Fugitive Slave Law was unconstitutional, and having talked resistance to the law for over a year, the group agreed that time for action had arrived. Gerrit Smith is reported to have said: "It is not unlikely the Commissioner will release Jerry if the examination is suffered to proceed—but the moral effect of such an acquittal will be as nothing to a bold and forcible rescue. A forcible rescue will demonstrate the strength of public opinion against the possible legality of slavery and this Fugitive Slave Law in particular. It will honor Syracuse and be a powerful example everywhere." [20] After a course of action was determined, the meeting adjourned.

After adjournment of the fugitive slave hearing, the crowd outside the police station began to disperse. At that time, the rescue plan conceived in Dr. Hoyt's office was put into effect. A mob of Negroes and abolitionists broke into the police station and rescued the fugitive. Jerry was placed in a carriage and driven away. After a few

19. *Trial of Henry W. Allen*, p. 3; *National Intelligencer*, October 7, 1851; Harlow, *Gerrit Smith*, pp. 297–98.
20. Earl Evelyn Sperry, *The Jerry Rescue, October 1, 1851, . . . Delivered Before the Onandaga Historical Association, October, 1921. . . . Additional Jerry Rescue Documents and Rescue of Harriet Powell in Syracuse, September, 1839*, comp. and ed. Franklin H. Chase (Syracuse: Onandaga Historical Association, 1924), p. 24.

days, he was sent to Kingston, Ontario where he lived until his death two years later.[21]

After two weeks of intensive investigation, the district attorney attempted to make a case of constructive treason against Gerrit Smith, Charles A. Wheaton, Samuel Joseph May, and five other defendants. He had hoped also to find sufficient evidence to indict sixteen others for aiding and abetting the rescue of a fugitive slave. According to Samuel J. May, the district court refused to issue warrants for the alleged offenders because of a lack of evidence.[22] By early November, however, thirteen of the alleged rescuers had been arrested. Each was required to post a two-thousand-dollar bond to insure his presence before the federal grand jury in Buffalo. On November 19, the grand jury indicted twenty-six persons, but they were charged with being "engaged in the Syracuse riots," not with treason.[23] In a letter to William Lloyd Garrison, May said that twelve of the defendants were Negroes, and all but three escaped into Canada. Four of the white men had also gone to Canada to avoid prosecution.[24]

The trials began January 21, 1852, in the United States District Court at Albany, New York. Because of the importance of the issues, the indictments were transferred to the circuit court for the same district, but for various reasons the cases were postponed until January, 1853. The case of Enoch Reed was the first to go to the jury. The verdict was guilty as charged.[25] A second case resulted in acquittal. The jury was divided on two other defendants, and the remaining cases were dropped.[26]

To bring further opprobrium on the Fugitive Slave Law, the abolitionists in Syracuse had Deputy Marshal Henry W. Allen indicted for violation of a New York statute of May 6, 1840, "An Act to extend the right of trial by jury." Marshal Allen went on trial in the New York Supreme Court on June 21, 1852. Gerrit Smith, as

---

21. Harlow, *Gerrit Smith*, p. 299; *Boston Liberator*, October 10, 1851.
22. May to W. L. Garrison, October 15, 1851, in Garrison, *William Lloyd Garrison*, 3:335.
23. *National Intelligencer*, November 21, 1851.
24. Samuel Joseph May to W. L. Garrison, November 23, 1851, Garrison, *William Lloyd Garrison*, 3:336.
25. *National Intelligencer*, February 3, 1852; February 1, 1853. See also U.S. v. Reed, 27 Federal Cases 727 (1852). This was a motion to quash the indictment, which was denied. There is no record showing Reed's sentence.
26. Harlow, *Gerrit Smith*, pp. 300–301.

special counsel for the prosecution, presented a seven-hour argument against the constitutionality of the Fugitive Slave Law. Messrs. S. D. Dillaye and George F. Comstock defended Allen. At the conclusion of the arguments, Judge Marvin reviewed the constitutional question, declared that the Fugitive Slave Law was constitutional, and advised the jury "to bring in a verdict for the defendant of Not Guilty." The jury complied and acquitted Marshal Allen without leaving their seats.[27]

From the abolitionist point of view, the Jerry rescue had been a resounding success. A fugitive slave had been taken from the custody of a federal marshal, and the government was able to secure only one conviction for violation of the Fugitive Slave Law. Each year thereafter until the Civil War, Syracuse commemorated the Jerry rescue on its anniversary date. As a result of the rescue, public opinion in the South was highly incensed. With regard to the Jerry rescue, a correspondent to the *Savannah Republican* said: "These scenes are too common at the North, and, if persisted in, will lead eventually, from sectional jealousy, to the bitterest hate and revenge. . . . We warn the press and the people of the North that there is a point, not far distant, when forbearance on our part will cease to be virtuous or honorable, and that they, and they alone, will be responsible for all the ills that may betide this Government." [28] Despite the fact that the great majority of slaves claimed in federal tribunals in 1851 were returned, extensive damage had been done.[29]

In March, 1854, Deputy United States Marshal Charles C. Cotton, accompanied by Benjamin S. Garland, of St. Louis, Missouri, and three other men, broke into the shanty of Joshua Glover, a Negro who was working in Racine, Wisconsin. After a fierce struggle, Glover was subdued and lodged in the county jail at Milwaukee. Glover, claimed as the slave of Garland, had allegedly escaped in 1852.[30]

27. *Trial of Henry W. Allen,* pp. 115–22; *National Intelligencer,* July 1, 1852; Harlow, *Gerrit Smith,* pp. 301–2.

28. *National Intelligencer,* October 20, 1851, quoting the *Savannah Republican.*

29. Most of the people in the country had no way of knowing that in forty-seven cases brought before fugitive tribunals in 1851, over 82 percent of the fugitives were remanded to their owners or were returned at government expense. See Appendix II.

30. *Boston Liberator,* March 24, 1854. See also United States *ex rel.* Garland v. Morris, 26 Federal Cases 1318 (1854).

As soon as word got out that a fugitive slave had been arrested, hundreds of men flocked to the jail. The courthouse bell was rung, and the throng which assembled in the courthouse square increased to over a thousand. The assemblage was organized by James H. Paine, and a committee was appointed to draft resolutions. Participating on the resolutions committee were Paine, William Whitnall, John Furlong, Sherman M. Booth, and Dr. E. Wunderly. The signers pledged to stand by the prisoner and do their "utmost to secure for him a fair and impartial trial by jury." A vigilance committee of twenty-five persons was appointed to watch the jail to prevent the prisoner from being moved secretly.[31]

During the morning after the arrest, Milwaukee's Sheriff Page was served with a writ of habeas corpus directing him to produce Glover before Judge Jenkins of the state court. In his answer to the writ, Sheriff Page said that Glover was not in his custody. The fugitive was being held by the United States District Court; it would therefore be impossible for him to present Glover before the court.[32]

Late that afternoon, a steamboat arrived from Racine carrying about one hundred men who had rushed to Milwaukee upon hearing that Glover had been arrested. They marched straight to the jail and demanded that the Negro be released. When the demand was refused, the jail was rushed, the door was broken down, and Glover was taken from his cell. He was placed in a carriage and sent to Racine; later he escaped into Canada.[33]

Sheriff Morris of Racine County had arrived on the same boat with the rescuers. He had a warrant for the arrest of Garland and four other men on a charge of assault and battery. Garland was taken into custody and committed to jail. Judge Miller, of the United States District Court, issued a writ of habeas corpus demanding Sheriff Morris to show why Garland should not be released. Morris answered that Garland was being held on a warrant issued by the mayor of Racine. Nevertheless, Judge Miller ordered Garland's release on the ground that "he was aiding the marshal in the service of a warrant, at the officer's request. . . . The law under which the fugitive was apprehended, is a law of the United States. . . ." Furthermore, the "judges, commissioners, marshals, or claimants are

31. *Boston Liberator*, March 24, 1854.
32. Ibid.
33. *Boston Liberator*, March 24, 1854.

not to be interfered with, in its [the law's] administration or execution, by the state courts or officers." [34]

Sherman M. Booth, who was to remain in the center of the jurisdictional dispute between state and federal courts for the next seven years, was arrested in March on a warrant issued by Commissioner Winfield Smith. Charged with "aiding, abetting, and assisting" in the escape of a fugitive slave, Booth was apprehended by United States Marshal Ableman. [35] Booth petitioned the Supreme Court of Wisconsin for a writ of habeas corpus, and the writ was granted on the grounds that the Fugitive Slave Law was unconstitutional; he was discharged. [36] Marshal Ableman arrested Booth again on July 20 after indictment by the grand jury of the United States District Court at Madison. He declined to give bail and petitioned the Wisconsin Supreme Court again for a writ of habeas corpus. The application was denied on the grounds that, in this instance, the federal courts had jurisdiction. [37] John Rycraft, a member of the vigilance committee which had participated in the attack on the jail, was also indicted for having assisted in Glover's escape. At his trial before the United States District Court in November, Rycraft was found guilty as charged, fined two hundred dollars, and imprisoned for ten days. [38] Rycraft appealed to the Wisconsin Supreme Court.

Booth was brought to trial in January, 1855. The jury found Booth guilty. He was fined one thousand dollars and sentenced to prison for one month. He was lodged in the county jail at Milwaukee and was not to be freed until the fine was paid. [39] With Rycraft, Booth once again applied to the Wisconsin Supreme Court for a writ of habeas corpus. The writ was granted, and both Rycraft and Booth were freed on the grounds that the charges upon which the petitioners had been convicted did not indicate an offense over which the federal courts had jurisdiction. [40] Although a minor victory for Booth, his problems were still to come.

34. United States *ex rel.* Garland v. Morris, 26 Federal Cases 1318 (1854). See Catterall, *Judicial Cases,* 5:90.
35. *National Intelligencer,* July 27, 1854; *Boston Liberator,* March 24, 1854.
36. Ableman v. Booth, 21 Howard 508 (1858). See also Catterall, *Judicial Cases,* 5:89.
37. *National Intelligencer,* July 27, 31, 1854.
38. United States v. Rycraft, 27 Federal Cases 918 (1854).
39. Ableman v. Booth, 21 Howard 510 (1858) ; *National Intelligencer,* January 24, 1855.
40. Ibid., 21 Howard 511 (1858). See also *In re* Booth and Rycraft, 3 Wisconsin 157 (1855), and the *National Intelligencer,* February 7, 8, 13, 1855.

On July 13 and 14, 1855, the case of *Garland* v. *Booth* was heard in the United States District Court at Madison. Garland had brought suit against Booth for one thousand dollars in damages, the value of the slave Joshua Glover, as permitted under the Fugitive Slave Act. According to the *Madison Democrat*, the jury was not out over ten minutes; the verdict was unanimous for the plaintiff.[41] The cost of the suit ruined Booth financially.

On April 21, 1855, Attorney General Jeremiah S. Black petitioned the United States Supreme Court for a writ of error in the Booth case.[42] After the writ was issued, it was served on the clerk of the Wisconsin Supreme Court by the United States district attorney. He was informed by the clerk "that the court had directed the clerk to make no return to the writ of error, and to enter no order upon the . . . records of the court concerning same. . . ."[43] No return having been made by February 27, 1857, the attorney general asked permission to file a certified copy of the record of the Wisconsin Supreme Court. In 1858, after many delays, the case was finally heard by the United States Supreme Court.

Chief Justice Roger B. Taney delivered the majority opinion. The court ruled that the Fugitive Slave Law "in all of its provisions" was constitutional. The conduct of the Wisconsin Supreme Court was therefore illegal. It was the right and the duty of the federal marshal to resist by force any interference by the states. "The judgment of the Supreme Court of Wisconsin," said Taney, "must therefore be reversed in each of the cases now before the court."[44]

The United States District Court ordered Booth's arrest on February 20, 1860. He was apprehended on March 1 and confined in the Custom House in Milwaukee. Booth petitioned for a writ of habeas corpus, but on this occasion the Wisconsin Supreme Court declined to act. A last minute effort was made by the court of Racine County to release Booth on April 4, but the marshal refused to answer the writ. Booth remained in custody until August 1 when he was forcibly taken from the Custom House by ten armed men. The

41. *National Intelligencer*, July 18, 1855, citing the *Madison Democrat*.
42. *In re* United States v. Booth, 18 Howard 476 (1855).
43. Ableman v. Booth, 21 Howard 512 (1858).
44. Ibid. See also Catterall, *Judicial Cases*, 5:95–96, and the *National Intelligencer*, March 11, 1859. For a good discussion of the constitutional aspects of the case, see Yanuck, "Fugitive Slave Law," pp. 190–95.

marshal and his deputies had gone out to dinner, and the jailer was silenced by "'threats of violence.'" [45]

On August 6, Booth spoke before a group of antislavery sympathizers at Ripon, Wisconsin. He announced during his remarks that there was a marshal in the room and dared the officer to arrest him. Deputy United States Marshal McCarty, of Fond du Lac, stepped forward and presented his warrant. The reaction of the crowd was violent; McCarty's clothing was nearly torn off. "No shots were fired, although revolvers and bowie knives were handled carelessly," said the *Milwaukee Sentinel.*[46]

During the first week in September, Marshal McCarty made a second attempt to arrest Booth. With six men, McCarty went to the home of a man named Pickett where it had been reported that Booth was hiding. This move was repulsed by sixty-two armed men. Booth remained at large until October 8, 1860, when he was arrested at Berlin, Wisconsin. Taken into custody by Deputy United States Marshal Taylor, he was removed to Milwaukee and once again confined in the Custom House.[47]

On March 2, 1861, two days before the end of his term, President James Buchanan directed Edwin M. Stanton to have a pardon issued to Sherman M. Booth. Having been in prison for ten months, Booth was unable to pay the fine and costs resulting from his conviction. Because the "confinement already suffered by . . . Booth is deemed sufficient punishment to satisfy the ends of Justice in his case," said Stanton in his letter to the attorney general, the pardon was issued and Booth was set free.[48]

Near Mechanicsburg, Ohio, on May 21, 1857, an unsuccessful attempt was made to arrest a fugitive slave named Addison White. For several months, White had been living with and working for Udney H. Hyde. White's master, Daniel G. White, had learned of his slave's whereabouts through letters Addison had written to his wife, a free Negro woman who had remained in Kentucky. Accompanied by five Kentuckians, Deputy United States Marshals B. P. Churchill

45. *National Intelligencer*, March 6, 9, 12, April 6, August 3, 1860.
46. Ibid., August 11, 1860.
47. Ibid., September 5, October 12, 1860.
48. Edwin M. Stanton to Jeremiah S. Black, March 2, 1861, Letter Book B-2, Attorney General's Office, National Archives, Justice and Executive Branch, Washington, D.C.

and John C. Elliot appeared early on the morning of May 21 to arrest the fugitive slave. Having seen the marshals and their party approaching, Addison took refuge in the loft of the house. But White was seen climbing the ladder into the loft and was followed by Marshal Elliot. White was armed, and, when the marshal's head appeared in the loft, the Negro fired. Fortunately for the marshal, the bullet hit the barrel of his shotgun and ricocheted.[49] Elliot came down the ladder and left White in the loft.

In the meantime, Hyde had sent his daughter to Mechanicsburg to warn his son of what was happening. Soon thereafter, twenty or thirty heavily armed people gathered in Hyde's yard to prevent the arrest. After a heated argument, the marshals and their party decided to withdraw without the fugitive. Addison was then moved to a place of safety, and Hyde went into hiding for the next six months.[50]

On May 27, Deputy Marshals Churchill and Elliot returned to Mechanicsburg with a posse. Their purpose was to arrest Udney H. Hyde. After their arrival at Hyde's home, the federal officers became engaged in a controversy with Russell Hyde, son of the man whom they sought, Charles and Edward Taylor, and Hiram Gutridge. These four men were arrested and charged with obstructing federal officers in the performance of their duty and with harboring Addison White.[51]

Not wishing to see these men prosecuted, friends procured a writ of habeas corpus from Samuel V. Baldwin, judge of the Probate Court of Champaign County, but before Sheriff Clark could serve the writ the federal officers had passed beyond his jurisdiction. Another writ was then obtained and placed in the hands of Sheriff John E. Layton of Clark County. Sheriff Layton met Churchill and Elliot at South Charleston and attempted to serve the writ, but Churchill was in no mood to accept it and resisted with considerable force. According to the *Cincinnati Gazette,* Sheriff Layton was knocked down with a Colt revolver during the melee and was badly beaten.[52] As a result

49. *New York Weekly Tribune,* June 6, 1857.
50. Ibid.; Benjamin Franklin Prince, "The Rescue Case of 1857," *Ohio Archaeological and Historical Society Publications* 16 (January 1907) : 293–306 (hereafter cited as Prince, "Rescue Case of 1857") ; May, *Fugitive Slave Law and Its Victims,* p. 68.
51. Prince, "Rescue Case of 1857," p. 293; *New York Weekly Tribune,* June 6, 1857.
52. *National Intelligencer,* June 1, 1857, citing the *Cincinnati Gazette.*

of the violence, Justice of the Peace J. A. Houston issued a warrant for the arrest of the marshal and his posse. The charges were assault and battery with intent to kill.[53]

A warrant having been issued in Greene County, Sheriff Samuel Lewis of Greene County overtook the marshals in the little village of Lumberton. After stubborn resistance, the officers and their prisoners were taken into custody by Sheriff Lewis's superior force and returned to South Charleston. Arraigned before Justice of the Peace Houston's court, the marshals were bound over to the Probate Court of Clark County and were held overnight in the Springfield jail. Hyde, Gutridge, and the Taylors were returned to Champaign County and released by Judge Baldwin. On May 29, the marshals appeared before the Probate Court of Clark County and, after posting $150 bail each, were discharged. After their release, they were rearrested on a warrant issued by Justice of the Peace James S. Christie, and trial was set for May 30.[54]

Meanwhile, an appeal had been made to Judge Leavitt of the United States District Court. He ordered that the prisoners be released and brought to Cincinnati.[55] In this conflict between state and federal courts, the latter remained firm. When United States Marshal Lewis W. Sifford wired Washington for instructions, the secretary of the interior is reported to have replied: "Consult the District Attorney, and execute the law. The President desires you to do your duty, and he will do his." [56]

On June 9, the case came before the district court in Cincinnati. George E. Pugh, United States senator from Ohio, and Congressman Clement Laird Vallandigham joined United States Attorney Stanley Matthews as counsel for the deputy marshals. Sheriff Layton was represented by Ohio's Attorney General Christopher P. Walcott, Rodney Mason, and James C. Good.[57] Defense counsel severely condemned interference with the arrest of persons charged with violations of the Fugitive Slave Law. Even though the state had issued a writ of habeas corpus, the federal officers were under no obligations

53. *New York Weekly Tribune,* June 6, 1857; Prince, "Rescue Case of 1857," pp. 293–306.
54. Prince, "Rescue Case of 1857," pp. 305, 303.
55. *Ex Parte* Sifford, 22 Federal Cases 105 (1857).
56. *New York Weekly Tribune,* June 6, 1857.
57. Prince, "Rescue Case of 1857," p. 302.

to obey it. Sheriff Layton admitted that when the writ was placed in his hands for service he was told that "the persons having the custody of the prisoners were deputy marshals, and held the prisoners under authority of the United States." Despite arguments by the state that the federal courts could not review the action of a state court, Judge Leavitt freed the marshals from prosecution by the state of Ohio. The judge ruled that, at the time of their arrest, the federal officers were attempting to discharge their duty and were therefore not liable to arrest by state officers. Having acted under a law of the United States, the marshals could use any degree of force necessary to retain the custody of their prisoners. The federal officers had been arrested illegally and were now discharged.[58]

The United States district attorney now retaliated. He ordered the arrest of all those persons who had tried to prevent enforcement of the Fugitive Slave Law in the Addison White case. Not only were the sheriffs and constables arrested, but so were the state judges who had issued the writs of habeas corpus and warrants for the arrest of the federal officers. Charged with resisting federal officers in the discharge of their duties, they were bound over for trial in October.[59]

When it became clear that the United States attorney intended to prosecute these cases energetically, Governor Chase sought a compromise with the national government. It was finally agreed that one thousand dollars would be raised by private subscription which would be paid to Daniel White for the loss of his slave. In return, President Buchanan would order the United States attorney to discontinue the prosecution of all cases both criminal and civil.[60] While Addison White was rescued, Southerners could not argue that in this case federal officers did not vigorously prosecute the violators of the Fugitive Slave Law.

The last important and widely publicized fugitive slave rescue occurred at Wellington, Ohio. In September, 1858, Anderson D. Jennings arrived in Oberlin, Ohio in search of a fugitive slave. During the course of his investigation, he saw a Negro whom he recognized as the slave of John G. Bacon, a neighbor of his in Macon County, Kentucky. Jennings wrote Bacon informing him of the

---

58. *Ex Parte* Sifford, 22 Federal Cases 110 (1857).

59. Prince, "Rescue Case of 1857," p. 303.

60. Ibid., p. 306. For a good discussion of the legal issues involved in the case, see Yanuck, "Fugitive Slave Law," pp. 179–86.

Negro's whereabouts and received from Bacon a power of attorney to act in his behalf. On Jenning's complaint, the United States commissioner issued a warrant for the slave's arrest. United States Marshal Lowe, accompanied by R. P. Mitchell who knew Bacon's slave, went to Oberlin to make the arrest. Apparently afraid to apprehend the Negro in town, the marshal hired the young son of a local farmer to decoy the fugitive out of town on the pretext that he was wanted to dig potatoes. The slave, named John, was seized and taken to Wellington, a village nine miles from Oberlin, to await the train for Columbus. The slave was confined in a local tavern. When word was spread in Oberlin that a Negro had been kidnapped, many of the residents armed themselves and hurried to Wellington. After conferring with the deputy marshal, they discovered that there was no hope that the Negro would be released. After two exciting hours during which the mob became increasingly belligerent, the fugitive was forcibly taken from an upper room in the tavern, put in a wagon, and presumably driven to Canada.[61]

Embarrassed by such open contempt for federal law, the government moved quickly. Determined to punish those who had participated in the rescue, a federal grand jury at Cleveland indicted thirty-seven persons for violations of the Fugitive Slave Law. Among those indicted were the Reverend Henry Peck, a professor at Oberlin College, the Reverend James M. Fitch, former missionary to Jamaica, "several theological students, five fugitive slaves, and thirty other citizens" including whites, blacks, and mulattoes. By December 8, fourteen of the participants in the Oberlin rescue had appeared in the United States District Court and posted one-thousand-dollar bonds assuring their appearance for trial.[62]

While the officers of the federal court were preparing their cases and gathering witnesses, the grand jury of Loraine County returned indictments against Anderson D. Jennings, R. P. Mitchell, Samuel Davis, another witness to the arrest, and Deputy Marshal Lowe for kidnapping a Negro.[63]

The case against the rescuers went to trial in Cleveland in April,

---

61. *New York Weekly Tribune,* April 23, 1859; *National Intelligencer,* December 11, 1858; May, *Fugitive Slave Law and Its Victims,* pp. 103–4. See also Rhodes, *History of the United States,* 2:362.

62. *National Intelligencer,* December 11, 15, 1858.

63. *National Intelligencer,* April 9, 1859; May, *Fugitive Slave Law and Its Victims,* p. 106.

1859. The first person tried was Simeon Bushnell, a clerk in a store at Cleveland who had driven the wagon in which the fugitive made his escape. The jury before whom Bushnell was tried, according to the *New York Weekly Tribune*, was made up "entirely of Buchanan Democrats." [64] There was no question about the law, the evidence was clear, and the verdict was guilty as charged. Bushnell was sentenced to pay a fine of six hundred dollars and costs and was imprisoned in the county jail for sixty days. [65] The next person to be prosecuted was Charles Langston, but his counsel objected to his being tried before the same jury that had convicted Bushnell. After considerable bickering, a new jury was impanelled, and the trial continued. Despite the fact that Langston was a Negro and had elicited a great deal of sympathy, the new jury found him guilty. He was fined one hundred dollars and costs and sentenced to twenty days imprisonment. [66]

The trials were proceeding much too slowly. Already more than thirty days had elapsed since the trials began. According to an editorial in the *Cleveland Plain Dealer*, the costs of prosecution were skyrocketing. "If a new jury is allowed in each case . . . it will take three hundred and twelve jurors to complete the list, and some five hundred and twenty days to finish the term, at an expense of some twenty thousand dollars to somebody." [67] Because the defendants were suffering a self-imposed martyrdom by refusing to post bail or pledge that they would appear in court, the marshal was forced to keep them in jail. Public opinion was aroused by the fact that obviously honorable men were being kept in prison. Seven of the men from Wellington, however, decided that they had had enough of martyrdom and requested that they be allowed to plead guilty so they could pay their fines and go home. The district attorney agreed and asked the court to make their punishment as light as possible. Each was sentenced to pay a fine of twenty dollars and costs and imprisonment in the county jail for twenty-four hours. [68]

64. *New York Weekly Tribune*, April 23, 1859.
65. *Ex Parte* Simeon Bushnell, 9 Ohio State Reports 77 (1859) ; *National Intelligencer*, May 13, 1859.
66. *Ex Parte* Charles Langston, 9 Ohio State Reports 77 (1859). See also, Wilbur Greeley Burrough, "Oberlin's Part in the Slavery Conflict," *Ohio Archaeological and Historical Publications* 20 (1911) : 219–334.
67. *National Intelligencer*, May 6, 1859, quoting the *Cleveland Plain Dealer*.
68. *National Intelligencer*, May 6, 11, 16, 1859.

Meanwhile, Bushnell and Langston had filed a petition for habeas corpus with the Supreme Court of Ohio to test the constitutionality of the Fugitive Slave Law. The writ was issued returnable at Columbus on May 25. C. P. Walcott, attorney general of Ohio, represented Bushnell and Langston at the hearing. Despite his impassioned argument that "under the federal constitution Congress had no power to enact the act of 1850," the court, by a vote of three to two, remanded the two rescuers to the custody of the United States marshal to complete their sentences.[69]

The time was now approaching for the trial of Jennings, Lowe, Mitchell, and Davis. It appeared certain that the defendants would be convicted. To resolve the dilemma, a compromise was agreed to whereby the United States district attorney would file *nolle prosequis* in the remaining cases if the state of Ohio would drop the charges against the four prisoners charged with kidnapping. The prisoners of both sides were released. On their return to Oberlin, the rescuers received "an enthusiastic reception." This ended the Oberlin-Wellington slave rescue case.[70]

According to criterion established at the beginning of the previous chapter, to measure effectively the enforcement of the Fugitive Slave Law, one must compare the number of slaves remanded to their owners by the federal tribunals with the number of claims made by the owners for fugitive slaves. During the period 1850 through 1860, 191 slaves were claimed in the federal courts under the Fugitive Slave Law. The efficiency of the courts responsible for enforcing the law in this period was 82.3 percent. At considerable trouble and expense, a minority of the cases, or 43.3 percent, required the return of the slaves by federal marshals. In some parts of the nation, hostility to the institution of slavery was so high that recovery of fugitive slaves was even more difficult. No claims were made upon federal tribunals in the New England states after the rendition of Anthony Burns, but only three claims had been made before 1854.

69. *Ex Parte* Simeon Bushnell and Charles Langston, 9 Ohio State Reports 77–325 (1859) ; Catterall, *Judicial Cases*, 5:1; *National Intelligencer*, June 2, 1859.

70. For a contemporary account of the case, see Jacob R. Shipherd, *History of the Oberlin-Wellington Rescue* (Boston: John P. Jewett and Company, 1859). In the 191 known cases tried before fugitive slave tribunals in the decade before the Civil War, only 22 slaves were rescued. See Appendices I–XII.

That no slaves were returned from New England by due process of law after the Burns case may be attributed indirectly to the personal liberty laws. As will be made clear in the next chapter, these laws seem to have had little effect upon the will or the ability of federal officials to enforce the Fugitive Slave Law. Indeed, there is not a single instance on record in which federal jurisdiction in fugitive slave cases was finally lost because of action taken by abolitionist lawyers under the personal liberty laws or any other laws.

On the other hand, the degree of cooperation between state and federal officials, even in the states without personal liberty laws, left much to be desired. Little was done by the states to curb harassment of federal officers in the performance of their duty under the Fugitive Slave Law. Because of increased expenses resulting from court fees and retention of lawyers, enforcement in some areas was difficult, if not prohibitive, but the recovery of any kind of property in courts of law was expensive. The additional expenses made necessary by the personal liberty laws discouraged many slaveholders from attempting to recover their runaway slaves. Considering the propaganda spread by the abolitionist press, and other news media, about the personal liberty laws, it is not difficult to understand why the slaveholder might have been reluctant to attempt recovery of his fugitive property. If the slave did not make the long pull for Canada and settled in one of the northern states, particularly Illinois, Indiana, Ohio, Pennsylvania, or eastern New York, and his master made a claim upon the fugitive slave tribunals as provided under the Fugitive Slave Law, the record shows that most officers of the federal courts would go to almost any lengths to enforce the law.

To argue that the Fugitive Slave Law was persistently enforced is not to argue that the law itself was effective. Indeed, the Fugitive Slave Law was an extremely inadequate law. Its effectiveness, however, had little to do with the will of federal officers to enforce it. It has been estimated that somewhere between eight thousand and fifteen thousand slaves escaped from their owners in the decade before the Civil War. The number which escaped to the North is impossible to calculate for reasons already ·explained. Only a small percentage of these slaves was recovered. The fact that so few slaves were recovered cannot be attributed to lack of enforcement; rather, the failure was inherent in the law itself. The South got the law it wanted; the bill submitted by Senator Mason and supported by Senators Clay, Webster, and Douglas was amended minimally in its essentials. Under the circumstances, perhaps no law could have provided effectually for the return of fugitive slaves. By mid-nineteenth century, slavery was a dying institution in the western world. In many parts of that world the institution had become morally indefensible. The fact was probably not apparent to most southerners, but by 1860 abolitionist propaganda had made great inroads upon northern public opinion. An adequate Fugitive Slave Law would have required the great majority of northern citizens to have been suspicious of every strange Negro whom they saw and to report his presence in the community to proper authorities. It would have provided machinery for the arrest and extradition of slaves upon the same basis as criminals. However, a distinction had been made between the extradition of criminals and the return of fugitive slaves in the Constitution, and it would have been unrealistic to expect that distinction to be breached in the 1850's. Many Southerners railed against the North for its failure to enforce the Fugitive Slave Law, but the North had no responsibility for enforcement of the law. When the charges that the law was not enforced are subjected to systematic analysis, they have no substance in fact. Claims by historians that the law was not and could not be enforced have been based on insufficient research. Secessionists who justified secession on the grounds that the Fugitive Slave Law had not been enforced were, perhaps unknowingly, using a false issue.

Perhaps more exasperating to Southerners than the few instances of rescue was the enactment of the personal liberty laws by northern legislatures. Southerners referred to the personal liberty laws more than to any other single issue as evidence of hostility to the South. These laws seemed to demonstrate that the North refused to abide by the Constitution or the law.

Chapter VIII

The Personal Liberty Laws and Enforcement of the Fugitive Slave Law

The statutes known as personal liberty laws, passed by some of the northern legislatures in the decade following enactment of the Fugitive Slave Law of 1850, were considered by Southerners as extremely hostile to their interests, and many felt that the laws were unconstitutional.[1] But Southerners entertained numerous misconceptions about the personal liberty laws. While the statutes to protect personal liberty in many instances ran counter to the spirit of the Constitution

1. For a typical example of the Southern attitude toward the personal liberty laws, see the "Report of the Joint Committee on the Harpers Ferry Outrages," in *Virginia Documents, 1858–1859*, Document No. 57, pp. 1–40. The appendix to that report contains an incomplete compilation of the personal liberty laws, titled "Hostile Legislation of the North. A Collection of State Laws Unrepealed, and of Legislative Resolves Hostile to Rights of Slave Owners and to the Slaveholding States; Especially to the Recovery of Fugitive Slaves" (pp. 41–102).

and laws of the United States, there were few provisions in those statutes which contradicted the Constitution or the Fugitive Slave Law. Indeed, an analysis of the personal liberty laws reveals the small extent to which they were intended to interfere with enforcement of the Fugitive Slave Law. With few exceptions, the personal liberty laws enacted prior to 1850, which were applicable to the Fugitive Slave Law of 1793, did not apply to the Fugitive Slave Law of 1850. It should also be remembered that the personal liberty laws affecting the Act of 1850 were not passed until after passage of the Kansas-Nebraska Act and the repeal of the Missouri Compromise in 1854. This chapter concerns not northern justification for passage of the laws, but the degree to which they acted as a deterrent upon enforcement of the Fugitive Slave Law.

Rather than trace chronologically the passage of the personal liberty laws in the various states, one might more usefully compare the many provisions of those laws topically. The provisions of the statutes to safeguard personal liberty can be classified under eight headings: (1) laws barring state officers from enforcing the Fugitive Slave Law; (2) laws prohibiting the use of state jails to house fugitive slaves; (3) laws preventing kidnapping free Negroes and removing fugitives slaves from the states without due process of law; (4) laws extending the writ of habeas corpus to fugitive slaves; (5) laws extending trial by jury to fugitive slave cases; (6) laws requiring certain state officers to defend fugitive slaves; (7) laws excluding federal officers enforcing the Fugitive Slave Law from prosecution under the personal liberty laws; and (8) miscellaneous provisions.

Before 1860, the laws of only three states prohibited state officers from participating in the enforcement of the Fugitive Slave Law. The model for these statutes was the Latimer Law enacted in Massachusetts in 1843. In June, 1854, after the rendition of Anthony Burns and the repeal of the Missouri Compromise, the Rhode Island legislature extended its personal library law enacted in 1848 to apply to the Act of 1850. This statute provided that "No judge of any court of record of this State, and no justice of the peace, shall hereafter take cognizance or grant a certificate in cases" arising under the Fugitive Slave Law "to any person who claims any other person as a fugitive slave within the jurisdiction of this state." Any state officer who violated the law was subject to a five-hundred-dollar fine, or six months in prison.[2] In March, 1855, Maine's legislature enacted an almost identical statute. In this law, however, the fine and prison term were doubled.[3] Two months later, the legislature in Massachusetts re-enacted the 1843 statute over the governor's veto and made it applicable to the Fugitive Slave Law of 1850.[4] Furthermore that statute was considerably strengthened.

To ensure that no state officer would again remand a fugitive slave to his owner, as Commissioner Loring had done in the Burns case, the 1855 statute provided that any person holding a state office and who should grant a certificate of removal "shall be deemed to have resigned any commission from the Commonwealth which he may possess, his office shall be deemed vacant, and he shall be forever thereafter ineligible to any office of trust, honor or emolument, under the laws of this Commonwealth." Any attorney holding a commission under the constitution of the state and who represented the claimant of a fugitive slave was thereafter barred from appearing in the state courts. Any person, serving as judge in the Commonwealth, who issued a certificate of removal would violate "good behavior" and would be liable for impeachment, and any judicial officer of the state, who continued to hold office as United States commissioner ten days after passage of the law, was liable for impeachment and removal from office. Finally, the state militia was prohibited from acting in any capacity in the rendition of fugitive slaves.[5] In March, 1860, the state of Pennsylvania enacted a law removing jurisdiction in fugitive slave cases from the state courts.[6]

The provisions of the personal liberty laws in Rhode Island, Maine, and Pennsylvania barring state officers from participating in the rendition of fugitive slaves did not conflict with the Constitution. Although they might be interpreted, and indeed were interpreted, as

2. *Public Laws of the State of Rhode Island, and Providence Plantations, Passed at the Sessions of the General Assembly, From May, 1853, to January, 1855, Inclusive* (Providence: Knowles & Anthony, 1855), p. 1100 (hereafter cited as *Laws of Rhode Island* [1853–1855]).

3. *Acts and Resolves Passed by the Thirty-Fourth Legislature of the State of Maine, 1855* (Augusta: Stevens & Blaine, 1855), pp. 207–8 (hereafter cited as *Acts and Resolves of Maine* [1855]).

4. *Acts and Resolves Passed by the General Court of Massachusetts, in the Year 1855* (Boston: William White, 1855), pp. 924–29 (hereafter cited as *Acts and Resolves of Massachusetts* [1855]).

5. *Acts and Resolves of Massachusetts* (1855), sect. 10, 11, 12, 14, 16, p. 927.

6. *National Intelligencer,* December 11, 1860.

hostile to the South, these provisions conformed to the decision of the Supreme Court of the United States in *Prigg* v. *Pennsylvania*. In that decision the Court had held that state courts and magistrates were excluded from responsibility in the enforcement of the Fugitive Slave Law of 1793. The Court's decision made void any state statutes designed to aid in the enforcement of the law, but it did not hinder the states from enacting laws prohibiting state officers from acting in any way to return fugitives from labor. The Massachusetts statute went considerably beyond the laws of her three sister states, however, and, while not strictly unconstitutional, its provisions were far more vindictive. The intent of the Massachusetts legislators was obviously to hinder enforcement of the Fugitive Slave Law, but these provisions were directed at least in part against United States Commissioner Edward Loring for his decision to return Anthony Burns, and under the law's terms he was removed from office.[7]

The prohibitions against civil and military servants of the state from acting under the Fugitive Slave Law applied "only to acts done by them in their official and military capacities," and they were "not intended to apply to acts done by them in their private capacity as citizens of the United States."[8] Hence it was argued that these provisions were not unconstitutional. While one might doubt the validity of these arguments, the Massachusetts Personal Liberty Law was never tested before the Court.[9] Since these provisions did not provide for the actual interference with federal process in the enforcement of the law, they did not deter the law's enforcement by federal authorities.

A second class of provisions in the personal liberty laws prohibited the use of state jails or prisons to house fugitive slaves. Pennsylvania, Ohio, Massachusetts, Michigan, and Rhode Island had such statutes on their law books at some period during the 1850's. In March, 1847, the legislature of Pennsylvania enacted a personal

7. Leonard W. Levy, *The Law of the Commonwealth and Chief Justice Shaw* (Cambridge: Harvard University Press, 1957), p. 106 (hereafter cited as Levy, *Chief Justice Shaw*). See also "The Removal of Judge Loring," *Monthly Law Reporter*, n.s. 8 (1856): 8. The provisions concerning removal from office of judicial officers were repealed in 1858. *Acts and Resolves of Massachusetts* (1858), p. 151.

8. Joel Parker, *Personal Liberty Laws, (Statutes of Massachusetts,) and Slavery in the Territories* (Boston: Wright & Potter, 1851), p. 15.

9. Levy, *Chief Justice Shaw*, p. 106.

liberty law which forbade state officers from remanding fugitives from labor to their owners. Section 6 of that statute made it unlawful

to use any jail or prison of this commonwealth, for the detention of any person claimed as a fugitive from servitude or labor, except in cases where jurisdiction may lawfully be taken by any judge, under the provisions of this act; and any jailor or keeper of any prison, or other person, who shall offend against the provisions of this section, shall, on conviction thereof, pay a fine of five hundred dollars; one-half thereof for the use of the commonwealth, and the other half to the person who prosecutes; and shall, moreover, thenceforth be removed from office, and be incapable of holding such office of jailor or keeper of a prison, at any time during his natural life.[10]

This section of the law was applicable to all fugitive slaves. Hence, those slaves arrested under the Act of 1850 could not be lodged in Pennsylvania jails. As public opinion in favor of the Compromise of 1850 increased, pressure to repeal the law began to rise. On April 8, 1852, despite "an immense number of remonstrances," [11] this section of the law was repealed.[12] But between 1855 and 1857, Rhode Island, Massachusetts, Michigan, and Ohio enacted similar laws which forbade fugitive slaves from being incarcerated in county jails.[13] The Ohio law remained on the statute books only ten months. Enacted on April 17, 1857, it was repealed on February 23, 1858. Moreover, on April 4, 1859, the Ohio legislature made it mandatory upon the sheriffs and jailers in the state to receive prisoners committed under the authority of the United States, provided the United States pay the expenses of imprisonment and pay a fee to the county commissioner of fifty cents per month for the use of the jail.[14]

10. *Laws of the General Assembly of the Commonwealth of Pennsylvania, Passed at the Session of 1847* (Harrisburg: J. M. G. Lescure, 1847), pp. 206–8 (hereafter cited as *Laws of Pennsylvania* [1847]).

11. Edward Raymond Turner, *The Negro in Pennsylvania: Slavery-Servitude-Freedom 1639–1861* (Washington: American Historical Association, 1911), pp. 244–45.

12. *Laws of Pennsylvania* (1852), p. 295.

13. *Laws of Rhode Island* (1853–1855), p. 1100; *Acts and Resolves of Massachusetts* (1855), pp. 928–29; *Acts of the Legislature of the State of Michigan, Passed at the Regular Session of 1855* (Lansing: Geo. W. Peck, 1855), p. 414 (hereafter cited as *Acts of Michigan* (1855); *Acts of a General Nature and Local Laws and Joint Resolutions, Passed by the Fifty-Second General Assembly, of the State of Ohio* (Columbus: Statesman Steam Press, 1857), p. 170 (hereafter cited as *Session Laws of Ohio* [1857]).

14. *Session Laws of Ohio* (1858), p. 10; (1859), pp. 158–59. On March 26, 1860, the fee paid to the county commissioner was raised to $1.00 per month. *Session Laws of Ohio* (1860), pp. 108–9.

The laws which forbade the use of state jails to hold fugitive slaves made it extremely inconvenient for federal officers in the performance of their duty under the Fugitive Slave Law. When local jails were not available, suitable quarters to house the fugitives from labor while they were being processed had to be rented, and that was sometimes very difficult. Because violence was frequently coincident with the arrest of fugitive slaves, owners of buildings that might be used for such purposes were reluctant to expose their property to the effects of riot. Since the jails were not to be used, the danger that the fugitive slave might be more easily rescued was apparent not only to the federal marshals but to the abolitionists as well. Nothing in the Constitution required the state to cooperate with the national government in providing jails for housing federal prisoners, but the laws closing the jails made enforcement of the Fugitive Slave Law more difficult.

The third category of laws was designed to prevent the kidnapping of free Negroes and the removal of fugitive slaves from the states without due process of law. From the time that the debates on the Fugitive Slave Law of 1850 began in the Congress, a constant fear prevailed in many of the northern states that adequate protection of free Negroes in the North would not be provided for in the new law. Northern fears were justified because a hearing before a fugitive slave commissioner under the new act was summary in nature, and the evidence of ownership was *ex parte*; it was therefore possible that a free Negro might be remanded to slavery. Furthermore, because the Act of 1850 permitted the slaveholder to pursue his fugitive slave into the free states, capture him, and return him without due process of law, the possibilities that free Negroes would be kidnapped and sold into slavery posed a constant threat.[15] To meet that threat, six of the northern states enacted antikidnapping laws during the decade before the Civil War.

The first state to enact an antikidnapping law applicable to the Act of 1850 was Connecticut. In response to repeal of the Missouri Compromise in 1854, the legislature in Connecticut enacted a law

15. The Dred Scott decision in 1857 upheld the right of the slaveholder to pursue his runaway slaves into the free states and capture them. This right was not unlimited, however. Section 6 of the Fugitive Slave Law provided that the slaveholder could "seize or arrest his fugitive where the same can be done without process. . . ." *U.S. Statutes at Large*, 9:463.

which stated: "Every person who shall falsely and maliciously declare, represent or pretend, that any free person entitled to freedom is a slave, or owes service or labor to any person or persons, with intent to procure or to aid or assit in procuring the forcible removal of such free person from this state as a slave, shall pay a fine of five thousand dollars and be imprisoned five years in the Connecticut state prison." Furthermore, any fugitive slave case withess who testified falsely that a free Negro was a slave was subject to the same fine and term of imprisonment.[16] Five other states passed similar antikidnapping laws.

Michigan and Massachusetts included such provisions in their personal liberty laws passed in 1855. Michigan's law was similar to the law in Connecticut, but the penalty for violation of the law was not as great.[17] Massachusett's law was more sweeping in its provisions. To prevent kidnapping of free Negroes and the removal of fugitive slaves from the state without due process of law, the Massachusetts statute provided:

If any person shall remove from the limits of this Commonwealth, or shall assist in removing therefrom, or shall come into the Commonwealth with the intention of removing or of assisting in the removing therefrom, or shall procure or assist in procuring to be so removed, any person being in the peace thereof who is not "held to service or labor" by the "party" making the "claim" or whose "service or labor" is not "due" to the "party" making "claim," within the meaning of those words in the constitution of the United States, on the pretence that such person is so held or has so escaped, or that his "service or labor," is so "due," or with the intent to subject him to such "service or labor," he shall be punished by a fine not less than one thousand, nor more than five thousand dollars, and by imprisonment in the State Prison not less than one, nor more than five years.[18]

Moreover, any person who was falsely claimed as a fugitive slave was permitted by the law to "maintain an action and recover damages therefor in any court competent to try the same." [19]

Ohio and Wisconsin passed antikidnapping laws in 1857. The state

16. *Resolutions and Private Acts of the General Assembly of the State of Connecticut, May Session, 1854* (New Haven: Babcock & Wildman, 1854), pp. 123–24, 798–99 (hereafter cited as *Session Laws of Connecticut* [1854]).
17. *Acts of Michigan* (1855), sect. 6–7, p. 414.
18. *Acts and Resolves of Massachusetts* (1855), p. 926.
19. Ibid.

of Ohio enacted two laws to prevent kidnapping, but they were designed to force the slaveholder, searching for his fugitive property, into the fugitive slave tribunals and to prevent the practice of coming into the state and removing Negroes without due process of law. The law said that no "black or mulatto person" who was claimed as a fugitive slave could be forcibly removed from the state "without first taking such black or mulatto person or persons before the court, judge or commissioner of the proper circuit, district or county having jurisdiction, according to the laws of the United States . . . and there, according to the laws of the United States, establishing by proof his or their property in such person." The law also prohibited the arrest and removal of free Negroes from the state without due process under the laws of Ohio. Any person convicted under these provisions was liable to imprisonment at hard labor for "not less than three years nor more than eight years at the discretion of the court. . . ." Like the other provisions of Ohio's personal liberty laws, the antikidnapping statutes were repealed in February, 1858.[20] The Wisconsin law was designed primarily to protect free Negroes from molestation and arrest as fugitive slaves, and anyone convicted of forcibly removing a free Negro from the state was liable to a fine of one thousand dollars and imprisonment for "not more than five nor less than one year: *provided,* that nothing in this chapter shall be construed as applying to any claim of service from an apprentice for a fixed time." [21] Ostensibly, a Negro serving an apprenticeship could not claim the protection of this law if he had run away.

Vermont did not enact an antikidnapping law until 1858. According to her law of 1858, "No person within this State shall be considered as property, or subject as such to sale, purchase, or delivery; nor shall any person within the limits of this State, at any time, be deprived of liberty or property without due process of law." Due process of law was defined as the "usual process and forms in

20. *Session Laws of Ohio* (1857), pp. 221–22, 186; (1858), p. 19.
21. *The Revised Statutes of the State of Wisconsin: Passed at the Annual Session of the Legislature Commencing Jan. 13, 1858, and Approved May 17, 1858* (Chicago: W. B. Kenn, 1858), pp. 912–14 (hereafter cited as *Revised Statutes of Wisconsin* [1858]). The laws of Connecticut and Michigan also excluded apprentices from protection under the Personal Liberty Laws. *Session Laws of Connecticut* (1854), p. 799; *Acts of Michigan* (1855), p. 415.

force by the laws of this State, and issued by the courts thereof.
. . ." [22] This law did not take cognizance, therefore, of due process
under the laws of the United States.

With the exception of Vermont's antikidnapping law, these
provisions of the personal liberty laws were not contrary to the
Constitution of the United States. The states had the right, indeed the
obligation, to protect the personal liberty of free persons within their
jurisdictions. But since the Fugitive Slave Laws, supported by the
Prigg decision in 1842 and the Dred Scott decision in 1857, permitted the slaveholder to pursue his fugitive property into the free states
and return his slaves where such could be done without due process
of law, the antikidnapping provisions may have been in conflict with
the laws of the United States, and thus unconstitutional. But they
were never tested before the Court. These laws were, however, hostile
to the intent of the Fugitive Slave Law, and while they did not
prevent due process under the laws of the United States, they had the
effect of increasing the cost of returning fugitive slaves from the free
states. Forcing the slaveholder to recover his runaway slaves through
the fugitive slave tribunals required him to hire lawyers and pay the
fees which resulted from due process under the laws of the United
States. If the hearing before the fugitive slave commissioner was
protracted, as in many cases it was, the expenses became prohibitive.
Indeed, it was better never to attempt to recover the slave than it was
to pay more than he was worth to secure his rendition.

Vermont's statute to prevent kidnapping was another matter.
These provisions of the law of Vermont were clearly unconstitutional. By maintaining that no person within the state should be
"considered as property, or subject as such to sale, purchase, or
delivery," the legislature seemed to be saying that merely by coming
into the state the slave became free.[23] With reference to fugitive

22. *The Acts and Resolves Passed by the General Assembly of the State of
Vermont, at the October Session, 1858* (Bradford: Joseph D. Clark, 1858), pp.
42–44 (hereafter cited as *Acts and Resolves of Vermont* [1858]).

23. In fact section 6 of the act stated: "Every person who may have been
held as a slave, who shall come or be brought or be in this State, with or without the consent of his or her master or mistress, or who shall come or be
brought, or be involuntarily, or in any way, in this State, shall be free." *Laws
of Vermont* (1858), p. 44. New Hampshire had a similar statute. *Laws of the
State of New Hampshire, Passed June Session,* 1857 (Concord: George G.
Fogg, 1857), p. 1876 (hereafter cited as *Laws of New Hampshire* [1857]).

slaves, the Constitution of the United States stated: "No person held to service or labor in one State, under the laws thereof, escaping into another, shall, in consequence of any law or regulation therein, be discharged from such service or labor, but shall be delivered up on claim of the party to whom such service or labor may be due." [24] Thus, no law enacted in Vermont, or any other free state, could change the status of a slave who had escaped his master's service. On its face, this provision of Vermont's law was void and of no force.

The fourth and fifth categories which extended the writ of habeas corpus and the right of trial by jury to fugitive slaves worked in conjunction with the antikidnapping laws. The personal liberty laws of only four states extended the benefits of habeas corpus to Negroes arrested as fugitives from labor. They were Vermont, Massachusetts, Michigan, and Wisconsin.

Under the Personal Liberty Law of Vermont, the authority to issue writs of habeas corpus, formerly held by justices of the state supreme court, was extended to the circuit judges within the state. The law also provided that upon application in writing by state attorneys, "stating in substance the name of the prisoner and the persons detaining him, if known, and that the person arrested, claimed or imprisoned, is arrested, claimed or imprisoned as a fugitive slave," the judges were authorized to grant the writ of habeas corpus. The law provided further that if the prisoner should not be discharged after a hearing, "such person shall be entitled to an appeal to the next stated term of the County Court in the country where the hearing was had" merely by furnishing bail in an amount determined by the judge.[25] The more extensive Personal Liberty Law of Massachusetts provided:

> The writ of *habeas corpus* may be issued by the supreme judicial court, the court of common pleas, by any justice's court or police court of any town or city, by any court of record, or by any justice of either of said courts, or by any judge of probate; and it may be issued by any justice of the peace, if no magistrate above named is known to said justice of the peace to be within five miles of the place where the party is imprisoned or restrained, and it shall be returnable before the supreme judicial court, or any one of the justices thereof, whither the court may be in session or not, and in term time or vacation.[26]

24. U.S. Constitution, Art. 4, Sec. 2, par. 3.
25. *Acts and Resolves of Vermont* (1850), pp. 9–10.
26. *Acts and Resolves of Massachusetts* (1855), pp. 924–25.

Michigan's act "to protect the rights and liberties" of her citizens said that anyone "arrested and claimed as a fugitive slave" shall be "entitled to all the benefits of the writ of habeas corpus. . . ." Like the Massachusetts statute, the Michigan law provided that, if the fugitive slave should not be discharged after a hearing, by paying "reasonable and proper" bail he was entitled to an appeal to the circuit court of the county in which the hearing had been held.[27] Habeas corpus proceedings in fugitive slave cases under Wisconsin's personal liberty law were virtually the same as those of Massachusetts. The judges of both the supreme court and the circuit courts were given authority to grant the writ in cases where inhabitants of the state were arrested as fugitive slaves. The writ would be issued upon the written application of the district attorneys.[28]

The same four states provided for trial by jury in fugitive slave cases. Vermont in 1850 and 1858, Massachusetts and Michigan in 1855, and Wisconsin in 1857 enacted laws which either permitted or required trial by jury in cases where Negroes were arrested as fugitive slaves. The trial by jury provisions in the personal liberty laws of Vermont, Michigan, and Wisconsin were almost identical. In habeas corpus proceedings involving fugitive slaves, Vermont's law provided that the court "may and shall, on application of either party to such proceeding, allow and direct a trial by jury, on all questions of fact in issue between the parties, . . . and the taxable costs of such trial shall be chargeable to the State, whenever the same would be otherwise chargeable to the person arrested or claimed as a fugitive slave." [29] On the one hand, the fugitive slave who had been arrested could, at the habeas corpus hearing, demand a trial by jury to determine the facts of the case. On the other hand, if the claimant were willing to submit to due process under the state laws, he too could request a trial by jury. But in doing so the claimant would have been working against his own best interests because of the added costs and the constant danger that he might lose his slave. His alternative in such a case was to appeal to the federal courts which had jurisdiction in fugitive slave cases.

27. *Acts of Michigan* (1855), pp. 413–14.

28. *Revised Statutes of Wisconsin* (1858), pp. 912–14.

29. *Acts and Resolves of Vermont* (1850), p. 10; (1858), pp. 42–44. For the trial by jury provision of the other two states, see *Acts of Michigan* (1855), p. 414, and *Revised Statutes of Wisconsin* (1858), p. 913.

Like the two previous categories, the sixth category of laws which required certain state officers to come to the defense of fugitive slaves presented still another problem for the owners of fugitives from labor or service. Vermont, Massachusetts, Michigan, Maine, and Wisconsin included such provisions in their personal liberty laws. Vermont's law provided: "It shall be the duty of state's attorneys, within their respective counties, whenever any inhabitant of this State is arrested or claimed as a fugitive slave, on being informed thereof, diligently and faithfully to use all lawful means to protect, defend, and procure to be discharged every such person so arrested or claimed as a fugitive slave." [30] The Massachusetts statute required the governor, "by and with the advice and consent of the council," to appoint commissioners in every county to "use all lawful means to protect, defend and secure to such alleged fugitive a fair and impartial trial by jury. . . ." [31] The trial by jury provisions in the personal liberty laws of Michigan, Maine, and Wisconsin were identical.[32] In Maine and Massachusetts, the legal fees of the person arrested as a fugitive slave were to be paid by the state.[33]

Unlike the first three, the fourth, fifth, and sixth categories of personal liberty laws were designed not only to frustrate the efforts of the slave owner, but also to interfere with enforcement of the Fugitive Slave Law by federal authorities. These laws appeared to conflict with the Constitution of the United States and with the Fugitive Slave Law. The operation of these laws, however, depended upon the ability of the state courts to obtain jurisdiction in the fugitive slave cases. In the face of a determined policy on the part of the federal government to enforce the law, obtaining jurisdiction was manifestly impossible.

The duty of the state officers under these laws was to protect persons within their jurisdiction from unlawful arrest. The personal liberty laws could not lawfully be exercised to prevent a fugitive from labor from apprehension and arrest under the Fugitive Slave Law. These provisions of the personal liberty laws became operable

30. *Acts and Resolves of Vermont* (1850), p. 9.
31. *Acts and Resolves of Massachusetts* (1855), p. 928.
32. *Acts of Michigan* (1855), p. 413; *Revised Statutes of Wisconsin* (1858), p. 912; *Acts and Resolves of Maine* (1857), p. 28.
33. *Acts and Resolves of Massachusetts* (1855), p. 928; *Acts and Resolves of Maine* (1857), p. 28.

only after the fugitive slave had been arrested. Through habeas corpus proceedings, the state courts had legal authority only to inquire into the legality of the arrest of the fugitive slave. But the Fugitive Slave Law guaranteed the claimant that the certificate of removal issued by the United States commissioner "shall be conclusive of the right of the person or persons in whose favor granted, to remove such fugitive to the State or Territory from which he escaped, and shall prevent all molestation of such person or persons by any process issued by any court, judge, magistrate, or other person whomsoever." [34] Furthermore, the attorneys general consistently held that habeas corpus should not be issued if it appeared that the decision to deliver the fugitive was made by the proper authority. The fugitive slave tribunal had exclusive jurisdiction, therefore, and its decision was "conclusive upon every other tribunal." [35]

The states did have authority to inquire into the legality of a fugitive slave's arrest, but if it were shown that the fugitive was held under authority of the United States, the state court could proceed no further. [36] Even though state officers were required to "use all lawful means" to protect and defend every person arrested as a fugitive slave, once federal jurisdiction was established in the case, the authority of these officers was exhausted. The provisions requiring trial by jury were therefore superfluous because federal jurisdiction would not and could not yield to that of the states. Because the federal courts did insist upon the supremacy of the laws of the United States, these provisions of the personal liberty laws were ineffective in deterring enforcement of the Fugitive Slave Law by officers of the federal government.

The seventh category of provisions in the personal liberty laws explicitly recognized the jurisdiction of the federal government in fugitive slave cases by excluding federal officers from prosecution under the personal liberty statutes. Maine's statute, enacted in 1855, provided: "Nothing in this act shall be construed to hinder or obstruct the marshal of the United States, his deputy or any officer of the United States from executing or enforcing the laws of the United

---

34. *U.S. Statutes at Large,* 9:463–64.

35. Hall, *Opinions of the Attorneys General,* 5:286. See also, Justice Grier's reasoning in *Ex Parte* Jenkins, 13 Federal Cases 969 (1855), and Justice McLean's opinion in *Ex Parte* Robinson, 20 Federal Cases 445 (1853).

36. Ableman v. Booth, 21 Howard 560 (1859).

States. . . ."[37] The New Hampshire law contained a proviso that "any act lawfully done by any officer of the United States, or other person, in the execution of any legal process," was exempt from prosecution.[38] Ohio's law was more generous. The law stated that its provisions did not apply to any person acting "under authority of the constitution of the United States, made in pursuance thereof."[39] When the state of Massachusetts modified its personal liberty laws in March, 1861, a similar provision was added which denied to state officers the authority to remove a fugitive slave from the legal custody of the United States marshal.[40]

The significance of these provisions in the personal liberty laws was that they explicitly announced the acquiescence of the states concerned with enforcement of the Fugitive Slave Law by the federal government. Designed to prevent the illegal removal of Negroes from the state without due process of law, these statutes recognized the duty and responsibility of the federal government to carry out the constitutional and statutory requirement to capture and return fugitive slaves when called upon to do so. The slave-holder was prevented from capturing and returning his own slave but was not prevented from recovering his slave by due process under the laws of the United States.

Finally, under the miscellaneous provisions of the personal liberty laws, the state of Wisconsin went further than any other state in her efforts to nullify the Fugitive Slave Law. Her law provided that judgments recovered against anyone convicted of violating the Fugitive Slave Law should not constitute a lien on "any real estate" within the state, and any sale of real estate or personal property to recover such judgments was prohibited.[41] This statute was enacted because of the judgments rendered against Sherman M. Booth in the Joshua Glover rescue and because of reaction in the state against the decision of the Supreme Court in the Dred Scott case.[42] Despite the law, Booth was kept in prison until March, 1861 because of his

37. *Acts and Resolves of Maine* (1855), p. 208.
38. *Laws of New Hampshire* (1857), p. 1876.
39. *Sesssion Laws of Ohio* (1857), p. 186.
40. *Acts and Resolves of Massachusetts* (1861), p. 399.
41. *Revised Statutes of Wisconsin* (1858), p. 914.
42. Ames, *State Documents*, 6:63–64. See also Mason, *Fugitive Slave Law in Wisconsin*, p. 142.

unwillingness or inability to pay the judgments rendered against him by the federal courts.

Largely in response to the Dred Scott decision, New Hampshire and Vermont enacted statutes which provided that no person, because of descent from an African, would be disqualified from becoming a citizen of their states with full rights and privileges.[43] These statutes had little to do with the rendition of fugitive slaves except that they tended to make more explicit the presumption of freedom of every person within their respective jurisdictions. Their real effect was to create greater mistrust in the South, but they did not really hinder enforcement of the Fugitive Slave Law.

There was limited diminution of the number of slaves returned from the free states by federal officers after the personal liberty laws were enacted. It is true that no fugitive slaves were returned from the New England states by due process after the rendition of Anthony Burns in 1854, but only three slaves had been returned from there before Burns's rendition. One must conclude, therefore, that some other reason must be found to explain why so few slaves were returned from that area. The most obvious reasons, and the ones already suggested, were the distance of the New England states from the slave states and the proximity of the northeastern states to the Canadian border. It was a simple matter for a fugitive slave to slip across the border into Canada at the first hint of danger, and there were many people in New England eager to help him escape. But if he were captured, even by federal officers, the costs involved in due process and in returning fugitive slaves over such great distances became prohibitive. Because of the misconceptions held by Southerners about the personal liberty laws, these laws seemed a greater deterrent than they really were. An already costly process, however, had become prohibitively expensive, and the slaveholders despaired of recovery of their property. The same thing can be said for Michigan and Wisconsin, two states where virtually the same conditions prevailed as in New England.

By denying the slave owner the right to capture and return his fugitive slave without due process of law, the states that enacted personal liberty laws were able to discourage the kidnapping of free

43. *Laws of New Hampshire* (1857), p. 1876; *Laws of Vermont* (1858), p. 44.

Negroes. By forcing the owner of fugitive slaves to resort to federal process under the Fugitive Slave Law, the costs of rendition increased considerably. Therefore, rather than face the danger and expense involved in returning fugitive slaves themselves, many slave owners did not even attempt to recover their lost property. Where the danger of rescue was acute, the fugitive slave commissioner could order the slave returned at government expense. But the government did not pay the cost of hiring lawyers, paying the expense of witnesses, posting bail, paying the necessary fees incurred in the process, or the expenses of the owner or his agent. This may account in large part for the small number of slaves that were captured and returned to their owners in the decade before the Civil War, particularly from New England and the states along the Canadian border. If the Fugitive Slave Law was a dead letter in New England, Michigan, and Wisconsin, it was not because the law could not be enforced; it was because it was not economically feasible to trace, capture, and returned to their owners in the decade before the Civil War, particularly from New England and the states along the Canadian border. If the Fugitive Slave Law was a dead letter in New England, Michigan, and Wisconsin, it was not because the law could not be enforced; it was because it was not economically feasible to trace, capture, and return fugitive slaves from there. In fact, it never had been. As regards the states bordering the slave states, however, the story was quite different.

During the 1850's, New York, New Jersey, Indiana, Illinois, and Minnesota enacted no personal liberty laws. Pennsylvania's law prohibiting the use of her jails to house fugitive slaves was repealed in 1852. Ohio's personal liberty laws were repealed after being in force less than ten months. Where the distance was not too great, the record shows that throughout the decade preceding the war runaway slaves were captured and returned without due process of law. In the border states, the federal government had its greatest success in enforcing the Fugitive Slave Law. The law could be enforced in these states, not because they had no personal liberty laws, but because the slave owners could afford to file claims with the fugitive slave tribunals. Because there was less hostility in these states to enforcement of the law, expenses could be kept within reasonable limits. Even where there were personal liberty laws, the prior jurisdiction of the federal courts in fugitive slave cases rendered them inapplicable to federal officers. The federal marshals and slaveholders were in some instances harassed where federal jurisdiction was questioned by the states, but in no case of record were the personal liberty laws used successfully to prevent the return of a fugitive slave by due process under the Fugitive Slave Law. Despite the popular view that the personal liberty laws rendered the Fugitive Slave Law a dead letter, the law was enforced when claims were initiated by the slaveholders in the fugitive slave tribunals. The Fugitive Slave Law was not a dead letter in the border states.

Chapter IX

The Fugitive Slave Law:
From Secession
*to Repeal**

O nce the Southern states had seceded from the Union and the Civil War had begun, the responsibility of the federal government for the return of fugitive slaves became radically complicated. If the states in the Confederacy were no longer in the Union, it would seem that they had forfeited their right under the Constitution of the United States to have fugitive slaves delivered up on claim. But what of the fugitive slaves escaping from states still loyal to the Union? What were the rights of the loyal slaveholder? And what were the obligations of the government at Washington with regard to fugitive slaves now that the Union was torn asunder? As the Union armies

---

* After the Southern states had seceded from the Union, the Fugitive Slave Law lost much of its significance. A majority of the people in the free states had acquiesced in the law's enforcement in order to preserve the Union. Now that hope was dead. President Lincoln would continue to enforce the law, but only as a means of holding the border states in the Union. The history of the law's enforcement from secession to the law's repeal on June 28, 1864 was quite different from enforcement before the war because of the complications arising from the problem of contraband slaves who flocked behind Union lines. Because of that difference, this chapter will present only a brief synopsis rather than an exhaustive treatment.

penetrated slave territory, many slaves, thinking that they had been liberated, flocked behind the lines. What disposition must be made of them? Despite the great effort to keep the slavery question in abeyance, these were problems that plagued the Lincoln administration. Both the president and Congress had to deal with them.

It soon became apparent to many of the fugitive slaves residing in the Union that they were by no means free from arrest as fugitives from service or labor. On January 23, 1861, a fugitive slave girl named Lucy, arrested in Cleveland, Ohio, was remanded to her owner and returned to Virginia.[1] A fugitive slave named Harris, his wife, and two children were apprehended in Chicago on April 3 and sent to Springfield for a hearing before a United States commissioner. Harris was owned by one man, his wife and children by another, both residents of St. Louis County, Missouri. After the hearing, the slaves were remanded to their owners and quietly returned to Missouri. The reaction of the Negro communities in Illinois to these arrests was not quiet. As a result of the arrests in Chicago, a veritable stream of fugitive slaves headed for the Canadian border. On April 8, 106 fugitive slaves were counted boarding the Michigan Southern and Northern Indiana Railroad. Their destination was Canada and freedom from arrest. About three hundred Negroes passed through Detroit the same day, most of them from Illinois. In Cincinnati, a Negro named George Lee was arrested by a United States marshal and taken before the United States commissioner without opposition. Following the hearing, he was remanded to the custody of his claimant and taken across the river to Covington, Kentucky to await return to his owner in Clarksburg, Virginia.[2] Despite the fact that the states of the Deep South had seceded from the Union, and confrontation between the North and South was imminent, the Fugitive Slave Law was still being enforced by the federal marshals.

In his inaugural address, President Lincoln once again disclaimed any intention of interfering with slavery in the states.[3] The president had not changed his mind with regard to the power of Congress to

1. *National Intelligencer*, January 24, 1861.
2. Ibid., April 10, 1861.
3. James Garfield Randall, *Constitutional Problems Under Lincoln*, rev. ed. (Urbana: The University of Illinois Press, 1951), p. 351 (hereafter cited as Randall, *Constitutional Problems*).

abolish slavery in the states, nor had his views about the Fugitive Slave Law changed. On August 27, 1858, Lincoln had expressed his view of the Fugitive Slave Law. Although he wished that some of the more controversial features of the law had been amended, he said: ". . . I have never hesitated to say, and I do not now hesitate to say, that I think, under the Constitution of the United States, the people of Southern States are entitled to a Congressional Fugitive Slave Law." [4] Congress took a similar position about interference with slavery on July 22, 1861 when it adopted, "almost without dissent," the Crittenden resolution. In that resolution, the Congress declared that "this war is not waged . . . in any spirit of oppression, or for any purpose of conquest or subjugation, or . . . of overthrowing or interfering with the rights or established institutions" of the states which had seceded from the Union. Rather the purpose of the war was "to defend and maintain the supremacy of the Constitution, and to preserve the Union with all the . . . rights of the several States unimpaired." [5] Before the year ended, however, the exigencies of war forced both the president and Congress to come to grips with the fugitive slave problem.

The nation had been engaged in Civil War less than three months before the Union government was forced to find some solution to the problem created by fugitive slaves. As early as May 27, General Benjamin F. Butler, commanding general at Fortress Monroe, reported to the War Department that slaves worth sixty thousand dollars had come within his lines.[6] Three of the slaves were the property of a Confederate colonel in command of the rebel forces in the region, and, under a flag of truce, Butler was asked if he did not feel bound by his "constitutional obligations to deliver up fugitives under the Fugitive Slave Act." Butler replied that the Fugitive Slave Law did not apply to "a foreign country, which Virginia claimed to be," and refused to give them up.[7]

The matter was reported to Washington, and Secretary of War

4. *New York Weekly Tribune*, June 2, 1860.
5. Randall, *Constitutional Problems*, p. 352.
6. Rhodes, *History of the United States*, 3:466.
7. Randall, *Constitutional Problems*, p. 355. From this affair came the term "contraband slaves." For a discussion of the controversial origin of this term, see pp. 354–56.

Simon Cameron sent explicit instructions to General Butler with regard to the disposition of fugitive slaves. Cameron said:

It is the desire of the President that all existing rights, in all the States, be fully respected and maintained. The war now prosecuted on the part of the Federal Government is a war for the Union, and for the preservation of all constitutional rights of States and the citizens of the States in the Union. Hence no question can arise as to fugitives from service within the States and Territories in which the authority of the Union is fully acknowledged. The ordinary forms of judicial proceedings, which must be respected by military and civil authorities alike, will suffice for the enforcement of all legal claims.[8]

Because of the war, and the embarrassment and injuries which might result from the substitution of military for judicial proceedings, General Butler was instructed to receive within his lines the fugitive slaves of both loyal and disloyal masters and to employ them "under such organizations and in such occupations as circumstances may suggest or require." The instructions stated further that a record was to be kept "showing the name and description of the fugitives, the name and the character, as loyal or disloyal, of the master, and such facts as may be necessary to a correct understanding of the circumstances of each case after tranquillity shall have been restored." Cameron was confident that Congress would provide "just compensation to loyal masters." Finally Butler was ordered neither to "authorize or permit any interference, by the troops under your command, with the servants of peaceful citizens, in house or field, nor will you, in any way, encourage such servants to leave the lawful service of their masters; nor will you, except in cases where the public safety may seem to require it, prevent the voluntary return of any fugitive to the service from which he may have escaped." [9]

According to Professor James G. Randall, some of the generals in the early part of the war followed Butler's course while others, including General Henry W. Halleck in Missouri and General Thomas Williams in Louisiana, "refused to receive such fugitives into their lines." [10] On November 20, 1861, an order went out from General Halleck's headquarters which said: "It has been represented that important information, respecting the number and condition of

8. Camerson to Butler, August 8, 1861, quoted in *National Intelligencer,* August 12, 1861.
9. Ibid.
10. Randall, *Constitutional Problems,* p. 356.

our forces, is conveyed to the enemy by means of fugitive slaves who are admitted within our lines. In order to remedy this evil, it is directed that no such person be hereafter permitted to enter the lines of any camp, or of any forces on the march; and that any now within such lines be immediately excluded therefrom." [11] Realizing the importance of the problem to the border states, President Lincoln was forced to intervene when one of his generals exceeded his authority. On August 30, 1861, General John C. Fremont instituted martial law throughout the state of Missouri and declared that the property of all persons taking up arms against the United States would be confiscated and their slaves freed. In a letter to General Fremont on September 2, Lincoln overruled the proclamation and requested that the order be made to conform to existing law.[12] Because of Fremont's defiance, and complaints that the general was militarily incompetent, Lincoln removed Fremont from his command at St. Louis on November 2, 1861.[13] The president would let no military commander force his hand in matters concerning military emancipation.

While the president and the military were seeking solutions to the problems created by fugitive slaves, Congress went about solving the problem in its own way. On August 6, 1861, Congress enacted the first confiscation act. This law provided that whenever slaves were permitted or required "to take up armes against the United States," or were employed "in any military or naval service . . . against the Government and lawful authority of the United States," the owners of such slaves would forfeit their claims to the service or labor of the slaves. The second confiscation act, enacted on July 17, 1862, went even further. Under this law, if any person owning slaves committed treason, he should "suffer death, and all his slaves" would be declared free. At the discretion of the court, a fine and imprisonment might be imposed instead of the death penalty; in any case, the slaves were to be freed.[14] As regards the return of fugitive slaves, Congress passed a

11. Quoted in *National Intelligencer*, December 12, 1861. A similar order was issued from Headquarters Department of Washington on July 17, 1861, quoted in the *Intelligencer* July 20, 1861.

12. Rhodes, *History of the United States*, 3:470–71; Randall, *Constitutional Problems*, p. 354.

13. James Garfield Randall, *The Civil War and Reconstruction* (Boston: D. C. Heath and Company, 1937), p. 480.

14. *U.S. Statutes at Large*, 12:319, 589–92. Since this law specified no pro-

law on March 13, 1862, that prohibited anyone in the military or naval service "from employing any of the forces . . . for the purpose of returning fugitives from service or labor, who may have escaped." On July 17, Congress passed a law which said that no slave escaping from one state into another would be delivered up except for a crime unless the slave belonged to a *loyal owner*. The slaves of *disloyal owners* who came into the Union lines were declared free.[15]

In the meantime, the Fugitive Slave Law remained in force and was executed by the federal marshals in the border states. When United States Marshal J. L. McDowell wrote to Attorney General Edward Bates for instructions about enforcing the law in Missouri, Bates replied:

> It is the President's constitutional duty to 'take care that *the laws* be faithfully executed.' That means *all* laws. He has no right to discriminate —no right to execute the laws he likes and leave unexecuted those he dislikes. And of course you and I, his subordinates, can have no wider latitude of discretion than he has. Missouri is a State *in the Union*. The insurrectionary disorders in Missouri are but individual crimes, and do not change the legal *status* of the State, nor change its rights and obligations as a member of the Union.
>
> A refusal by a ministerial officer to execute *any* law which properly belongs to his office is official misdemeanor, of which I do not doubt the President would take notice.[16]

In October, 1861, the *Louisville Journal* was pleased to report that a resident of Louisville had recovered his fugitive slave from the state of Indiana by due process of law. The federal marshal had acted promptly, and the fugitive slave tribunal performed efficiently in remanding the slave to his owner.[17]

In May, 1862, the Superior Court of the District of Columbia ruled that the Fugitive Slave Law was as applicable to the District of Columbia as it was to any of the states.[18] The docket of the court for 1862 listed the claims of twenty-eight different slave owners for 101

---

cedure by which the slaves were to be freed, the sections of the law providing for the sale of property were not applicable to the slaves who were to be freed. Randall, *Constitutional Problems*, pp. 357–63.

15. *U.S. Statutes at Large*, XII, 354, 589.

16. Bates to McDowell, July 23, 1861, quoted in *National Intelligencer,* September 4, 1861.

17. *National Intelligencer*, October 19, 1861, citing *Louisville Journal.*

18. U.S. v. Copeland, 25 Federal Cases 646 (1862) ; see also Catterall, *Judicial Cases*, 4:208.

runaway slaves. In the two months following the court's decision, 26
fugitive slaves were returned to their owners from the fugitive slave
tribunal in the nation's capital.[19] As late as June, 1863, six months
after the Emancipation Proclamation went into effect, fugitive slaves
were still being returned to their masters in the loyal states. On June
12, for example, 3 women and 4 children were arrested as fugitive
slaves and taken before United States Commissioner Walter S. Coxe,
in Washington. After a hearing they were remanded to the claimant
from Prince George County, Maryland, and on June 18, Commissioner Coxe remanded 2 fugitive slaves to claimants from the same
county in Maryland.[20]

The thousands of "contraband Negroes" and fugitive slaves who
found their way behind Union lines created problems that almost
defied solution. If the Negroes were claimed as fugitive slaves, the
Fugitive Slave Law provided an easy solution to the problem. But if
they were part of the multitude of destitute Negroes roaming about
the northern states where few people wanted them, or if they were in
camps maintained by the army, their agony was almost unbearable.
For example, a large number of contraband Negroes had fled to
Cairo, Illinois. Seeking help for them, Brigadier General T. W. Tuttle
wrote to Mayor Sherman of Chicago, saying: "I have a large number
of applications from your city for negro servants. Will you appoint a
committee to see that they are properly put out to work? Will send as
soon as the committee is appointed and I am notified." [21] Mayor
Sherman seemed to be horrified at such a suggestion, and to Tuttle's
letter he quickly replied: "Your proposition to send negroes to
Chicago to work *would be in violation of the laws of this State*, and a
great injustice to the laboring population. *I cannot give* my consent
by appointing a committee as you propose, *or in any other way*." The
city of Chicago which in many ways had been a haven for fugitive
slaves during the 1850's had undergone a change of heart. The
Common Council, supporting the action of the mayor, resolved:
"That we, Aldermen of the city of Chicago, heartily approve of the
action of our Mayor relative to the proposal to send negroes to this

19. Circuit Court, District of Columbia Case Papers, Fugitive Slave Cases,
1851–1863, National Archives, Justice and Executive Branch, Washington, D.C.

20. *National Intelligencer*, June 12, 20, 1863.

21. Tuttle to Sherman, September 22, 1862, quoted in the *National Intelligencer*, October 3, 1862.

city, and that his answer to that proposal meets our unqualified approbation." [22]

When the *Boston Post,* on October 30, 1862, reported that five hundred families of contraband Negroes were to be sent to Massachusetts, Governor John Albion Andrew promptly refused to permit them to come.[23] With regard to the governor's refusal to accept the Negroes into the state, the editor of the *National Intelligencer* wrote:

It . . . seems that the introduction of members of this oppressed race into a State where they are supposed to have so many sympathizing friends is not regarded with favor by the people of Massachusetts. So unpropitious to 'loyal blacks' is the social atmosphere that it is precisely because Governor Andrew 'does not wish their new freedom to become license, corruption, and infamy,' that he respectfully declines to aid or countenance their transportation to the North. The 'African' is a 'brother,' but South Carolina, not Massachusetts, is left to be the 'brother's keeper.' [24]

It was ironic that two areas in the country which had been so hostile to slavery and opposed to enforcement of the Fugitive Slave Law were so reluctant to accept into their midst Negro families who were faced with disease and starvation and in need of help.

By the summer of 1863 the Fugitive Slave Law had lost its usefulness, and henceforth there seems to have been no great desire to see it enforced. The statute which had caused so much bitterness remained effective, however, until June 28, 1864. As early as December, 1861, Senator Timothy Otis Howe of Wisconsin had introduced into the Senate a bill for the repeal of the Fugitive Slave Law. The bill was referred to the Judiciary Committee which reported in February, 1863 against repeal.[25] Because of a great many difficulties, the Thirty-seventh Congress adjourned without taking action on the repeal of the law.

When Congress assembled in December, 1863, the subject of repeal was discussed without delay. In the House of Representatives, Thaddeus Stevens introduced a bill on December 14, 1863 to repeal the fugitive slave laws of 1793 and 1850. James Mitchell Ashley of Ohio and George Washington Julian of Indiana also introduced such

22. *National Intelligencer,* October 3, 1862.
23. Ibid., November 4, 5, 1862.
24. Ibid., November 4, 1862.
25. Wilson, *Rise and Fall of Slave Power,* 3:395; *National Intelligencer,* December 27, 1861.

bills. They were referred to the Committee on the Judiciary which finally reported them out in June, 1864. At the instigation of Charles Sumner, a select committee was appointed in the Senate on January 13, 1864 "to consider all propositions concerning slavery and the freedmen." Early in February, Sumner introduced a bill to repeal the Fugitive Slave laws, and the bill was referred to the select committee of which he was a member. The majority report of the committee favored repeal.[26]

When the bill came up for consideration on February 19, Senator John Sherman of Ohio expressed his doubts about the wisdom of repealing the Act of 1793. He moved an amendment to the bill which would prevent the repeal of the earlier law, and it was adopted.[27] An extended and confused debate followed during which several other amendments were offered. Discussion of the bill was then deferred until April 27, but it never came up for consideration.[28]

In the House of Representatives, the Committee on the Judiciary reported a substitute bill "to repeal the Fugitive Slave Act of 1850, and all acts and parts of acts for the rendition of fugitive slaves." An attempt to recommit the bill failed. On the demand for the previous question, a sharp debate followed in which the advocates and opponents of the law had a chance to speak. But the previous question was finally ordered, and the bill was adopted by a vote of eighty-two to fifty-seven.[29]

The bill reached the floor of the Senate on June 21 but met with spirited opposition from senators representing the slave states. Despite all efforts to thwart its passage, however, the bill was finally passed by a vote of twenty-seven to twelve, and it was approved by the president on June 28, 1864.[30]

The Fugitive Slave Law of 1850 had been on the statute books three months less than fourteen years. Its passage had created bitter animosity in many northern communities, and the belief that the law was not being enforced created an even greater degree of misunderstanding in the South. The initial ground swell of opposition to enforcement of the Fugitive Slave Law had subsided by midsummer

26. Wilson, *Rise and Fall of Slave Power*, 3:396.
27. Ibid., p. 398.
28. Wilson, *Rise and Fall of Slave Power*, 3:399.
29. Ibid.
30. Ibid., pp. 401–2; *U.S. Statutes at Large*, 13:200.

1851. By election time in 1852, the Compromise of 1850 had been accepted hopefully by the majority as a final settlement of the slavery question. Although opposed to slavery and its extension into the free territories, the majority in the North reluctantly acquiesced in the enforcement of the Fugitive Slave Law. But passage of the more stringent law had not resulted in the wholesale return of fugitive slaves. The inadequacy of the law is not questioned, but many Southerners believed that the Fugitive Slave Law had not been enforced. Some southern leaders justified secession from the Union on grounds that the refusal of citizens in the northern states to aid in the recovery of runaway slaves posed a threat to the institution of slavery. But residents in the free states were obliged only not to interfere with the rendition of fugitive slaves. Officers of the federal courts were charged with the responsibility for enforcing the law. That the institution of slavery was not endangered by the fugitive slave problem is demonstrated simply by pointing out the small number of slaves that escaped each year as compared with the over-all slave population. Secessionist leaders in the South may have felt that their cause was just, but the assertion that the failure to recover a few hundred fugitive slaves was grounds for severing the Union rings hollow upon closer examination.

Appendix

Bibliography

Index

Appendix

TABLE 1. FUGITIVE SLAVE CASES: 1850

Names	Number of Cases	Date	Place	Disposition
James Hamlet	1	9/28	New York, N.Y.	1 remanded by fed. tribunal at gov't. expense
Fugitive slaves	2	9/30	Harrisburg, Penn.	2 remanded by fed. tribunal
Fugitive slaves	8	10/5	Bedford, Penn.	8 returned without due process
Fugitive slave	1	10/18	Detroit, Mich.	1 released
Henry Garnett	1	10/18	Philadelphia, Penn.	1 released
Fugitive slaves	3	11/14	Quincy, Ill.	3 remanded by fed. tribunal
Fugitive slaves	3	12/2	New Albany, Ind.	3 remanded by fed. tribunal
Fugitive slave		12/10	Marion, Ill.	1 returned without due process
Adam Gibson	1	12/21	Philadelphia, Penn.	1 remanded by fed. tribunal
Fugitive slave	1	12/28	Springfield, Mass.	1 remanded by fed. tribunal

TABLE 2. FUGITIVE SLAVE CASES: 1851

Names	Number of Cases	Date	Place	Disposition
Fugitive slave	1	?	Shawneetown, Ill.	1 returned without due process
Henry Long	1	1/8	New York, N.Y.	1 remanded by fed. tribunal at gov't. expense
Fugitive slave	1	1/20	Ripley, Ohio	1 remanded by fed. tribunal
Fugitive slave	1	1/30	Harrisburg, Penn.	1 remanded by fed. tribunal
Tamar Williams	1	2/14	Philadelphia, Penn.	1 released
Shadrack	1	2/21	Boston, Mass.	1 rescued from fed. custody
Thomas Hall		3/?	Sandy Hill, Penn.	1 returned without due process
Mitchum	1	3/7	Vernon, Ind.	1 remanded by fed. tribunal
Sam Wilson and George Brocks	2	3/8	Harrisburg, Penn.	2 remanded by fed. tribunal at gov't. expense
David	1	3/10	Harrisburg, Penn.	1 remanded by fed. tribunal at gov't. expense

TABLE 2. CONTINUED

Names	Number of Cases	Date	Place	Disposition
Woodson	1	3/13	Pittsburgh, Penn.	1 remanded by fed. tribunal at gov't. expense
Richard Gardner	1	3/15	Pittsburgh, Penn.	1 remanded by fed. tribunal
Woman and child	2	3/15	Philadelphia, Penn.	2 remanded by fed. tribunal
Moses Johnson	1	4/?	Chicago, Ill.	1 released
Thomas Sims	1	4/11	Boston, Mass.	1 remanded by fed. tribunal at gov't. expense
Fugitive slaves	4	4/26	Vincennes, Ind.	4 remanded by fed. tribunal
Daniel, Ally, and Carolina Franklin	3	5/21	Harrisburg, Penn.	3 remanded by fed. tribunal at gov't. expense
Elizabeth Williams	1	7/?	West Chester, Penn.	1 remanded by fed. tribunal
Fugitive slaves	18	7/8	New Athens, Ohio	18 returned without due process
Daniel Hawkins	1	7/26	Lancaster, Penn.	1 remanded by fed. tribunal
William Smith	1	8/19	Harrisburg, Penn.	1 remanded by fed. tribunal at gov't. expense
Daniel Davis	1	8/19	Buffalo, N.Y.	1 remanded by fed. tribunal
John Bolding	1	8/26	Poughkeepsie, N.Y.	1 remanded by fed. tribunal at gov't. expense
Fugitive slaves	2	9/17	Christiana, Penn.	2 rescued from fed. custody
Harrison	1	9/26	Buffalo, N.Y.	1 remanded by fed. tribunal at gov't. expense
Fugitive slaves	2	9/30	Harrisburg, Penn.	2 remanded by fed. tribunal
Fugitive slave	1	10/7	Buffalo, N.Y.	1 remanded by fed. tribunal
Jerry	1	10/7	Syracuse, N.Y.	1 rescued from fed. custody
Martha Rouse	1	10/17	Chestnut Hill, Ind.	1 remanded by fed. tribunal
Jesse Whiten	1	10/22	Hazeltown, Penn.	1 remanded by fed. tribunal at gov't. expense
Macubbins, Coe, Sen, and Lee	4	10/23	Harrisburg, Penn.	4 remanded by fed. tribunal at gov't. expense
Henry Pierce	1	10/24	Philadelphia, Penn.	1 remanded by fed. tribunal
Henry	1	11/1	Harrisburg, Penn.	1 remanded by fed. tribunal
Fugitive slave	1	11/7	Ottowa, Ill.	1 rescued from fed. custody
Henry Cromwell	1	11/11	Harrisburg, Penn.	1 remanded by fed. tribunal at gov't. expense
Fugitive slave	1	11/21	Illinois	1 released
John Maynard	1	12/5	Harrisburg, Penn.	1 remanded by fed. tribunal at gov't. expense
William Kelly	1	12/19	Harrisburg, Penn.	1 remanded by fed. tribunal at gov't. expense

TABLE 3. FUGITIVE SLAVE CASES: 1852

Names	Number of Cases	Date	Place	Disposition
James Tasker	1	2/?	New York, N.Y.	1 remanded by fed. tribunal at gov't. expense
Horace Preston	1	4/9	New York, N.Y.	1 remanded by fed. tribunal at gov't. expense
James Phillips	1	5/24	Harrisburg, Penn.	1 remanded by fed. tribunal at gov't. expense
Fugitive slaves	14	8/17	Hagerstown, Penn.	14 returned without due process
Fugitive slaves	2	9/?	Petersburg, Penn.	2 returned without due process
Fugitive slaves	3	9/21	Sandusky, Ohio	3 rescued from fed. custody
George Bordley	1	11/9	Philadelphia, Penn.	1 remanded by fed. tribunal

TABLE 4. FUGITIVE SLAVE CASES: 1853

Names	Number of Cases	Date	Place	Disposition
Richard Neal	1	1/29	Chester, Penn.	1 remanded by fed. tribunal
Charles Wesley	1	2/18	Wilmington, Del.	1 remanded by fed. tribunal
Fugitive slaves	10	3/5	Indiana	10 returned without due process
Fugitive slave	1	3/?	Alton, Ill.	1 remanded by fed. tribunal
Amanda	1	3/17	St. Louis, Mo.	1 remanded by fed. tribunal
Fugitive slaves	2	3/?	Columbus, Ohio	2 returned without due process
Edmin Brook	1	4/1	Uniontown, Penn.	1 remanded by fed. tribunal at gov't. expense
George	1	4/?	Washington, Ind.	1 remanded by fed. tribunal
William Thomas	1	5/19	Wilkesbarre, Penn.	1 escaped from fed. custody
Basil White	1	6/1	Philadelphia, Penn.	1 remanded by fed. tribunal
George Smith	1	7/26	Philadelphia, Penn.	1 remanded by fed. tribunal
George McQuerry	1	8/17	Troy, Ohio	1 remanded by fed. tribunal
Fugitive slaves	2	8/27	Chicago, Ill.	2 returned without due process
Hannah and child	2	8/27	Cincinnati, Ohio	2 remanded by fed. tribunal
Edward	1	8/27	Cincinnati, Ohio	1 remanded by fed. tribunal
John Freeman	1	9/3	Indianapolis, Ind.	1 released
Fugitive slaves	3	9/?	Uniontown, Penn.	3 remanded by fed. tribunal

TABLE 5. FUGITIVE SLAVE CASES: 1854

Names	Number of Cases	Date	Place	Disposition
Joshua Glover	1	3/5	Racine, Wisc.	1 rescued from fed. custody
Edward Davis	1	3/?	Newcastle, Del.	1 remanded by fed. tribunal
Stephen, Bob, and Jake Pembroke	3	5/29	New York, N.Y.	3 remanded by fed. tribunal at gov't. expense
Anthony Burns	1	6/3	Boston, Mass.	1 remanded by fed. tribunal at gov't. expense
Shadrack, Susan, Lee, Wesley, Anderson, John, Almeda, Lewis, Sarah, and Jane	10	6/11	Ohio	10 remanded by fed. tribunal
Alvin Adams	1	7/?	Madison, Ind.	1 remanded by fed. tribunal
Fugitive slaves	2	7/?	Chicago, Ill.	2 returned without due process
Fugitive slave	1	9/18	Byberry, Penn.	1 returned without due process
Harvey	1	9/22	Cumminsville, Ohio	1 remanded by fed. tribunal
Henry Massey	1	9/?	Philadelphia, Penn.	1 remanded by fed. tribunal
Jane Moore	1	11/?	Cincinnati, Ohio	1 released

TABLE 6. FUGITIVE SLAVE CASES: 1855

Names	Number of Cases	Date	Place	Disposition
John Anderson	1	1/12	Boston, Mass.	1 rescued from fed. custody
George Clark	1	2/23	Norristown, Penn.	1 rescued from fed. custody
Fugitive slaves	2	2/?	Harrisburg, Penn.	2 remanded by fed. tribunal
Rosetta Armstead	1	3/12	Columbus, Ohio	1 remanded by fed. tribunal
Fugitive slaves	2	3/20	Cincinnati, Ohio	2 returned without due process
Fugitive slave	1	6/13	Dayville, Conn.	1 rescued from fed. custody
Dick	1	6/?	Burlington, Iowa	1 released
Celeste	1	7/7	Cincinnati, Ohio	1 released
Fugitive slaves	2	8/31	Illinois	2 returned without due process
Fugitive slaves	2	9/?	Vernon, Ind.	2 returned without due process
Jack	1	10/18	Boston, Mass.	1 returned without due process
Fugitive slaves	2	10/?	Greensburg, Ind.	2 returned without due process
Fugitive slaves	2	12/30	Baltimore, Md.	2 remanded by fed. tribunal

TABLE 7. FUGITIVE SLAVE CASES: 1856

Names	Number of Cases	Date	Place	Disposition
Fugitive slave	1	1/?	Blair Co., Penn.	1 returned without due process
Fugitive slaves	7	1/27	Cincinnati, Ohio	7 remanded by fed. tribunal at gov't. expense
Fugitive slaves	9	1/29	Northern Ohio	9 remanded by fed. tribunal at gov't. expense
Fanny	1	1/?	Chicago, Ill.	1 returned without due process
Ralls and Logan	2	3/?	Cincinnati, Ohio	2 returned without due process
Fugitive slave	1	4/?	Decatur, Ill.	1 returned without due process
Fugitive slave	1	6/?	Cincinnati, Ohio	1 returned without due process
John	1	6/10	Arrested at sea	1 returned without due process
Fugitive slave	1	10/5	New York, N.Y.	1 returned without due process
Fugitive slave	1	10/10	New York, N.Y.	1 returned without due process
Fugitive slaves	3	10/17	Carlisle, Penn.	3 remanded by fed. tribunal at gov't. expense
Hird	1	10/31	Philadelphia, Penn.	1 returned without due process
Fugitive slaves	4	11/21	Indiana	4 returned without due process
Fugitive slaves	2	12/3	New Albany, Ind.	2 returned without due process
Mary Ann Willaims	1	12/17	Washington, D.C.	1 remanded by fed. tribunal

TABLE 8. FUGITIVE SLAVE CASES: 1857

Names	Number of Cases	Date	Place	Disposition
Michael Brown	1	1/18	Philadelphia, Penn.	1 remanded by fed. tribunal
John Tatson	1	2/7	Jeffersonville, Ind.	1 remanded by fed. tribunal
Addison White	1	5/21	Mechanicsburg, Ohio	1 rescued from fed. custody
Irwin and Angela	2	6/13	Cincinnati, Ohio	2 remanded by fed. tribunal at gov't. expense
Fugitive slave	1	7/3	Cincinnati, Ohio	1 returned without due process
Fugitive slaves	4	7/15	Camp Point, Ill.	4 returned without due process
Fugitive slave	1	8/?	Springfield, Ill.	1 remanded by fed. tribunal
Fugitive slaves	2	8/?	Martinsville, Ohio	2 returned without due process
Wither's slaves	3	10/7	Cincinnati, Ohio	3 remanded by fed. tribunal
Benjamin Chelsom	1	10/26	Cincinnati, Ohio	1 returned without due process
Fugitive slave	1	10/?	Syracuse, N.Y.	1 rescued from fed. custody
Fugitive slaves	2	11/19	Cleveland, Ohio	2 remanded by fed. tribunal
Fugitive slaves	3	11/21	Cincinnati, Ohio	3 remanded by fed. tribunal
Fugitive slave	1	11/26	Naples, Ill.	1 remanded by fed. tribunal at gov't. expense
John Smith	1	12/12	Brooklyn, N.Y.	1 released
Fugitive slaves	11	12/?	St. Joseph, Mo.	11 returned without due process
West	1	12/12	Indianapolis, Ind.	1 remanded by fed. tribunal at gov't. expense
Jacob Dupen	1	12/18	Philadelphia, Penn.	1 remanded by fed. tribunal

TABLE 9. FUGITIVE SLAVE CASES: 1858

Names	Number of Cases	Date	Place	Disposition
Fugitive slaves	3	1/25	Sandoval, Ill.	3 returned without due process
George Farris	1	2/13	St. Louis, Mo.	1 remanded by fed. tribunal
Fugitive slave	1	4/16	Blairsville, Penn.	1 rescued from fed. custody
Fugitive slave	1	6/12	Sandusky, Ohio	1 rescued from fed. custody
Fugitive slave	1	8/?	Terre Haute, Ind.	1 remanded by fed. tribunal at gov't. expense
Fugitive slave	1	8/15	Shawneetown, Ill.	1 returned without due process
Ingram slaves	2	8/28	Cincinnati, Ohio	2 remanded by fed. tribunal
Fugitive slaves	2	9/?	Wilmington, Del.	2 returned without due process
John	1	9/11	Oberlin, Ohio	1 rescued from fed. custody
Weaver	1	11/13	Harrisburg, Penn.	1 returned without due process

TABLE 10. FUGITIVE SLAVE CASES: 1859

Names	Number of Cases	Date	Place	Disposition
Fugitive slaves	2	3/?	Indiana	2 returned without due process
Mason Barbour	1	3/26	Columbus, Ohio	1 remanded by fed. tribunal at gov't. expense
Lewis Early	1	3/29	Cincinnati, Ohio	1 remanded by fed. tribunal at gov't. expense
Daniel Dangerfield	1	4/6	Harrisburg, Penn.	1 released
Jackson	1	5/?	Zanesville, Ohio	1 remanded by fed. tribunal at gov't. expense
Columbus Jones	1	6/24	Hyannis, Mass.	1 returned without due process
Fugitive slaves	5	6/?	Detroit, Mich.	5 returned without due process
Butler, wife, child	3	6/?	Holly Springs, Penn.	3 returned without due process
Agnes Robinson, child	2	6/24	Washington, D.C.	2 remanded by fed. tribunal
Washington and James Anderson and Henry Scott	3	7/21		3 returned without due process
Burton Ellis	1	9/2	Belleville, Ill.	1 returned without due process
Fugitive slave	1	8/30	Cincinnati, Ohio	1 returned without due process
Oliver Anderson	1	10/12	Chillicothe, Ohio	1 remanded by fed. tribunal
Henry Seaton	1	11/12	Cleveland, Ohio	1 remanded by fed. tribunal at gov't. expense
John Tyler	1	11/18	Columbus, Ohio	1 remanded by fed. tribunal
John Rice	1	11/12	Mt. Gilead, Ohio	1 remanded by fed. tribunal at gov't. expense
Jim	1	?	Ottowa, Ill.	1 rescued from fed. custody

TABLE 11. FUGITIVE SLAVE CASES: 1860

Names	Number of Cases	Date	Place	Disposition
James Waggoner	1	1/?	Cincinnati, Ohio	1 returned without due process
Fugitive slave	1	2/17	Centralia, Ill.	1 remanded by fed. tribunal
Fugitive slave	1	3/3	Springfield, Ill.	1 remanded by fed. tribunal at gov't. expense
John Brown	1	3/?	Lancaster, Penn.	1 returned without due process
Moses Horner	1	4/7	Philadelphia, Penn.	1 remanded by fed. tribunal at gov't. expense
Charles Nalle	1	4/27	Troy, N.Y.	1 rescued from fed. custody
Tom Bishop	1	4/30	New Albany, Ind.	1 remanded by fed. tribunal at gov't. expense
Allen Graff, Josiah Hay	2	5/5	New York, N.Y.	2 remanded by fed. tribunal
Fugitive slaves	2	5/10	Aurora, Ill.	2 returned without due process
Fugitive slaves	3	6/3	Clifton, Ill.	3 returned without due process
John Marshall	1	6/27	Washington, Ohio	1 returned without due process
George Armstrong	1	7/5	Albany, N.Y.	1 returned without due process
Fugitive slave	1	9/23	Iberia, Ohio	1 remanded by fed. tribunal
Fugitive slaves	2	9/23	Iberia, Ohio	2 rescued from fed. custody
Johnny Boyd, wife, and child	3	9/?	Galena, Ill.	3 returned without due process
Henson	1	10/?	Cincinnati, Ohio	1 remanded by fed. tribunal
Marshall, wife, Hutchins, wife, 2 children	6	10/15	Sandusky, Ohio	6 remanded by fed. tribunal at gov't. expense
Eliza	1	11/24	Chicago, Ill.	1 rescued from fed. custody
John Thomas	1	12/1	New York, N.Y.	1 remanded by fed. tribunal at gov't. expense
Fugitive slave	1	12/29	Cincinnati, Ohio	1 remanded by fed. tribunal

TABLE 12. SUMMARY OF FUGITIVE SLAVE CASES

Years	Total Cases	Cases before Fed. Trib.	Remanded by Fed. Trib.	Remanded at Gov't. Exp.	Returned without Due Process	Rescued from Fed. Cust.	Escaped from Fed. Cust.	Released
1850	22	13	11	1	9	–	–	2
1851	67	47	39	20	20	5	–	3
1852	23	7	4	3	16	3	–	–
1853	31	17	15	1	14	–	1	1
1854	23	19	18	4	3	1	–	1
1855	19	10	5	–	9	3	–	2
1856	36	21	20	19	16	–	–	–
1857	38	19	16	4	19	2	–	1
1858	14	7	4	1	7	3	–	–
1859	27	11	9	5	16	1	–	1
1860	32	20	16	10	12	4	–	–
Totals	**332**	**191**	**157**	**68**	**141**	**22**	**1**	**11**
Percentage of total cases		57.5	47.3	20.5	42.5	6.6	–	–
Percentage of cases before Federal Tribunals		100.0	82.2	35.6	–	11.5	0.5	5.8
Percentage of cases remanded by Federal Tribunals		–	100.0	43.3	–	14.0	0.6	–

Bibliography

I. PRIMARY SOURCES

A. Manuscripts: National Archives, Justice and Executive Branch, Washington, D.C.

Attorney General's Papers, Letters Received, Massachusetts, 1842–1861. Includes the letters of United States Attorney Benjamin F. Hallet to President Franklin Pierce concerning the failure of prosecutions in the Anthony Burns case.

Attorney General's Papers, Letters Received, New York, 1848–1861. Contains a few valuable letters dealing with the problem of enforcing the Fugitive Slave Law of 1850.

Circuit Court, District of Columbia Case Papers: Fugitive Slave Cases, 1851–1863. Valuable for the study of enforcement during the Civil War in Washington. Includes the docket of the District Court for 1862.

Department of the Interior, Letter Book, Judiciary No. 1, 1849–1853. Contains an exchange of letters between Secretary of the Interior A. H. H. Stuart and United States Attorney George W. Ashmead concerning prosecutions in the Christiana riot.

Letter Book, A-2, Attorney General's Office, 1817–1858. A few letters in this collection, are of real value for the study of the Fugitive Slave Law of 1850.

Letter Book, B-2, Attorney General's Office, 1859–1861. Contains the instructions of Attorney General Jeremiah S. Black to United States Attorneys and United States marshals in Ohio concerning enforcement of the Fugitive Slave Law of 1850.

Letters Concerning Judiciary Expenses, 1849–1884, 24 vols. Of limited usefulness, but does provide an insight into the operation of the federal courts.

Solicitor of the Treasury, Letters Received: United States Attorneys,

Clerks of Courts, and Marshalls, Massachusetts, 1843–1859. Includes inquiries concerning judicial expenses.

Solicitor of the Treasury, Letters Written, 1849–1865. Of little use for the study of the Fugitive Slave Law of 1850.

United States District Court, Southern Districts of New York, Records of the United States Commissioners: Fugitive Slave Cases, 1837–1860. Especially useful for the study of enforcement in New York City.

United States District Courts, Pennsylvania, Eastern District, Circuit Court, Fugitive Slave Cases, 1850–1860. A valuable collection, but it does not include all of the cases.

United States District Courts, Pennsylvania, Eastern District, Circuit Court, Habeas Corpus Cases, 1848–1862. Contains the manuscript opinions of Associate Justice Robert C. Grier, and Judge John Kane in the case of *Ex Parte* Jenkins et al.

B. Manuscripts: National Archives, Fiscal Branch, Washington, D.C.

Secretary of the Treasury, Warrant Division, Treasury Appropriation Ledger Nos. 15–17, July 1, 1849 to June 30, 1864. Record Group 39, Records of the Bureau of Accounts. Contains the pay warrants to the United States marshals for returning fugitive slaves under the Fugitive Slave Law of 1850. Especially useful for checking the number of slaves returned at government expense.

Treasury Department, Register of Audits, vols. 6–9, April 3, 1850 to June 30, 1860. Record Group 217, Records of the United States Accounting Office. An indispensable cross reference for determining the amount of money appropriated for the return of fugitive slaves at government expense.

C. Federal Documents

Biographical Directory of the American Congress 1774–1927. Washington: Government Printing Office, 1928.

Congressional Globe, Containing the Debates and Proceedings, 1833–1873, 109 vols. Washington: Blair and Reeves, et al., editors and publishers, 1834–1873.

The Constitution of the United States of America (Annotated) *Annotations of Cases Decided by the Supreme Court of the United States to January 1, 1938. Senate Document,* No. 232, 74th Cong., 2d sess. Washington: Government Printing Office, 1938.

"Expenditures and Receipts of the Government for the Year Ending June 30, 1853." *Executive Document,* No. 112, 33rd Cong., 1st sess., vol. 14.

Hall, Benjamin F., *comp., Official Opinions of the Attorneys General of the United States, etc., 1791–1948,* vol. 5. Washington: n.p., 1852–1949.

"Letter of the Secretary of the Treasury, Transmitting a Statement of the Receipts and Expenditures of the Government During the Year Ending June 30, 1858." *House Executive Document,* No. 20, 35th Cong., 2d sess., vol. 4.

Receipts and Expenditures, 1850, An Account of the Receipts and Ex-penditures of the United States, for the Fiscal Year Ending June 30, 1850. [n.p., n.d.].

———. *1851, An Account of the Receipts and Expenditures of the United States, for the Fiscal Year Ending June 30, 1851.* [n.p., n.d.]

———. *1852, An Account of the Receipts and Expenditures of the United States, for the Fiscal Year Ending June 30, 1852.* [n.p., n.d.]

"Report Regarding Posse Comitatus." *Senate Reports,* No. 320, 31st Cong., 2d sess., vol. 1.

"Resolution for Repeal of Fugitive Slave Law." *Senate Miscellaneous Documents,* No. 54, 34th Cong., 1st sess., vol. 1.

"Resolutions on Compromise Measures." *House Miscellaneous Documents,* No. 13, 32nd Cong., 1st sess., vol. 1.

"Resolutions on the Compromise Measures." *House Miscellaneous Documents,* No. 65, 32nd Cong., 1st sess., vol. 1.

"Resolutions on Enforcement of the Laws." *Senate Miscellaneous Documents,* No. 4, 36th Cong., 2d sess.

"Resolutions on Extension of Slavery." *Senate Miscellaneous Documents,* No. 70, 33rd Cong., 1st sess., vol. 1.

"Resolutions on New States and Slavery." *Senate Miscellaneous Documents,* No. 15, 34th Cong., 1st sess., vol. 1.

"Resolutions on Property in Slaves." *Senate Miscellaneous Documents,* No. 6, 36th Cong., 2d sess.

"Resolutions on Slavery and Kansas." *House Miscellaneous Documents,* No. 50, 34th Cong., 3rd sess., vol. 1.

"Resolutions on Slavery and Slave Law." *Senate Miscellaneous Documents,* No. 11, 34th Cong., 1st sess., vol. 1.

"Resolutions Relating to Compromise Measures." *House Miscellaneous Documents,* No. 20, 32d Cong., 1st sess., vol. 1.

"Resolutions Relating to Fugitives from Labor." *House Miscellaneous Documents,* No. 60, 36th Cong., 1st sess., vol. 6.

Richardson, James D., *A Compilation of the Messages and Papers of the Presidents 1789–1897,* Washington: Government Printing Office, 1899. vol. 5.

"Statement of Receipts and Expenditures of the Government for the Year Ending June 30, 1854." *House Executive Document,* No. 10, 33rd Cong., 2d sess., vol. 4.

"Statement of Receipts and Expenditures of the Government for the Year Ending June 30, 1855." *House Executive Document,* No. 40, 34th Cong., 1st sess., vol. 8.

"Statement of the Receipts and Expenditures of the United States During the Year Ending June 30, 1856." *House Executive Document,* No. 86, 34th Cong., 3rd sess., vol. 11.

"Statement of the Amount of Receipts and Expenditures of the Government During the Year Ending June 30, 1857." *House Executive Document,* No. 13, 35th Cong., 1st sess., vols. 1, 4.

Statutes at Large of the United States . . . 1789–1873, 17 vols. Boston: Little, Brown and Company, 1845–73.

D. State Documents

Connecticut. *Resolutions and Private Acts, Passed by the General Assembly of the State of Connecticut, May Session, 1849.* Hartford: Courant Office Press, 1849.

———. *Resolutions and Private Acts of the General Assembly of the State of Connecticut, May Session, 1854.* New Haven: Babcock & Wildman, 1854.

Illinois. *General Laws of the State of Illinois Passed by the Eighteenth General Assembly, Convened January 3, 1853.* Springfield: Lamphier & Walker, 1853.

Indiana. *The Revised Laws of Indiana, Adopted and Enacted by the General Assembly at their Eighth Session.* Corydon: Carpenter & Douglass, 1824.

———. *The Revised Statutes of the State of Indiana, Passed at the Thirty-Sixth Session of the General Assembly,* 2 vols. Indianapolis: J. P. Chapman, 1852.

Maine. *Acts and Resolves Passed by the Thirty-Fourth Legislature of the State of Maine, 1855.* Augusta: Stevens & Blaine, 1857.

———. *Acts and Resolves Passed by the Thirty-Sixth Legislature of the State of Maine, 1857.* Augusta: Stevens & Blaine, 1857.

Massachusetts. *Acts and Resolves Passed by the Legislature of Massachusetts in the Year 1843.* Boston: Dutton & Wentworth, 1843.

———. *Acts and Resolves Passsed by the General Court of Massachusetts, in the Year 1855.* Boston: William White, 1855.

———. *Acts and Resolves Passed by the General Court of Massachusetts, in the Year 1858.* Boston: William White, 1858.

———. *Acts and Resolves Passed by the General Court of Massachusetts, in the Year 1861.* Boston: William White, 1861.

Michigan. *Acts of the Legislature of the State of Michigan, Passed at the Regular Session of 1855.* Lansing: George W. Peck, 1855.

———. *The Compiled Laws of the State of Michigan, 1897,* 4 vols. Compiled by Lewis Miller. Lansing: Robert Smith Printing Company, 1899.

New Hampshire. *Laws of the State of New Hampshire, Passed June Session, 1857.* Concord: George G. Fogg, 1857.

New York. *Statutes at Large of the State of New York, Comprising the Revised Statutes, As They Existed on the 1st Day of January, 1867.* 2d ed., vol. 1. Edited by John W. Edmonds. Albany: Weed, Parsons and Company, 1869.

Ohio. *Acts of a General Nature Passed by the Fifty-First General Assembly of the State of Ohio.* Columbus: Osgood, Blake & Knapp, 1854.

———. *Acts of a General Nature and Local Laws and Joint Resolutions, Passed by the Fifty-Second General Assembly of the State of Ohio.* Columbus: Statesman Steam Press, 1857.

———. *Acts of a General Nature and Local Laws and Joint Resolutions, Passed by the Fifty-Third General Assembly, of the State of Ohio.* Columbus: Richard Nevins, 1858.

———. *Acts of a General Nature and Local Laws and Joint Resolutions,*

Passed by the Fifty-Third General Assembly, of the State of Ohio. Columbus: Richard Nevins, 1859.

————. *Acts of a General Nature and Local Laws and Joint Resolutions, Passed by the Fifty-Fourth General Assembly, of the State of Ohio.* Columbus: Richard Nevins, 1860.

Pennsylvania. *Laws of the General Assembly of the Commonwealth of Pennsylvania, Passed at the Session of 1847.* Harrisburg: J. M. G. Lescure, 1847.

————. *Laws of the General Assembly of the Commonwealth of Pennsylvania, Passed at the Session of 1852.* Harrisburg: Theo. Fenn & Company, 1852.

Rhode Island. *Public Laws of the State of Rhode Island, and Providence Plantations, Passed at the Sessions of the General Assembly, From May, 1853, to January, 1855, Inclusive.* Providence: Knowles & Anthony, 1855.

————. *Supplement to the Revised Statutes, Being the Public Laws of the State of Rhode Island and Providence Plantations, Passed at the General Assembly, From January 1859, to April 1861, Inclusive.* Providence: A. Crawford Greene, 1861.

Vermont. *The Acts and Resolves Passed By the Legislature of the State of Vermont, at the October Session, 1850.* Montpelier: E. P. Walton & Son, 1850.

————. *The Compiled Statutes of the State of Vermont, 1839–1850.* Compiled by Charles L. Williams. Burlington: Chauncey Goodrich, 1851.

Vermont. *The Acts and Resolves Passed By the General Assembly of the State of Vermont, at the October Session, 1858.* Bradford: Joseph D. Clark, 1858.

Virginia. *Acts of the General Assembly of Virginia, Passed at the Extra and Regular Sessions in 1849 & 1850, and in the Seventy-Third and Seventy-Fourth Years of the Commonwealth.* Richmond: William F. Ritchie, 1850.

————. *Acts of the General Assembly, Passed in 1855–6, in the Eightieth Year of the Commonwealth.* Richmond: William F. Ritchie, 1856.

————. *Virginia Documents, 1858–1859.* Document No. 57. "Report of the Joint Committee on the Harpers Ferry Outrages, February 1860."

Wisconsin. *General Acts Passed By the Legislature of Wisconsin, in the Year Eighteen Hundred and Fifty-Seven.* Madison: Atwood & Rublee, 1857.

————. *The Revised Statutes of the State of Wisconsin: Passed at the Annual Session of the Legislature Commencing Jan. 13, 1858, and Approved May 17, 1858.* Chicago: W. B. Keen, 1858.

E. Cases Cited

Ableman v. Booth, 21 Howard 506 (1859).

Benner v. Porter, 9 Howard 235 (1850).

Bennett v. Butterworth, 11 Howard 669 (1850).

In re Booth, 3 Wisconsin 1 (1854).

In re Booth and Rycraft, 3 Wisconsin 157 (1855).

Cauffman v. Oliver, 10 Barr (Pa.) 514 (1848).

Cohens v. Virginia, 5 Wheaton 264 (1821).

Commonwealth v. Aves, 18 Pickering (Mass.) 193 (1836).

Commonwealth *ex rel.* Wright v. Deacon, 5 Sergeant & Rawle (Pa.) 62 (1819).

Fenn v. Holme, 21 Howard 481 (1859).

Freeman v. Robinson, 7 Indiana Reports 321 (1855).

Fugitive Slave Law, 30 Federal Cases 1015 (1851).

Giltner v. Gorham, 10 Federal Cases 424 (1848).

Glen v. Hodges, 9 Johnson (N.Y.) 67 (1817).

Graves v. The State, 1 Carter (Ind.) 368 (1849).

Irvine v. Marshall, 20 Howard 558 (1858).

Jack v. Martin, 12 Wendell (N.Y.) 311 (1834).

Jack v. Martin, 14 Wendell (N.Y.) 507 (1836).

Ex Parte Jenkins, 13 Federal Cases 969 (1855).

Ex Parte Jenkins et al., 13 Federal Cases 445 (1853).

Jones v. Van Zandt, 5 Howard 215 (1847).

In re Kaine, 14 Howard 120 (1853).

Kentucky v. Dennison, 24 Howard 66 (1861).

Miller v. McQuerry, 17 Federal Cases 335 (1853).

Murray's Lessee v. Hoboken, 18 Howard 272 (1856).

Oliver et al. v. Kaufman, Weakley, and Breckbill, 18 Federal Cases 657 (1853).

Parsons v. Bedford et al., 3 Peters 433 (1830).

Prigg v. The Commonwealth of Pennsylvania, 16 Peters 539 (1842).

Ex Parte Robinson, 20 Federal Cases 969 (1855).

Ex Parte Robinson, 20 Federal Cases 965 (1856).

Ex Parte Sifford, 22 Federal Cases 105 (1857).

Ex Parte Simeon Bushnell, 9 Ohio State Reports 77 (1859).

State v. Hoppess, 2 Western Law Journal (Ohio) 289 (1845).

Thomas Sims's Case, 7 Cushing 285 (1851).

In re Thornton, 11 Illinois 332 (1849).

Trial of Thomas Sims, An Issue of Personal Liberty, on the Claim of James Potter, of Georgia, Against Him, As An Alleged Fugitive From Service. Reported by James W. Stone. Boston: William S. Damrell & Co., 1851.

In re United States v. Booth, 18 Howard 476 (1855).

United States v. Buck, 24 Federal Cases 1289 (1860).

United States *ex rel.* Garland v. Morris, 26 Federal Cases 1318 (1854).

United States v. Rycraft, 27 Federal Cases 918 (1854).

United States *ex rel.* Wheeler v. Williamson, 28 Federal Cases 682 (1855).

Van Metre v. Mitchell, 28 Federal Cases 1036 (1853).

Ex Parte Van Orden, 28 Federal Cases 1060 (1854).

Weimer v. Sloane, 29 Federal Cases 599 (1854).

Weston v. Charleston, 2 Peters 449 (1829).

F. Legal Authorities

Bouvier's Law Dictionary. Revised and edited by Francis Rawle. 2 vols. Boston: The Boston Book Co., 1897.

Catterall, Helen Turncliff, ed. *Judicial Cases Concerning American Slavery and the Negro.* 5 vols. Washington: Carnegie Institution of Washington, 1926–37.

Hurd, John Codman. *The Law of Freedom and Bondage in the United States.* 2 vols. Boston: Little, Brown and Company, 1858, 1862.

Story, Joseph. *Commentaries on the Constitution of the United States: With A Preliminary Review of the Constitutional History of the Colonies and States, Before the Adoption of the Constitution.* 2d ed., vol. 2. Boston: Charles C. Little and James Brown, 1851.

G. Newspapers and Periodicals

Boston Advertiser, 1850–51.

Boston Liberator, 1850–64.

Christian Examiner and Religious Miscellany, vols. 49–69. Boston, 1850–60.

Christian Review, vols. 15–25. Boston: 1849–60.

De Bow's Review, vols. 18–32. New Orleans, 1850–64.

Friend's Review; A Religious, Literary, and Miscellaneous Journal, vols. 3–4. Philadelphia, 1847–60.

The Monthly Law Reporter, vols. 2–12. Boston, 1850–60.

New Englander, vol. 8. New Haven, 1850.

New York Tribune, 1850–51.

New York Weekly Tribune, 1850–64.

The United States Magazine, and Democratic Review, vols. 27–28. New York, 1850–51.

Washington Daily National Intelligencer, 1850–64.

H. Contemporary Books and Pamphlets

American and Foreign Anti-Slavery Society. *The Annual Report of the American Anti-Slavery Society, Presented at New York, May 6, 1851.* New York: William Harned, 1851.

———. *The Fugitive Slave Bill: Its History and Unconstitutionality: With an Account of the Seizure and Enslavement of James Hamlet, and His Subsequent Restoration to Liberty.* New York: William Harned, 1850.

American Anti-Slavery Society. *Annual Reports* (1855–61). New York: American Anti-Slavery Society, 1855–61.

———. *Proceedings of the American Anti-Slavery Society, at Its Second Decade, Held in the City of Philadelphia, Dec. 3d, 4th and 5th, 1853.* New York: American Anti-Slavery Society, 1854.

Barnes, Albert. *The Church and Slavery.* Philadelphia: Parry & McMillan, 1857.

Barton, Seth. *The Randolph Epistles.* Washington: n.p., 1850.

Bayly, Thomas Henry. *Speech of Mr. Bayly of Accomack, on the Bill to Prevent Citizens of New York from Carrying Slaves Out of This Commonwealth, and to Prevent the Escape of Persons Charged with the Commission of any Crime, and in Reply to Mr. Scott of Fauquier, Delivered in the House of Delegates of Virginia, on the 25th and 26th of February 1841.* Richmond: Shepard and Colin, 1841.

Beecher, Charles. *The Duty of Disobedience to Wicked Laws. A Sermon on the Fugitives Slave Law.* New York: J. A. Gray, 1851.

Booth, Sherman M. *Unconstitutionality of the Fugitive Slave Act. Argument of Byron Paine, Esq. and Opinion of Hon. A. D. Smith, Associate Justice of the Supreme Court of the State of Wisconsin.* Milwaukee: n. p., 1854.

Burleigh, Charles Calistus. *No Slave-Hunting in the Old Bay State; Speech . . . at the Annual Meeting of Massachusetts A.S. Society, Friday, January 28, 1859.* Boston: Massachusetts A.S. Society, 1859.

Callicot, Theophilus Carey. *Speech . . . Against the Personal Liberty Bill.* Albany: Comstock & Cassidy, 1860.

Carter, William. *A Reply to Hon. William Thomas' Exposition and Defence of the Fugitive Slave Law.* Winchester, Ill.: Western Unionist, 1851.

Chittenden, L. E. *A Report of the Debates and Proceedings of the Conference Convention for Proposing Amendments to the Constitution of the United States Held at Washington, D.C. in February, A.D. 1861.* New York: D. Appleton & Co., 1864.

Church Anti-Slavery Society. *Second Annual Report to the Church Anti-Slavery Society, Presented at Boston, May 28th, 1861.* n.p., n.d.

Clark, Rufus Wheelwright. *Conscience and Law.* Boston: Tappan & Whittemore, 1851.

Cobleigh, Nelson E. *Iniquity Abounding. A Sermon.* Worchester: J. Burrill & Co., 1851.

Colver, Nathaniel. *The Fugitive Slave Bill: Or, God's Laws Paramount to the Laws of Men. A Sermon, Preached on Sunday, October 20, 1850, by Rev. Nathaniel Colver, Pastor of the Tremont St. Church.* Boston: J. M. Hewes & Co., 1850.

Dana, Richard Henry. *Remarks . . . Before the Committee on Federal Relations, on the Proposed Removal of Edward G. Loring, Esq. from the Office of Judge of Probate.* Boston: Alfred Mudge & Son, 1855.

Dewey, Orville. *The Laws of Human Progress and Modern Reforms.* New York: C. S. Francis & Company, 1852.

Dexter, Franklin. *A Letter to the Hon. Samuel A. Eliot, Representative in Congress from the City of Boston, in Reply to His Apology for Voting for the Fugitive Slave Bill.* Boston: W. Crosby & H. P. Nichols, 1851.

Dorr, James Augustus. *Objections to the Act of Congress, Commonly Called the Fugitive Slave Law Answered, in a Letter to Hon. Washington Hunt.* New York: n.p., 1850.

Douglas, Stephen Arnold. *Speech . . . on the "Measures of Adjustment," Delivered in the City Hall, Chicago, October 23, 1850.* Washington: Gideon & Co., 1851.

Forman, Jacob Gilbert. *The Christian Martyrs; Or, The Conditions of Obedience to Civil Government: A Discourse By J. G. Forman, Minister of the Second Congregational Church in Nantucket; Until Recently Minister of the First Church and Congregation in West Bridgewater, Mass. to Which is Added a Friendly Letter to Said Church and Congregation on the Pro-Slavery Influences that Occasioned His Removal.* Boston: W. Crosby and H. P. Nichols, 1851.

Foster, Stephen S. *Revolution the Only Remedy for Slavery.* New York: American Anti-Slavery Society, 1855.

The Fugitive Slave Law, Its Character Fairly Stated—Its Constitutionality and Reasonableness Vindicated—and the Duty of Maintaining and Enforcing it Established Against the Misrepresentations, Sophistry, and Seditious Agitations of Demagogues and Abolitionists. Washington: Gideon & Co., 1850.

Furness, William Henry. *Christian Duty. Three Discourses . . . With Reference to the Recent Execution of the Fugitive Slave Law in Boston and New York.* Philadelphia: Merrihew & Thompson, 1854.

———. *The Moving Power. A Discourse Delivered in the First Congregational Unitarian Church in Philadelphia, Sunday Morning, Feb. 9, 1851, After the Occurrence of a Fugitive Slave Case.* Philadelphia: Merrihew and Thompson, 1851.

Goodell, William. *Slavery and Anti-Slavery; A History of the Great Struggle in Both Hemispheres; With a View of the Slavery Question in the United States.* New York: William Goodell, 1853.

Grimes, James Wilson. *Speech . . . on the Surrender of Slaves by the Army.* Washington: Congressional Globe, 1862.

Hall, Nathaniel. *The Limits of Civil Obedience. A Sermon Preached in the First Church, Dorchester, January 12, 1851.* Boston: W. Crosby and H. P. Nichols, 1851.

Harris, Thomas Langrell. *Letter of Hon. Thos. L. Harris, of Illinois, Upon Repeal of the Fugitive Slave Law.* Washington: J. T. Towers, 1851.

Hosmer, William. *The Higher Law, in its Relation to Civil Government: With Particular Reference to Slavery, and the Fugitive Slave Law.* Auburn, N.Y.: Derby and Miller, 1852.

Hossack, John. *Speech of John Hossack, Convicted of a Violation of the Fugitive Slave Law, Before Judge Drummond, of the United States District Court, Chicago, Ill.* New York: American Anti-Slavery Society, 1860.

Joliffe, John. *In the Matter of George Gordon's Petition for Pardon.* Cincinnati: Gazette Company, 1862.

Junkin, George. *Political Fallacies: An Examination of the False Assumptions, and Refutation of the Sophistical Reasonings, Which Have Brought on the Civil War.* New York: Charles Scribner, 1863.

Kettell, George F. *A Sermon on the Duty of Citizens, With Respect to the Fugitive Slave Law.* White Plains, N.Y.: Eastern State Journal, 1851.

Krebs, John Michael. *The American Citizen. A Discourse on the Nature and Extent of Our Religious Subjection to the Government Under Which We Live: Including an Inquiry into the Scriptural Authority of that Provision of the Constitution of the United States, Which Requires the Surrender of Fugitive Slaves.* New York: C. Scribner, 1851.

Lord, John Chase. *"The Higher Law" in its Application to the Fugitive Slave Bill. A Sermon on the Duties Men Owe to God and to Governments. Delivered at the Central Presbyterian Church on Thanksgiving-Day.* New York: Union Safety Committee, 1851.

Love, Horace Thomas. *Slavery in its Relation to God. A Review of Rev. Dr. Lord's Thanksgiving Sermon, in Favor of Domestic Slavery, Entitled The Higher Law, in its Application to the Fugitive Slave Bill.* . . . Buffalo: A. M. Clapp & Co., 1851.

Love, William De Loss. *Obedience to Rulers—The Duty and its Limitations. A Discourse.* . . . New Haven: Storer & Stone, 1851.

McEwen, Abel. *A Sermon Preached in the First Congregational Church, New London, Conn., On the Day of Thanksgiving, November 28, 1850.* New London: Daniels & Bacon, 1851.

Mann, Horace. *Horace Mann's Letters on the Extension of Slavery into California and New Mexico; and on the Duty of Congress to Provide the Trial by Jury for Alleged Fugitive Slaves.* . . . [Washington]: Buell & Blanchard, [1850].

Marvin, Abijah Perkins. *Fugitive Slaves: A Sermon, Preached in the North Congregational Church, Winchendon, on the Day of the Annual Fast, April 11, 1850.* Boston: J. P. Jewett & Co., 1850.

May, Samuel Joseph. *The Fugitive Slave Law and Its Victims.* New York: American Anti-Slavery Society, 1861.

———. *Some Recollections of Our Antislavery Conflict.* Boston: Fields, Osgood & Co., 1869.

———. *Speech of Rev. Samuel J. May, to the Convention of Citizens, of Onandaga County, in Syracuse . . . Called "To Consider the Principles of the American Government, and the Extent to Which They are Trampled Under Foot by the Fugitive Slave Law." Occasioned by an Attempt to Enslave an Inhabitant of Syracuse.* Syracuse: Agan & Summers, 1851.

Myers, Emmanuel. *The Trial of Emmanuel Myers, of Maryland, for Kidnapping Certain Fugitive Slaves, Had at Carlisle, Pennsylvania November 1859.* Carlisle: n.p., 1859.

Newell, John. *"The Higher Law," in its Application to the Fugitive Slave Bill. Review of Dr. John C. Lord's Sermon, on the Duties Men Owe to God and to Governments.* . . . Syracuse: Journal Office, 1851.

Official Report of the Great Union Meeting, Held at the Academy of Music, in the City of New York, December 19th, 1859. New York: Davies & Kent, 1859.

Parker, Joel. *Personal Liberty Laws, (Statutes of Massachusetts,) and Slavery in the Territories.* Boston: Wright & Potter, 1861.

Patton, William Weston. *Conscience and Law; or, A Discussion of Our Comparative Responsibility to Human and Divine Government: With an Application to the Fugitive Slave Law.* New York: M. H. Newman & Co., 1850.

Peck, John Mason. *The Duties of American Citizens: A Discourse, Preached in the State-House, Springfield, Illinois, January 26, 1851.* . . . St. Louis: T. W. Ustick, 1851.

Plover, Hiram, Jr. *The Square Egg; Being a Cheap Dish for the Times; Served up for the Public Health, With Special Reference to Democrats and Whigs.* Boston: J. P. Jewett & Co., 1852.

Quincy, Josiah. *Speech Delivered . . . Before the State Whig Convention, Assembled at the Music Hall, Boston, Aug. 16, 1854*. Boston, J. Wilson & Son, 1854.

Rand, Asa. *The Slave-Catcher Caught in the Meshes of Eternal Law*. Cleveland: Smead and Cowles, 1852.

Rantoul, Robert. *The Fugitive Slave Law. Speech . . . Delivered Before the Grand Mass Convention of the Democratic Voters of the Second Congressional District of Massachusetts. Holden at Lynn, Thursday, April 3, 1851*. Lynn, Mass.: n.p., 1851.

Richardson, John G. *Obedience to Human Law Considered in the Light of Divine Truth. A Discourse Delivered in the First Baptist Meeting House, Lawrence, Mass. July 4, 1852*. Lawrence, Mass.: Homer A. Cooke, 1852.

Sheldon, Luther Harris. *The Moral Responsibility of the Citizen and Nation in Respect to the Fugitive Slave Bill. A Discourse Delivered April 10, 1851, On Occasion of the Public Fast, in the Orthodox Congregational Church, Townsend, Mass*. Andover: John D. Flagg, 1851.

Shipherd, Jacob R., comp. *History of the Oberlin-Wellington Rescue*. Boston: John P. Jewett and Company, 1859.

Smith, Gerrit. *Abstract of the Argument on the Fugitive Slave Law . . . On the Trial of Henry W. Allen, U. S. Deputy Marshall, for Kidnapping*. Syracuse: Daily Journal, 1852.

Spear, Samuel Thayer. *The Law-Abiding Conscience, and the Higher Law Conscience; With Remarks on the Fugitive Slave Question. A Sermon*. New York: Lambert & Lane, 1850.

Spencer, Charles S. *An Appeal for Freedom, Made in the Assembly of the State of New York, March 7, 1859*. Albany: Weed, Parsons & Company, 1859.

Spooner, Lysander. *A Defence for Fugitive Slaves, Against the Acts of Congress of February 12, 1793, and September 18, 1850*. Boston: Bela Marsh, 1850.

Stevens, Charles Emery. *Anthony Burns: A History*. Boston: John P. Jewett and Company, 1856.

Storrs, Richard Salter. *The Obligation of Man to Obey the Civil Law: Its Ground and Its Extent. A Discourse Delivered December 12, 1850, On Occasion of the Public Thanksgiving; in the Church of the Pilgrims, Brooklyn, N.Y. . . .* New York: M. H. Newman & Co., 1850.

Stuart, Moses. *Civil Government*. Princeton: n.p., 1851.

Talbot, Thomas H. *The Constitutional Provision Respecting Fugitives from Service or Labor, and the Act of Congress, of September 18, 1850*. Boston: Bela Marsh, 1852.

Thayer, William Makepeace. *A Sermon on Moses' Fugitive Slave Bill, Preached at Ashland, Mass., November 3, 1850*. Boston: C. C. P. Moody, 1850.

Thompson, Joseph Parrish. *The Fugitive Slave Law; Tried by the Old and New Testaments*. New York: Mark H. Newman & Co., 1850.

Trial of Henry W. Allen, U.S. Deputy Marshall, For Kidnapping, With Arguments of Counsel & Charge of Justice Marvin, on the Constitutionality of the Fugitive Slave Law, in the Supreme Court of New York. Syracuse: Daily Journal Office, 1852.

Tucker, Joshua Thomas. *The Citizen and the Commonwealth. A Discourse Delivered in the First Congregational Church in Holliston, Mass., on the Day of the Annual State Fast, April 10, 1851.* Holliston, Mass.: Parker & Plimpton, 1851.

Union Safety Committee. *Proceedings of the Union Safety Meeting Held at Castle Garden, October 23, 1850.* New York: Union Safety Committee, 1850.

———. *Selections from the Speeches and Writings of Prominent Men in the United States on the Subject of Abolition and Agitation, and Addressed to the People of the State of New York.* New York: Union Safety Committee, 1854.

Watkins, James. *Narrative of the Life of James Watkins, Formerly a "Chattel" in Maryland, U.S.; Containing an Account of His Escape from Slavery, Together with an Appeal on Behalf of Three Millions of "Such Pieces of Property," Still Held Under the Standard of the Eagle.* Boston: Kenyon and Abbot, 1852.

Willard, Samuel. *The Grand Issue: An Ethico-Political Tract.* Boston: John P. Jewett & Co., 1851.

I. Memoirs and Diaries

Bearse, Austin. *Reminiscences of Fugitive-Slave Law Days in Boston.* Boston: W. Richardson, 1880.

Coffin, Levi. *Reminiscences of Levi Coffin. . . .* 3rd ed. Cincinnati: The Robert Clarke Company, 1899.

Higginson, Thomas Wentworth. *Cheerful Yesterdays.* Boston: Houghton, Mifflin and Company, 1899.

———. *Contemporaries.* Boston: Houghton, Mifflin and Company, 1899.

Hoar, George F. *Autobiography of Seventy Years,* 2 vols. New York: Charles Scribner's Sons, 1903.

Ross, Alexander Milton. *Recollections and Experiences of an Abolitionist; From 1855 to 1865.* Toronto: Rowsell and Hutchison, 1875.

J. Collected Source Documents

Abel, Annie Heloise, and Klingberg, Frank J., eds. *A Side-Light on Anglo-American Relations, 1839–1858.* Lancaster, Pennsylvania: The Association for the Study of Negro Life and History, Inc., 1927.

Ames, Herman V., ed. *State Document on Federal Relations: The States and the United States.* Philadelphia: The Department of History, University of Pennsylvania, 1900.

Basler, Roy P., ed. *The Collected Works of Abraham Lincoln.* 8 vols. New Brunswick, New Jersey: Rutgers University Press, 1953.

Dumond, Dwight Lowell. *Letters of James Gillespie Birney 1831–1852.* 2 vols. New York: D. Appleton-Century Company, 1938.

Farrand, Max, ed. *Records of the Federal Convention of 1787.* 4 vols. Rev. ed. New Haven: Yale University Press, 1911–37.

"Papers of the Governors, 1845-1858," *Pennsylvania Archives.* 4th ser., 7:277-506. *Publications of the Buffalo Historical Society. Millard Fillmore Papers.* Edited by Frank H. Severance. Vols. 1-2. Buffalo: Buffalo Historical Society, 1907.

Higginson, Thomas Wentworth. *Letters and Journals of Thomas Wentworth Higginson, 1846-1906.* Edited by Mary Thatcher Higginson. Boston: Houghton Mifflin Company, 1921.

Mann, Horace. *Slavery: Letters and Speeches.* Boston: B. B. Mussey & Co., 1853.

Moore, John Bassett, ed. *The Works of James Buchanan.* Vols. 9-10. Philadelphia: J. B. Lippincott Company, 1908-11.

Sperry, Earl Evelyn. *The Jerry Rescue, October 1, 1851, . . . Delivered Before the Onandaga Historical Association, October, 1921. . . . Additional Jerry Rescue Documents and Rescue of Harriet Powell in Syracuse, September, 1839.* Collected and edited by Franklin H. Chase. Syracuse: Onandaga Historical Association, 1924.

Sumner, Charles, *The Works of Charles Sumner.* 15 vols. Boston: Lee and Shepard, 1875-83.

II. SECONDARY WORKS

A. General

Carson, Hampton L. *The History of the Supreme Court of the United States; With Biographies of All the Chief and Associate Justices.* 2 vols. Philadelphia: P. W. Ziegler and Company, 1902.

Channing, Edward. *A History of the United States.* 6 vols. New York: The Macmillan Company, 1905-25.

Crosskey, William Winslow. *Politics and the Constitution in the History of the United States.* 2 vols. Chicago: University of Chicago Press, 1953.

Galbreath, Charles B. *History of Ohio.* Vol. 2. Chicago: American Historical Society, 1925.

Nevins, Allan. *The Emergence of Lincoln.* 2 vols. New York: Charles Scribner's Sons, 1950.

———, *Ordeal of Union.* 2 vols. New York: Charles Scribner's Sons, 1947.

Nichols, Roy Franklin. *The Democratic Machine, 1850-1854.* New York: Columbia University, 1923.

Pierce, Bessie Louise. *A History of Chicago.* Vol. 2. New York: Alfred A. Knopf, 1959.

Rhodes, James Ford. *History of the United States from the Compromise of 1850 to the Final Restoration of Home Rule at the South in 1877.* Vols. 1-4. New York: The Macmillan Company, 1904-6.

Warren, Charles. *The Supreme Court in United States History.* Rev. ed., 2 vols. Boston: Little, Brown and Company, 1926.

Wilson, Henry. *History of the Rise and Fall of the Slave Power in America.* 3 vols. Boston: J. R. Osgood and Company, 1872-77.

B. Monographs and Special Studies

Buckmaster, Henrietta. *Let My People Go: The Story of the Underground Railroad and the Growth of the Abolition Movement.* New York: Harper & Brothers, 1941.

Craven, Avery. *The Coming of the Civil War.* Chicago: University of Chicago Press, Phoenix Books, 1966.

Dumond, Dwight Lowell. *Antislavery, the Crusade for Freedom in America.* Ann Arbor: The University of Michigan Press, 1961.

Filler, Louis. *The Crusade Against Slavery, 1830–1860.* New York: Harper & Brothers, 1960.

Fite, Emerson David. *The Presidential Campaign of 1860.* New York: The Macmillan Company, 1911.

Foner, Philip Sheldon. *Business and Slavery: The New York Merchants and the Irrepressible Conflict.* Chapel Hill: University of North Carolina Press, 1941.

Greeley, Horace, and Cleveland, John F., comps. *A Political Text-Book For 1860: Comprising A Brief View of Presidential Nominations and Elections: Including All the National Platforms Ever Yet Adopted: Also, A History of the Struggle Respecting Slavery in the Territories, And of the Action of Congress as to the Freedom of the Public Lands, with the Most Notable Speeches and Letters of Messrs. Lincoln, Douglas, Bell, Cass, Seward, Everett, Breckinridge, H. V. Johnson, etc., etc., Touching the Questions of the Day; and Returns of All Presidential Elections Since 1836.* New York: The Tribune Association, 1860.

Harris, N. Dwight. *The History of Negro Servitude in Illinois and of the Slavery Agitation in that State 1719–1864.* Chicago: A. A. McClurg & Co., 1904.

Hensel, W. U. *The Christiana Riot and the Treason Trials of 1851: An Historical Sketch.* Lancaster, Pa.: New Era Printing Company, 1911.

Howe, Daniel Wait. *Political History of Secession to the Beginning of the American Civil War.* New York: G. P. Putnam's Sons, 1914.

Levy, Leonard W. *The Law of the Commonwealth and Chief Justice Shaw.* Cambridge: Harvard University Press, 1957.

McDougall, Marion Gleason. *Fugitive Slaves 1619–1865.* Boston: Ginn & Company, 1891.

Pillsbury, Parker. *Acts of the Anti-Slavery Apostles.* Concord, N.H.: Clague, Wegman, Schlict, & Co., 1883.

Randall, James Garfield. *Civil War and Reconstruction.* Boston: D.C. Heath and Company, 1937.

———. *Constitutional Problems Under Lincoln.* Rev. ed. Urbana: The University of Illinois Press, 1951.

Shaw, Warren Choate. *The Fugitive Slave Issue in Massachusetts Politics, 1780–1837.* Urbana: The University of Illinois Press, 1938.

Siebert, Wilbur H. *The Underground Railroad from Slavery to Freedom.* New York: The Macmillan Company, 1898.

———. *Vermont's Anti-Slavery and Underground Railroad Record.* Columbus, Ohio: Spahr and Glenn Co., 1937.

Still, William. *Still's Underground Railroad Records.* Rev. ed. Philadelphia: J. W. Keeler & Co., 1883.

Thornbrough, Emma Lou. *The Negro in Indiana: A Study of a Minority.* Indianapolis: Indiana Historical Bureau, 1957.

Turner, Edward Raymond. *The Negro in Pennsylvania: Slavery-Servitude-Freedom 1639–1861.* Washington: American Historical Association, 1911.

Wilson, Henry. *History of the Antislavery Measures of the Thirty-Seventh and Thirty-Eighth United States Congresses, 1861–1864.* Boston: Walker, Wise, and Company, 1864.

Yanuck, Julius. "The Fugitive Slave Law and the Constitution." Ph.D. dissertation, Columbia University, 1953.

C. Biographies

Adams, Charles Francis. *Richard Henry Dana, A Biography.* Rev. ed., 2 vols. Boston: Houghton, Mifflin and Company, 1891.

Bancroft, Frederic. *The Life of William H. Seward.* 2 vols. New York: Harper & Brothers, 1900.

Barre, W. L. *The Life and Public Services of Millard Fillmore.* Buffalo: Wanzer, McKim & Co., 1856.

Brodie, Fawn M. *Thaddeus Stevens Scourge of the South.* New York: W. W. Norton & Company, Inc., 1959.

Commager, Henry Steele. *Theodore Parker.* Boston: Little, Brown and Company, 1936.

Donald, David Herbert. *Charles Sumner and the Coming of the Civil War.* New York: Alfred A. Knopf, 1961.

Foner, Philip Sheldon. *The Life and Writings of Frederick Douglass.* Vol. 2. New York: International Publishers, 1950–55.

Fuess, Claude M. *The Life of Caleb Cushing.* 2 vols. New York: Harcourt, Brace and Company, 1923.

Garrison, Wendell Phillips. *William Lloyd Garrison, 1805–1879: The Story of His Life Told By His Children.* 4 vols. Boston: Houghton, Mifflin and Company, 1894.

Harlow, Ralph Volney. *Gerrit Smith, Philanthropist and Reformer.* New York: Henry Holt and Company, 1939.

Higginson, Mary Thatcher. *Thomas Wentworth Higginson: The Story of His Life.* Boston: Houghton, Mifflin and Company, 1914.

Julian, George Washington. *The Life of Joshua Giddings.* Chicago: A. C. McClurg and Co., 1892.

Kirwan, Albert D. *John J. Crittenden: The Struggle for the Union.* Lexington: University of Kentucky Press, 1962.

Klein, Philip Shriver. *President James Buchanan: A Biography.* University Park: The Pennsylvania State University Press, 1962.

Merril, Walter M. *Against Wind and Tide: A Biography of Wm. Lloyd Garrison.* Cambridge: Harvard University Press, 1962.

Nichols, Roy Franklin. *Franklin Pierce: Young Hickory of the Granite Hills.* Philadelphia: University of Pennsylvania Press, 1931.

Rayback, Robert J. *Millard Fillmore: Biography of a President.* Buffalo: Buffalo Historical Society, 1959.

Thomas, Benjamin P., and Hyman, Harold M. *Stanton: The Life and Times of Lincoln's Secretary of War*. New York: Alfred A. Knopf, 1962.

Van Deusen, Glyndon G. *The Life of Henry Clay*. Boston: Little, Brown and Company, 1937.

Weiss, John. *Life and Correspondence of Theodore Parker, Minister of the Twenty-Eighth Congregational Society, Boston*. Vol. 2. New York: Appleton, 1864.

D. Periodical Articles

Alilunas, Leo. "Fugitive Slave Cases in Ohio Prior to 1850." *Ohio State Archaeological and Historical Quarterly* 49 (1940) : 160–84.

Burroughs, Wilbur Greeley. "Oberlin's Part in the Slavery Conflict." *Ohio Archaeological and Historical Publications*, 20 (1911) : 269–334.

Cochran, William C. "The Western Reserve and the Fugitive Slave Law: A Prelude to Civil War." *The Western Reserve Historical Society, Publication* No. 10 (January 1920).

Commager, Henry Steele. "Constitutional History and the Higher Law," *Pennsylvania Magazine of History and Biography* 62 (January 1938) : 20–40.

Cooley, Verna. "Illinois and the Underground Railroad to Canada," *Transactions of the Illinois State Historical Society, No. 23* (1917), pp. 76–98.

Ellis, Lewis Ethan. "A History of the Chicago Delegation in Congress, 1843–1925." *Transactions of the Illinois State Historical Society, No. 37* (1930), pp. 52–149.

Fishback, Mason McCloud. "Illinois Legislation on Slavery and Free Negroes, 1818–1865." *Transactions of the Illinois State Historical Society, No. 9* (1904), pp. 414–22.

Geffen, Elizabeth M. "William Henry Furness: Philadelphia Anti-slavery Preacher." *Pennsylvania Magazine of History and Biography* 82 (July 1958) : 259–92.

Greene, Evarts B. "Sectional Forces in the History of Illinois." *Transactions of the Illinois State Historical Society, No. 8* (1903), pp. 75–83.

Griffin, Clifford S. "The Abolitionists and the Benevolent Societies, 1831–1861." *Journal of Negro History* 44 (July 1959) : 195–216.

Harmon, George D. "Douglas and the Compromise of 1850." *Journal of the Illinois State Historical Society* 21 (January 1929) : 453–99.

Johnson, Allen. "The Constitutionality of the Fugitive Slave Acts." *Yale Law Journal* 31 (1921–1922) : 161–82.

King, Ameda Ruth. "The Last Years of the Whig Party in Illinois, 1847–1856." *Transactions of the Illinois State Historical Society, No. 32* (1925), pp. 108–54.

Land, Mary. "John Brown's Ohio Environment." *Ohio State Archaeological and Historical Quarterly* 57 (January 1948) : 24–47.

Landon, Fred. "The Negro Migration to Canada After the Passing of the Fugitive Slave Act." *Journal of Negro History* 5 (January 1920): 22–36.

Levi, Kate Everest. "The Wisconsin Press and Slavery." *The Wisconsin Magazine of History* 9 (June 1925): 423–34.

Levy, Leonard W. "Sims' Case: The Fugitive Slave Law in Boston in 1851." *Journal of Negro History* 35 (January 1950): 39–74.

Luthin, Reinhard H. "Pennsylvania and Lincoln's Rise to the Presidency." *The Pennsylvania Magazine of History and Biography* 67 (January 1943): 61–82.

Mann, Charles Wesley. "The Chicago Common Council and the Fugitive Slave Law of 1850." *Proceedings of the Chicago Historical Society* 2 (1903–5): 55–86.

Mason, Vroman. "The Fugitive Slave Law in Wisconsin, With Reference to Nullification Sentiment." *Proceedings of the State Historical Society of Wisconsin* (1895), pp. 117–44.

Money, Charles H. "The Fugitive Slave Law of 1850 in Indiana." *Indiana Magazine of History* 17 (June, September 1921): 159–98, 257–97.

Pendergraft, Daryl. "Thomas Corwin and the Conservative Republican Reaction, 1858–1861." *The Ohio State Archaeological and Historical Quarterly* 57 (January 1948): 1–23.

Prince, Benjamin Franklin. "The Rescue Case of 1857." *Ohio Archaeological and Historical Society Publications* 16 (January 1907): 292–309.

Ranck, James B. "The Attitude of James Buchanan Towards Slavery." *Pennsylvania Magazine of History and Biography* 51 (January 1927): 126–42.

Ryan, John H. "A Chapter From the History of the Underground Railroad in Illinois: A Sketch of the Sturdy Abolitionist, John Hossack." *Journal of the Illinois State Historical Society* 8 (April 1915): 23–30.

Schafer, Joseph. "Editorial Comment: Stormy Days in Court—The Booth Case." *The Wisconsin Magazine of History* 20 (September 1936): 89–110.

Schilling, David Carl. "Relation of Southern Ohio to the South During the Decade Preceding the Civil War." *Quarterly Publication of the Historical and Philosophical Society of Ohio* 8 (January 1913): 1–28.

Shapiro, Samuel. "The Rendition of Anthony Burns." *Journal of Negro History* 44 (January 1959): 34–51.

Siebert, Wilbur H. "A Quaker Section of the Underground Railroad in Northern Ohio." *Ohio State Archaeological and Historical Quarterly* 39 (July 1930): 479–502.

Spenning, John P. "The Know-Nothing Movement in Illinois." *Journal of the Illinois State Historical Society* 7 (April 1914): 7–33.

Thornbrough, Emma Lou. "Indiana and Fugitive Slave Legislation." *Indiana Magazine of History* 50 (September 1954): 201–28.

"Trial of Anthony Burns, 1854." *Proceedings of the Massachusetts Historical Society* 44 (December 1953): 353–90.

Van Bolt, Roger. "Fusion Out of Confusion, 1854." *Indiana Magazine of History* 49 (December 1953): 353–90.

———. "The Hoosiers and the 'Eternal Agitation,' 1848–1850." *Indiana Magazine of History* 48 (December 1952): 331–68.

Van Tassel, David D. "Gentlemen of Property and Standing: Compromise Sentiment in Boston in 1850." *New England Quarterly* 23 (September 1950): 307–19.

Williams, Irene E. "The Operation of the Fugitive Slave Law in Western Pennsylvania, From 1850 to 1860." *Western Pennsylvania Historical Magazine* 4 (July 1921): 150–60.

Yanuck, Julius. "The Garner Fugitive Slave Case." *Mississippi Valley Historical Review* 40 (June 1953): 47–66.

Index

AMERICAN HISTORY TITLES IN THE NORTON LIBRARY